P9-DMF-035

50 Hikes in Connecticut

Bantam Lake from Mount Tom Tower

50 *Hikes*

In Connecticut

Hikes and Walks From the Berkshires to the Coast

Fifth Edition

DAVID, GERRY, AND SUE HARDY

With Photographs by the Authors

Backcountry Guides

Woodstock, Vermont

AN INVITATION TO THE READER

Over time trails can be rerouted and signs and landmarks altered. If you find that changes have occurred on the routes described in this book, please let us know so that corrections may be made in future editions. The author and publisher also welcome other comments and suggestions. Address all correspondence to:

Editor
50 Hikes™ Series
Backcountry Publications
P.O. Box 748
Woodstock, VT 05091

LIBRARY OF CONGRESS CATALOGING-IN-PUBLICATION DATA

Hardy, David, 1959–
  50 hikes in Connecticut : hikes and walks from the Berkshires to the coast / David, Gerry, and Sue Hardy ; [photographs by author].–5th ed.
    p. cm.–(50 hikes series)
  Includes bibliographical references and index.
  ISBN 0-88150-496-3
  1. Hiking–Connecticut–Guidebooks.
2. Connecticut–Guidebooks. I. Title: Fifty hikes in Connecticut. II. Hardy, Gerry. III. Hardy, Sue. IV. Title. V. Fifty hikes series.
GV199.42.C8 H37   2002
917.46'0444–dc21   2001037554
                          CIP

Text and cover design by Glenn Suokko
New maps by Mapping Specialists, Ltd., Madison, WI, © 2002 The Countryman Press

© 1978, 1984, 1991 by Gerry and Sue Hardy.
© 1996 and 2002 by David, Gerry, and Sue Hardy.

Fifth Edition

All rights reserved. No part of this book may be reproduced in any form or by any electronic or mechanical means, including information storage and retrieval systems, without permission in writing from the publisher, except by a reviewer, who may quote brief passages.

Published by Backcountry Guides, a division of The Countryman Press
P.O. Box 748
Woodstock, Vermont 05091
www.countrymanpress.com

Distributed by W. W. Norton & Company, Inc.
500 Fifth Avenue
New York, NY 10110

Printed in the United States of America

10 9 8 7 6 5 4 3 2 1

DEDICATION

To the next generation, Nicholas, Anna, Julia, and Charles, too.

50 Hikes at a Glance

HIKE	REGION
1. Falls Village	Canaan
2. Great Pond	Simsbury
3. Dinosaur State Park	Rocky Hill
4. Mount Tom Tower	Morris
5. Rocky Neck	East Lyme
6. Larsen Sanctuary	Fairfield
7. Highland Springs and Lookout Mountain	Manchester
8. Wadsworth Falls	Middlefield
9. Audubon Center in Greenwich	Greenwich
10. Hurd State Park	East Hampton
11. Sunny Valley	Bridgewater
12. Bluff Point	Groton
13. Day Pond Loop	Colchester
14. Hartman Park	Lyme
15. Soapstone Mountain	Somers
16. Penwood	Bloomfield
17. Northern Metacomet	Granby
18. Gay City	Hebron
19. Mount Misery	Voluntown
20. Wolf Den	Pomfret
21. Collis P. Huntington State Park	Redding
22. Green Fall Pond	Voluntown
23. Northern Nipmuck	Ashford
24. Chatfield Hollow	Killingworth
25. Great Hill	East Hampton

D	Easy terrain; little or no elevation change
CD	Intermediate between C and D
C	Average terrain; moderate ups and downs
CB	Intermediate between C and B
B	Strenuous terrain; steep climbs, considerable elevation gain
AB	Intermediate between A and B
A	Very strenuous terrain; maximum elevation gain

DISTANCE (miles)	RATING	VIEWS	WATERFALLS	GOOD FOR KIDS	NOTES
1.0	D			★	Impressive white pines; river walk
1.5	D	★		★	Loop around pine shoreline
1.25	D			★	Nature walk; dinosaur trackways
1.5	C	★		★	Short uphill to stone tower
3.0	D	★		★	Ocean bayside walk to sandy beach
3.0	D			★	Nature walk
2.5	C	★		★	Hillside walk; springtime vernal pool
3.0	C		★	★	Old woods road leading to two waterfalls
3.0	CD			★	Nature center; woods ramble
3.5	C	★		★	Connecticut riverside walk
3.0	C	★		★	Rocky scrambles; riverside vista
4.5	D	★		★	Oceanside walk; old foundations
4.0	C	★		★	Summer swimming; glacial erratic boulders
4.0	C			★	Woods walk across narrow ridges; historic fortress
4.0	C	★		★	Ridgewalk to observation tower
4.75	C	★		★	Ridgewalk to rocky outcrop
4.0	C	★		★	Traprock ridge with clifftop views
5.0	CD			★	Woods walk through ghost town
5.25	CD	★		★	Rhododendron swamp boardwalk
5.0	CD			★	Rock formations; fabled wolf den cave
5.5	CD	★		★	Wood roads walk along pond shores
5.7	CD	★	★	★	Pond walk with approach through gorge
5.25	C	★		★	Rocky ridges and deep hemlock woods
5.5	C	★		★	Ledges and CCC-developed park
5.5	C	★	★	★	Rocky summit and ridgewalk to waterfall

50 Hikes at a Glance

HIKE	REGION
26. McLean Game Refuge	Granby
27. Northwest Park	Windsor
28. Mount Higby	Middlefield
29. Devils Den	Weston
30. White Memorial Foundation	Litchfield
31. Bullet and High Ledges	North Stonington
32. Chauncey Peak & Mount Lamentation	Meriden
33. Westwoods	Guilford
34. Cathedral Pines & Mohawk Mountain	Cornwall
35. Natchaug	Eastford
36. Peoples State Forest	Barkhamsted
37. West Peak and Castle Crag	Meriden
38. Bear Mountain	Salisbury
39. Macedonia Brook	Kent
40. Windsor Locks Canal	Suffield
41. Mansfield Hollow	Mansfield
42. Bigelow Hollow	Union
43. Devils Hopyard	East Haddam
44. Seven Falls	Middletown
45. Talcott Mountain	West Hartford
46. Ragged Mountain	Southington
47. Cockaponset	Chester
48. Tunxis Ramble	Burlington
49. Sleeping Giant	Hamden
50. Ratlum Mountain & Indian Council Cave	Barkhamsted

DISTANCE (miles)	**RATING**	**VIEWS**	**WATERFALLS**	**GOOD FOR KIDS**	**NOTES**
5.0	C	★		★	Barndoor Hill; great white pine woods
6.0	CD	★		★	Woods walk through old tobacco fields; nature center
5.0	B	★		★	Clifftop walk along traprock ridge
6.5	C	★			Woods ramble to highland vistas in nature preserve
6.7	D	★		★	Extensive boardwalk across shallow pond
6.0	C	★		★	Eastern Connecticut ledges
6.0	B	★		★	Traprock ridge walk
6.0	B	★			Scramble along rocky ledges
6.0	BC	★		★	Giant pines and observation tower
6.6	CD				Woods walk among remnants of 19th-century chestnut forest
7.0	BC	★			Woods ramble with rock outcrop views
6.4	B	★		★	Clifftop walk on traprock ridges
6.5	AB	★		★	Steady ascent to Connecticut's highest summit
6.7	A	★			Rugged hike around highland valley
9.0	D	★		★	Easy riverside walk along old canal
8.0	CD	★			Valley walk to local ledge
8.25	B	★			Woods walk over rocky ledges & along undeveloped shoreline
7.5	C	★	★		Hillside hike around a highland valley
8.0	C	★	★		Woods walk among cascades and rocky hillsides
8.5	C	★		★	Reservoir walk to traprock ridge with famous tower
6.0/9.1	A	★		★	Rocky trail along traprock clifftop and ridges
10.1	CD		★		Woods ramble
9.5	BC	★			Hike along the Mile of Ledges
4.8/9.0	A	★			Quarry views; rocky ledges
13.0	B	★			Visit reputed Native American gathering place

D	Easy terrain; little or no elevation change
CD	Intermediate between C and D
C	Average terrain; moderate ups and downs
CB	Intermediate between C and B
B	Strenuous terrain; steep climbs, considerable elevation gain
AB	Intermediate between A and B
A	Very strenuous terrain; maximum elevation gain

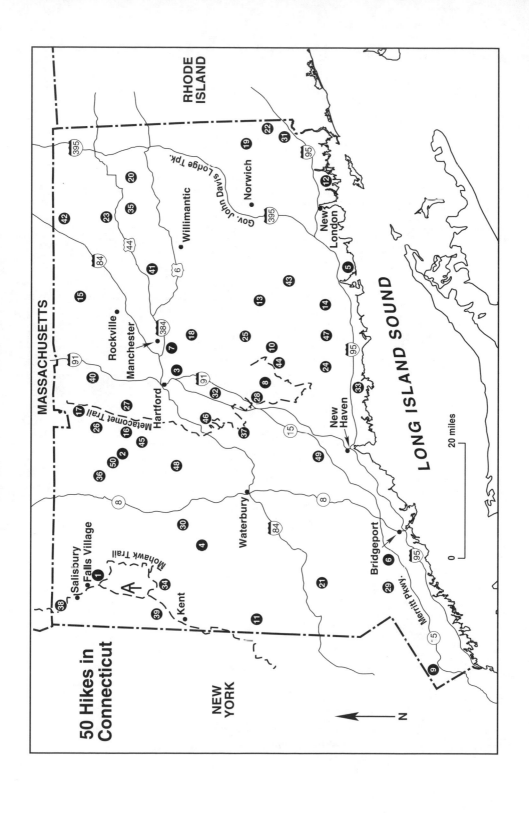

CONTENTS

Acknowledgments

Many of our thoughts were honed on our numerous hiking companions, to whom we are very grateful. The Appalachian Mountain Club groups we hike with provide an endless supply of wit and good fellowship. Above all, we would like to thank the dedicated volunteers of the Connecticut Forest and Park Association for the existence and maintenance of Connecticut's Blue Trails, members of the Connecticut Chapter of the AMC for managing and maintaining the Appalachian Trail in Connecticut, and all those who laid out and maintain the many other fine trails in our state. Especially we thank Carol for her endless patience with this project. We would also like to thank Ann Kraybill at The Countryman Press for her patience and perseverance in preparing this fifth edition.

Introduction

Contrary to popular opinion, Connecticut is not all cities and suburbs. A gratifyingly high proportion of our state's woodland is preserved as state parks and state forests. In fact, the only states in New England with more miles of hiking trails are Vermont and New Hampshire.

These 50 hikes represent all areas of the state and traverse almost all the existing natural habitats. Naturally, this selection is only a sampler and, of necessity, somewhat reflects our own preferences and prejudices. We chose the hikes with an eye to the hiking family; most are suitable for families with young children (who are usually far more capable physically than psychologically). But remember, a half-day hike for adults and teenagers may take all day with youngsters along, especially if they take time to examine their surroundings closely.

Revising a hiking guide is a never-ending task. A new edition becomes necessary due to changes in trails, whether caused by humans or by natural events. Outdated hiking guides can be particularly frustrating for new hikers.

This edition reflects trail changes in some hikes (Mount Misery, Northwest Park, Mount Higby, White Foundation, McLean, Westwoods, West Peak and Castle Crag, and Mansfield Hollow), a new hike in an old haunt (Chauncey Peak), several brand-new hikes (Falls Village, Dinosaur State Park, Devils Den, and Bigelow Hollow), and many minor adjustments. The hikes in this edition represent their trail status as of 2000; all were walked during that hiking season.

Written comments by interested hikers like you were considered and field-checked. Such notes are important in keeping this volume up to date, and any suggestions are appreciated.

This book is intended to please both the armchair and the trail hiker by fleshing out directions with photographs and snippets of natural history. We have also tried to answer some of the questions that you might ask while walking these trails. The phenomena we describe we actually saw on these 50 hikes (some hiked many times over many years); by being fairly observant you can see the same things. For this reason our descriptions are short on wildlife, which is seen only occasionally, and long on vegetation and terrain. Effective observation of animal life requires very slow movement (if any), blinds, and binoculars or scopes. In contrast, vegetation and terrain features require only an alert eye and an inquiring mind.

These hikes, which we feel represent some of the most attractive in the state, break longer trails into manageable sections. In addition to some of the best pieces of the Blue Trail System and more interesting state park trail networks, we have included a few hikes in wildlife sanctuaries and in city- and town-owned, open-space areas. We now try to avoid the world-famous Appalachian Trail, which is overexposed in other trail publications and overused as a result.

CHOOSING A HIKE

The hikes are presented in order of their estimated hiking time; the first hike, Falls

Village, is the shortest, and the last one, Ratlum Mountain, the longest. Since gauging difficulty is more subjective, however, owing to ruggedness of terrain, length, and vertical rise (as well as vertical drop), the order does not necessarily reflect the hikes' difficulty.

Total distance is the mileage walked if you complete the entire hike as described. Many of these hikes lend themselves readily to shortening if you desire an easier day. Some, with the help of local maps or the *Connecticut Walk Book,* can be lengthened. Trail distances are given in fractions of a mile for some hikes and in decimals for others. Fractional distances are estimates, while decimal distances have usually been measured with a wheel and are fairly accurate.

Hiking time is computed from a simple formula used all over the country: 2 miles an hour plus one-half hour for every 1,000 feet of vertical rise. Thus, a 6-mile hike on flat terrain would have a three-hour hiking time, but a 6-mile hike with 2,000 feet of climbing would take four hours. If you are a middle-aged, beginning hiker, you may not match "book time" for a while. A young, experienced hiker will consistently better these times. A word of caution—hiking time means just that and does not allow for lunch stops, rest breaks, sight-seeing, or picture taking.

The rating for each hike refers to the average difficulty of the terrain you traverse on the route we have described. The difficulty of a hike is relative. A tough section in Connecticut is far easier than a tough section in New Hampshire or Vermont. However, some of our rock scrambles, while shorter, can be just as difficult. The big difference between Connecticut and northern New England is our dearth of sustained climbs. Only Bear Mountain (see Hike 38) offers such an ascent.

Our rating system is the one used by the Connecticut Chapter of the Appalachian Mountain Club and is designed for Connecticut trails. It combines such factors as elevation gain, rock scrambling, footpath condition, and steepness. Hikes rated D are the easiest, and A the most difficult. The seven categories used in our rating system are:

D   Easy terrain; little or no elevation change, easy footing

CD   Intermediate between C and D

C   Average terrain; moderate ups and downs with some need to watch footing

CB   Intermediate between C and B

B   Strenuous terrain; steep climbs, considerable elevation gain or some poor footing or both

AB   Intermediate between A and B

A   Very strenuous terrain; maximum elevation gain, poor footing or hand-assisted scrambling up steep pitches or both

In an effort to limit grade inflation, an A rating is rarely given and *will* require the use of your hands on a steep pitch at some point in the hike. Where such a situation exists, it will be noted in the text.

When selecting a day's ramble, don't overdo it. If you haven't hiked before, try the shorter, easier hikes first and build up to the longer ones. Don't bite off more than you can chew—that takes all the pleasure out of hiking. As the saying goes, "Walk till you're half tired out, then turn around and walk back."

The *maps* listed are the United States Geological Survey (USGS) maps replicated as part of the route map provided in each hike description. You may wish to obtain some of these maps in their entirety to get a better sense of the region you're hiking in. They're available at some bookstores and outdoor equipment shops, from the Connecticut Department of Environmental Protection, and directly from the USGS.

ABOUT CONNECTICUT SEASONS

Hiking in Connecticut is a four-season avocation. Our winters are relatively mild—we rarely have temperatures below zero Fahrenheit or snow accumulations of more than a foot. In general, the snow deepens and the temperature drops as you travel north and west. Often the southeastern part of the state is snow-free much of the winter and is the first area in the state to experience spring.

Spring is usually wet and muddy, although there is frequently a dry period of high fire danger before the trees leaf out. Spring flowers start in April and peak in May. Days of extreme heat in the 90s can come anytime after the beginning of April—sometimes sooner!

The humid heat of summer demands short, easy, early-morning strolls and usually requires insect repellent. Beginners sometimes think summer is the best time to hike; veterans consider it the worst time! Still, in summer the foliage is lush and botanizing is at its best.

Fall is the ideal hiking season. Cool, crisp days let us forget the enervating heat of summer; the colorful foliage and clear air make New England's fall unsurpassed. A better combination of season and place may exist elsewhere, but we doubt it.

The color starts with a few shrubs and the bright reds of swamp maples. When other trees start to turn, the swamp maples are bare. Then tree follows tree—sugar maple, ash, birch, beech, and finally oak—turning, blending, fading, falling. There is no better way to enjoy a New England autumn than to explore the woods on foot.

HOW TO HIKE

We do not mean to tell you how to walk. Most of us have been walking from an early age. Rather, we offer a few hints to help you gain as much pleasure and satisfaction as possible from a hike.

First and most important, wear comfortable shoes that are well broken in. Children can often hike comfortably in good sneakers; adults usually shouldn't. We're heavier, and our feet need more support than canvas offers. On the other hand, you don't need heavyweight mountain boots in Connecticut. A lightweight hiking boot or a good work boot with a Vibram or lug sole is ideal. While these soles may be hard on the woods' trails, we do recommend them, because most Connecticut hiking alternates between woods and rocky ledges, where the lug soles are very helpful. Your boots should be worn over two pairs of socks, one lightweight and one heavyweight. Wool or a wool-polypropylene blend is preferable for both pairs, as it provides warmth even when wet.

Second, wear comfortable, loose clothes that don't bind, bunch, or chafe. Cotton T-shirts work well but can get chilly when wet with sweat; synthetic T-shirts are more comfortable. For our day hikes, except in winter, we favor cutoff jeans or hiking shorts; they're loose and have many pockets for storing a neckerchief, a handkerchief, insect repellent, film, tissues, and a pocketknife.

Establish a comfortable pace you can maintain for long periods of time. The hiker who charges down the trail not only misses the subtleties of the surroundings, but also frequently starts gasping for breath after 15

A trail runs along an earthen dam in Collis P. Huntington State Park

minutes or so of hiking. That's no fun! A steady pace lets you both see and cover more ground comfortably than the start-and-stop, huff-and-puff hiker. When you climb a slope, slow your pace so you can continue to the top without having to stop. Having to stop is different from choosing to stop at places of interest, although the clever hiker learns to combine the two. With practice you'll develop an uphill rhythm and cover ground faster by going slowly.

WHAT TO CARRY

You may have read articles on the portable household the backpacker carries. While the day-hiker needn't shoulder this burden, there are some things you should carry to ensure a comfortable and safe hike. Ideally you will always carry your emergency gear and never use it.

Items 2–10 below live in our day packs:

1.   Small, comfortable, lightweight-pack.

2.   First-aid kit containing at least adhesive bandages, moleskin (for incipient blisters), adhesive tape, gauze pads, aspirin, salt tablets, Ace bandage, and antibiotic lotion. We always carry both elastic knee and ankle braces and Ace bandages—we have used them more than any of our other first-aid equipment.

3.   Wool or polypro shirt or sweater and a nylon windbreaker. A fast-moving cold front can turn a balmy spring day into a blustery, snow-spitting disaster, and sun-warmed, sheltered valleys may contrast sharply with windswept, elevated, open ledges.

4.   Lightweight rain gear. In warm, rainy weather, hikers are of two minds about rainwear—some don it immediately and get wet from perspiration; others don't and get wet from the rain. In colder weather, wear it for warmth. In any case, if

the day is threatening it's wise to have dry clothes in the car. On a warm day, an umbrella may be preferable to rain gear. It may seem strange at first, but it's effective!

5.   Water. Water in southern New England is almost never safe to drink. Always carry at least 1 to 3 quarts (more on hot summer days) per hiker. On cool days, a thermos of hot tea, cocoa, or broth is a good thing to have along. Also, carry some water purifier or a filter in case you need to take water from a source in the woods.

6.   Food. In addition to your lunch, carry high-energy food for emergencies. Sometimes you may feel nauseated when you need a bite to eat for energy, so carry stuff you like to eat. Hiking is no time to diet aggressively or to experiment in the food department. Gorp (Good Old Raisins and Peanuts)—a hand-mixed combination of chocolate chips, nuts, and dried fruit—is a good choice.

7.   Flashlight with extra batteries and bulb. You should plan to return to your car before dark, but be prepared in case you're delayed. Be aware of the shorter daylight hours of autumn and winter.

8.   A well-sharpened pocketknife. This tool has a thousand uses.

9.   Map and compass (optional). These items are not necessary for day hikers in Connecticut who stay on well-defined trails and use a guidebook. However, if you want to do any off-trail exploring, you should learn to use a map and compass and carry them with you.

10.   Others: toilet paper (always); insect repellent (in season); a hat or sunscreen lotion (always, especially on bright days); a wool hat and mittens (in spring and fall).

Winter hiking requires much additional equipment and does not fall within the scope of this book. Nonetheless, it is a lovely time to hike, and we encourage you to hone your skills in mild weather, consult experienced winter hikers, and consider hiking on winter's clear, crisp, often snow-white days. For additional information on winter hiking, we recommend John Dunn's *Winterwise,* published by the Adirondack Mountain Club.

HIKING CONCERNS

Footing is the major difference between road walking and hiking. Roads present a minimum of obstacles to trip you; at times hiking trails seem to have a maximum. The angular traprock cobbles on many of Connecticut's ridges tend to roll beneath your feet, endangering ankles and balance. An exposed wet root acts as a super banana peel, and lichen on wet rock as a lubricant. Stubs of improperly cut bushes are nearly invisible obstacles that can trip or puncture. All these potential hazards dictate that you walk carefully on the trail.

It is far safer to hike with a companion than to venture out alone. Should an accident occur while you're alone, you're in trouble. If you must hike alone, be sure someone knows where you are, your exact route, and when you plan to return. Don't leave this information in a note on your windshield—it's only an invitation to a thief.

Every Eden has its serpent. Connecticut's, in warm weather, is its tiny biting pests. We've all seen horror pictures of hikers in the Far North, their shirts blackened with bloodsucking mosquitoes. Explorers of the Tropics fear not lions or tigers but biting insects most of all. In Connecticut you can avoid this problem by hiking in winter or on chilly fall and spring days, which are often ideal for hiking. For your summer excursions, understanding the problem and knowing its appropriate remedies will greatly enhance your enjoyment.

Most bugs can be kept at bay with insect repellent. Herbal repellents are quite effective for mosquitoes, while stronger concoctions, often containing DEET, are necessary for blackflies and are recommended for deer ticks. We recommend bug "juice" that contains a moderate amount of DEET, primarily for deer ticks, which can carry Lyme disease. Studies, while not fully conclusive, seem to indicate that DEET isn't safe to use frequently or in high concentrations. For deer ticks it is best applied to clothes from the knees down, where they're most likely to land.

Lyme disease was named for a Connecticut town near Long Island Sound, where it was first identified in 1975. Carried by the very small deer tick (only 0.25 inch in diameter even when fully engorged with blood), Lyme disease does not affect most nonhuman animals except for dogs, which may develop joint disorders. It is now the most prevalent tick-borne illness in the United States, and the number of cases increases yearly. Originally reported only in southern New England, Lyme disease has been found (using different tick carriers in different regions of the world) in 47 states and on all continents except Antarctica. European literature almost a century ago reported a similar group of symptoms. The airlines and similar forces that are "shrinking" the globe may have helped its dissemination, much as they have spread more highly publicized "plagues." Fortunately, only a small percentage of deer ticks are infected, so the chances of contracting the disease are not high for hikers and other outdoorspeople; suburbanites seem much more susceptible. Usually within a month of infection, a circular rash a few inches in diameter surrounds the tick bite location. If you are uncertain about a tick bite or find the telltale "bull's-eye" rash, contact your doctor. Proper treatment within a few weeks of infection is very effective. While not considered a fatal disease, untreated Lyme disease produces debilitating symptoms that can persist for a lifetime. Even at this stage, the illness is treatable with antibiotics.

The best way to protect yourself against Lyme disease is to wear long sleeves and long pants tucked into your socks, use insect repellent on clothing, and check yourself for ticks. If you have been bitten, contact a physician. Inspect yourself for ticks. Yes, Lyme disease should concern hikers in Connecticut, but with proper precautions and a reasonable level of care, it shouldn't keep you from enjoying the woods. To put things in perspective, we know literally hundreds of hikers, most of whom live in the Northeast. We know of only a few who have ever had Lyme disease, and one of them has had it three times—all before he started hiking! He's sure he got it working in his garden.

Other hiking dangers are more common but minor. You should learn to identify poison ivy; it's a very common shrub or vine that can cause quite a bit of discomfort. If you stay on the trail, it shouldn't be a problem. It's most often a vine with little rootlets clinging to the bark of a tree or a shrub along old stone walls or a patch of plants on the ground. Its shiny, three-leafed arrangement is fairly unmistakable. And yes, you can catch poison ivy from the bark of this shrub even in winter.

Snakes are overrated; they will not bite you unless you pick them up or step on them. Snakes by nature want nothing to do with humans and will quickly get away whenever possible. Some nonvenomous snakes can deliver a nasty bite, which will require only a good cleaning and maybe a tetanus shot. Connecticut has two native poisonous snakes and only rarely racks up a snakebite statewide, almost never among hikers. The northern copperhead and timber rattlesnake are very rare creatures and very effective "mousers," which we need more of to keep the rodent population down. Rodents are not only destroyers of crops (and stealers of hikers' carelessly placed candy bars) but also hosts for deer ticks, which are potentially infected with Lyme disease. Although rattlesnakes are considered much more venomous than copperheads, there have been *no* confirmed deaths from a New England timber rattlesnake bite. Ever. In all our years of hiking in the state, we've never seen a rattlesnake. If you should be lucky enough to see one, enjoy the sight from a safe distance, and let one of nature's most efficient rodent controls continue to grace its highland home.

Bees are more of a problem. If you are allergic, you should carry the kit to deal with anaphylactic shock. More than twice as many people succumb to allergic reactions to bees as die from snakebite nationwide. Some people react more than others. Many people experience little more than the local swelling usually associated with mosquito bites.

WATER WORRIES

Most of New England's open water sources probably contain *Giardia*. Warm-blooded creatures (like us) ingest tiny *Giardia* cysts (about 16,500 can fit on the head of a pin) from contaminated drinking water. In the gut they will hatch, multiply, attach to the upper small intestine, and then do their damage, which can include diarrhea, cramps, and visible bloating. The cysts infest many warm-blooded animals, including the now numerous beavers; some people call these symptoms Beaver Fever. However, much of the problem has been caused by improper disposal of human waste and that of another commonly seen trail beast, the family dog. Both people and dogs carry *Giardia,* often without exhibiting any symptoms, and travel far more widely than any beaver we're aware of. Human and dog wastes should be buried in a shallow hole 6 to 8 inches deep (a "cat hole") at least 200 feet from water and 50 feet from the trail to reduce the spread of disease organisms. Don't bother to burn the toilet paper; it breaks down quickly in our damp New England climate. Carrying a small trowel can make this chore easier. *Giardia* lurks in even the clearest, coldest running water. Therefore, never drink untreated water! This means carrying your own water while day hiking and properly treating your drinking water while backpacking, with either a filter or chemical purifier like iodine. Giardiasis, once correctly diagnosed, is easily treated—but the best treatment is prevention.

POTPOURRI

While hiking, don't litter. The AMC motto, "Carry In—Carry Out," is a good one. Carry a small plastic bag in your pack for garbage, and pick up any trash you find along the trail.

On any hike the minerals, plants, and animals you see have been left untouched by previous trekkers. You, in turn, should leave all things for the next hiker to admire. Remember to "take only pictures, leave only footprints, kill only time."

Connecticut has a limited-liability law to protect landowners who grant access to the general public free of charge. This saves property owners from capricious lawsuits and opens up more private lands for trails.

Hiking should be much more than a walk in the woods. Knowledge of natural and local history adds another dimension to your rambles. We dip lightly into these areas to give you a sampling to whet an inquiring mind. To aid further investigation, we offer a short, descriptive Further Reading section at the end of this Introduction. Using good field guides will add immeasurably to a hike.

Another fascinating aspect of hiking involves observing and considering your environment. Think about why some plants are found in southern but not in northern Connecticut. Why are our woods filled with old roads and stone walls and dotted with cellar holes? Why do some trees grow straight and tall, while others have outflung, low branches? Someone once said, "Ecology is more complicated than you think; in fact, it is more complicated than you think!" You will never run out of things to learn on your hikes! In these trail descriptions we have thrown in a smattering of natural history. We've only touched on a few things, and we've tried not to repeat ourselves from hike to hike. Much of what is described in one hike also applies to many of the others.

THE CONNECTICUT 400 CLUB

Many hikers collect attractive patches to signify completion of a goal. The AMC sponsors, among other things, the New Hampshire 4,000-Footer Club and the New England 4,000-Footer Club for those who have climbed the 48 mountains in New Hampshire or the 65 in northern New England that are more than 4,000 feet high. Special patches are awarded to applicants for a small fee.

Connecticut's peaks are less lofty. However, the Connecticut Chapter of the AMC has since 1976 sponsored the Connecticut 400 Club, whose members have hiked all the through trails (approximately 450 miles) described in the *Connecticut Walk Book*. Patches are awarded to applicants for a small fee. The Connecticut 400 Club was established not only to recognize those who have hiked the through trails but also, and perhaps more importantly, to encourage hikers to explore all the trails in the state, thus reducing traffic on the famous but overused Appalachian Trail. The chapter also sponsors an "East of the River Hiker" patch for individuals who complete a list of hiking trails east of the Connecticut River.

For the name and address of the current Connecticut 400 Club Patch chair, East of the River Hiker patch information, or for information on the Connecticut Chapter of the AMC, write to the Appalachian Mountain Club, 5 Joy Street, Boston, MA 02108.

ABOUT TRAILS

Hiking trails do not just happen for our healthy enjoyment, and as we in Connecticut are well aware, they are impermanent at best. When the first *Connecticut Walk Book* was published in 1937, all the major trails in Connecticut were interconnected. The pressures of change have long since isolated most of these trails from each other. The major reason we still have good hiking trails is that hikers like rough, hard-to-reach land for their hikes, while builders prefer easily developed land. However, as time passes and populations grow, trail corridors become more and more endangered. Let's examine the history of the Appalachian Trail (AT), which mirrors the problems that beset many hiking trails.

The bane of the hiker in our uncertain world is the continual loss of hiking trails to development, land-use change, or just plain unhappy landowners. The AT had been at the mercy of changes such as

these since its inception in the 1930s. By the late 1960s some 200 miles of this trail, once on private land, had been displaced onto paved roads. The volunteer Appalachian Trail Conference, located in Harpers Ferry, West Virginia, which coordinated the building and maintenance of the AT, was paying more and more attention to the loss of this "wild" land. Largely because of a major push by volunteers and pressure from the public, the U.S. Congress passed the National Trails System Act, which was signed into law on October 2, 1968. While this potentially made the AT a permanent entity, no money was appropriated at that time to make the dream a reality.

In 1978 the act was amended, authorizing the National Park Service to acquire a 1,000-foot-wide Appalachian Trail corridor on the private land where about half of the original trail was located. Fortunately, Congress also appropriated $90 million to effect the needed acquisitions. A number of parcels are still to be purchased, and hopes are that it can be completed in the near future. Much has been done, but the toughest acquisitions remain. With the escalating cost of land and the uncertain attitude of recent administrations, it may take more time to complete this vital public acquisition.

What can we, the hiking public, do about this persistent problem? The hikes in this book are a direct result of the efforts of thousands of volunteers like you. Most of us do not have the time, ability, or money to make major contributions. However, we can all vote, support conservation-oriented politicians, and do some sort of volunteer trail maintenance. We must work to create an atmosphere of trust and understanding with private landowners. The hiker's cause is damaged by vandalism, rowdiness, and lack of respect for landowners' rights. But we all benefit from courteous hikers, diligent volunteer trail workers, and an understanding of landowners' concerns.

For more information about helping out, contact the following:

Connecticut Forest and
    Park Association
16 Meriden Road
Rock Fall, CT 06481

Appalachian Mountain Club
5 Joy Street
Boston, MA 02108

Appalachian Trail Conference
P.O. Box 807
Harpers Ferry, WV 25425

FURTHER READING

Connecticut is a small state with pleasing outdoor diversity. The hikes in this book touch lightly on many aspects of its ever-fascinating scene: flora, fauna, geology, and history. Since this is basically a hiking book, we have had neither the space nor the time to go into great detail, but we hope we have piqued your interest so you will want to become more knowledgeable about the outdoors and the history of Connecticut. The following books and articles should enhance your understanding of Connecticut's outdoors and add to your experience with this book. The following hiking guides are invaluable.

Among recently published books, the *Connecticut Walk Book,* published by the Connecticut Forest and Park Association, covers all the Blue Trails and many others in the state. The *Appalachian Trail Guide to Massachusetts–Connecticut* covers the AT through the northwestern corner of Connecticut. Another guide to consider is the Hunter Travel Guide, *Adventure Guide to Massachusetts and Western Connecti-*

cut, which includes local attractions in addition to hiking trails.

A precursor to the *Connecticut Walk Book* was *Walks and Rides in Central Connecticut and Massachusetts* by C. R. Longwell and E. S. Dana, published by the Tuttle, Morehouse, & Taylor Company, New Haven, Connecticut. Because these Yale professors specialized in geology, this book is built around the forces that created and shaped the state's terrain.

Since this corner of the nation is composed of six diverse states, we often think of ourselves as New Englanders. A grounding in all of New England's changes certainly increases our understanding of Connecticut itself. We recommend *Changing Face of New England* by B. F. Thompson, Houghton Mifflin, 1958; *Changes in the Land* by W. Cronin, Hill & Wang, 1983; and *A Guide to New England's Landscape* by Neil Jorgensen, Pequot Press, 1977. Jorgensen's *A Sierra Club Naturalist Guide to Southern New England,* Sierra Club Books, 1978, examines a narrower section of the Northeast in greater detail, thus limiting the scope while broadening the understanding of our natural wonders.

Many of the Peterson field guides are invaluable aids in identifying the world met along the trail. Those of special value to us include: *A Field Guide to Wildflowers* by M. McKenney and R. T. Peterson; *A Field Guide to the Mammals* by W. H. Burl and R. P. Grossenheider; *A Field Guide to the Ferns and Their Related Families of Northeastern and Central North America* by B. Cobb; *A Field Guide to the Reptiles and Amphibians of the United States and Canada East of the l00th Meridian* by R. Conant; and *A Field Guide to Trees and Shrubs* by G. A. Petrides.

A special little softcover book, *Connecti-*

cut's *Notable Trees* by G. D. Dreyer (Memoir of the Connecticut Botanical Society #2– 1989), lists not only the dimensions and locations of all the known largest trees of each species in Connecticut, but also several large historic oaks and the largest known specimens of ash, eastern cottonwood, and elm.

Other good guides include *Stokes' Amphibians and Reptiles* by Tom Tyning, *Newcomb's Wildflower Guide,* National Geographic's *Birds of North America,* and *Tracking and the Art of Seeing* by Paul Rezendes. Audubon Society field guides are particularly helpful because of their extensive use of photographs.

If you want to go beyond the nuts and bolts of identification, the following books contain much of the lore that is so dear to the hearts of natural history buffs: *How to Know the Ferns* by F. T. Parsons, Dover, 1961; *A Natural History of Trees* by D. C. Peattie, Houghton Mifflin, 1950; *Trees of Eastern and Central United States and Canada* by W. M. Halow, Dover, 1957; and *How to Know the Wildflowers* by W. S. Dana, Dover, 1963.

The forces that shaped our land can also be found in *Underfoot: A Geological Guide to the Appalachian Trail* by V. C. Chew, Appalachian Trail Conference, 1988, which covers the trail's entire 2,000 miles, including the trail section that passes through northwestern Connecticut. Excellent geological coverage of all of Connecticut for the layperson is provided by M. Bell's *The Face of Connecticut: The People, Geology, and the Land,* State Geological and Natural History Survey of Connecticut, 1985.

Finally, there are several books published on other outdoor aspects of our state. These include *Connecticut Railroads: An Illustrated History,* Connecticut Historical Society, 1986, and *Fishery Survey of the Lakes and Ponds of Connecticut* by the State Board of Fisheries and Game.

——	main trail
• • •	side trail
Ⓟ	parking area
🛖	shelter
⚔	Appalachian Trail

1

Falls Village

Location: Canaan

Distance: 1 mile

Vertical rise: negligible

Time: ½ hour

Rating: D

Map: USGS 7.5-minute South Canaan

Volunteers maintain the Appalachian Trail (AT) in Connecticut for the Appalachian Trail Conference and the Appalachian Mountain Club (two different nonprofit cooperative groups). The conference works with the National Park Service to manage and maintain the AT from Georgia to Maine. Individual trail clubs, like the Appalachian Mountain Club (AMC), maintain sections of the trail. The Connecticut Chapter of the AMC maintains the AT in Connecticut and mobilizes volunteer work parties for construction projects such as staircases or basic maintenance like brushing and blazing. Volunteers also build shelters and bridges along the trail. Trail maintainers often start out simply as day hikers and eventually show their appreciation by volunteering and "giving something back" to the trail.

The Appalachian Trail offers some of Connecticut's finest, and most difficult, hiking. Since it has some of the most popular hiking destinations in the state, the trail gets more use than many of our other walkways. Consequently, we've reduced the number of hikes in this book that follow the AT. This hike, however, is special. Members of the AMC Connecticut Chapter, with a little help from their friends, have made a short piece of the Appalachian Trail accessible to folks with limited walking capabilities. They were able to achieve this feat with little change in the "trail experience," and the walk along the Housatonic River here is well worth the trip.

To reach the trailhead, take CT 126 west from its junction with US 7 east of Falls

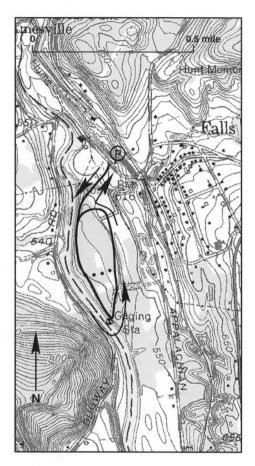

The work necessary to make this an accessible trail is hidden beneath the graded, hard-packed surface of the trail. Imagine trying to turn any stretch of hiking trail into a smooth-surfaced path. Mud spots needed filling, roots needed to be removed, and seemingly easy ups and downs had to be graded and packed down to allow wheelchairs to pass easily. With a little hiking experience in Connecticut it's easy to see that this is no simple feat!

After you enter the woods, cross a small stream over a bridge and follow the path, staying left on the white-blazed AT at a fork. You'll soon reach a view of the Housatonic River, and then parallel it among some giant oak and pine trees. The next fork is the junction of the AT and your return loop trail—stay to your right on the Appalachian Trail along the river. You'll pass between three great white pines and arrive at another fork. Here the AT continues straight, while the short loop option to the accessible trail turns left. You could follow the short loop counterclockwise and return to the parking lot in ½ mile, but our hike takes you straight again, toward Georgia.

A short distance farther your route bears left away from the river, and then the AT bears right off the accessible trail. Continue along the accessible trail, leaving further adventures on the fabled Appalachian Trail for another day. Pass the remains of a gauging station on your right and follow the raised pathway away from the river. Although the white blazes are gone, the hard-packed, graded surface leaves no doubt about your route through the forest. You'll find partridgeberry on both sides of the trail, and an extensive stand of white pine to your left. Some of this portion of the trail was once a harness-racing track, which saw its last race in 1911. Photographs of the track

Village ½ mile to a stop sign. Turn left and then immediately right to pass under a railroad bridge. Take Water Street to your right; the hiker's lot (with an information kiosk) is on your left.

Follow the white-blazed Appalachian Trail across a field. You are now hiking "south" on the AT, which continues another 1,300 or so miles to Springer Mountain in Georgia. If you are out for a summertime walk, you may meet hikers who started their treks two or three months ago and still have a couple more months of hiking to go to reach Maine before the fall snows begin.

mounted along your route show no trees growing nearby at all. What a difference a century makes!

Stay on the path straight ahead at the junction with the short loop option and head back toward the river. At the next three-way junction, bear right to follow the AT back to Water Street where you started.

2

Great Pond

Location: Simsbury

Distance: 1½ miles

Vertical rise: negligible

Time: ¾ hour

Rating: D

Map: USGS 7.5-minute Tariffville

This hike circles a delightful little body of water paradoxically called Great Pond. You will appreciate short hikes such as this one best when you take them slowly. Adopt a silent, hesitative step to enhance your chances of surprising wildlife. Try being first out on a Sunday morning to increase your chances even more.

From the junction of CT 167 and CT 10/US 202 in Simsbury, follow CT 167 south 0.2 mile to the next traffic light at Firetown Road and turn right. Proceed down this road for 0.7 mile and then fork left onto Great Pond Road. The dirt entrance road to Great Pond State Forest is on your right in another 1.6 miles. After passing an outdoor chapel, frequently used for weddings, the road soon ends at a parking lot with a wooden trail map in a dense grove of white pines.

We owe the preservation of this 280-acre state forest to James L. Goodwin, the forester and conservationist who established a tree nursery here in 1932. Twenty-four years later the nursery was designated Connecticut Tree Farm Number One by the American Tree Farm Program. The land was subsequently bequeathed to Connecticut by Mr. Goodwin and dedicated as a state forest in 1967.

Many unmarked trails crisscross near the parking lot. This hike starts at the far right corner of the lot and continues in the same direction as the entrance road. The wide (it was an old tote road), well-worn, horseshoe-pocked trail at first goes along the edge of the thick white pine grove and then passes through it. This pine plantation is so dense that no new pines have sprouted despite the millions of seeds shed by opening cones. Instead, the main understory tree is the shade-tolerant hemlock. In early summer pink lady's slippers add color to the soft carpet of pine needles.

Turn right at the first four-way junction onto a woods road. The pond is visible through the trees. Turn left to follow the trail around the pond; keep the pond to your right. Following this rule of thumb, you may take an occasional dead end to the water's edge without getting lost—these inadvertent side trips permit you to admire the pond from many viewpoints. Cross an aging bridge over an arm of the pond and then follow a boardwalk through a marsh. You will pass a bull white pine 4 feet in diameter with enormous branches. The size of the branches indicates that the pine matured in a clearing, without any competition for sunlight.

Shallow Great Pond is strewn with lily pads and bordered with emergent vegetation and tree stumps gnawed by beavers. The moisture-loving royal fern stands on water-girt hummocks and even grows in shallow water. Dragonflies dance around and alight with their four wings outspread. Iridescent damselflies flap awkwardly and then perch with wings clasped together above a long, thin abdomen. From numerous spots around the pond you can see pine-dotted islands rising from the pond's northern end—we noted that many pines have died in the last few years, probably from drowned roots.

In fall especially, the fallen pine needles on these tote roads create interesting patterns. If it has been dry of late, a nice fluffy carpet of freshly fallen needles covers the road. If there have been heavy rains, the fallen needles outline the flow of the runoff

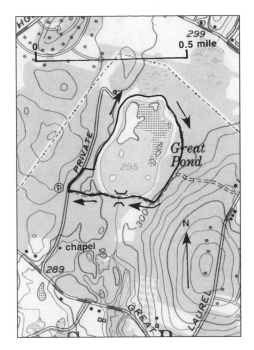

water. Where the water has pooled, an even layer of flattened needles tells the story.

Needles falling? But aren't pines evergreens? Yes, to both questions. A needle grows in the spring, stays on the tree the first winter—creating the evergreen effect—and is joined the next spring by a crop of fresh new needles. Finally, about a year and a half after emerging, the needles die and fall. If you walk through a pine grove in early October, every little puff of air causes the needles to drift downward.

As your path enters more swampy areas, watch for the tupelo (or black gum) tree. Found from Maine to northern Florida, it has an exceptionally wide range but is found growing naturally only in swampy areas. The tupelo has glossy, leathery leaves, slightly teardrop in shape, and deeply furrowed, crosshatched bark that somewhat resembles alligator skin. As the leaves change color in fall, this tree presents a deep burgundy red. A good-sized tree (1 or 2 feet in diameter, with

Great Pond through the trees

a record of 5 feet), the tupelo is unfit for most uses. It rots easily and its fibers are so intertwined that it is impossible to split. This tree is fairly common on the borders of the pond.

Just past a stand of great rhododendron—a native relative of our mountain laurel—and red pine, bear right at a woods road junction and continue around the pond. In July the evergreen rhododendrons boast impressive white flowers.

In this area we froze at the sight of a large doe feeding in a clearing. By moving only when she lowered her head to feed and freezing during her periodic surveillances, we came within 30 yards of her before our suspicious forms elicited a steady stare. Mosquitoes fed happily on our unmoving forms and finally forced us to push on. The highly visible flag of her upraised tail punctuated her instant flight.

At the next junction, turn right to cross a causeway offering views across the pond to the giant white pine stand and the red pine–rhododendron stand to its right. Pass an old beaver lodge on your right. Soon cross a bridge at the small cement dam on the south end of the pond. Notice the beaver lodge and evidence of activity just past the dam. We recently discovered small orange fungi growing on the abundant white pine branches on the forest floor, appropriately named witch's butter for an October visit! Shortly you come to another woods road to your left leaving the pond. Turn left and follow it uphill through the dense hemlock and pine grove to the parking lot.

3

Dinosaur State Park

Location: Rocky Hill

Distance: 1¼ miles

Vertical rise: negligible

Time: ¾ hour

Rating: D

Map: USGS 7.5-minute Hartford South

Located near the western edge of the Connecticut River, Dinosaur State Park provides a little oasis in an urban landscape–a small tract of land offering a quiet walk in the woods and, more important, a sanctuary for prehistoric footprints discovered in 1966 during excavations that were halted when officials realized what they had found. The Exhibit Center alone is worth a trip to the park, and a walk along Dinosaur's nature trail provides a welcome transition from the days of the dinosaurs back to the 21st century.

This site would have been just another large building in Rocky Hill if excavators hadn't noticed the tracks preserved in the shale and sandstone that had once been an ancient shoreline. Fortunately, Connecticut has its own dinosaur experts at Yale's Peabody Museum, and the trackway was rescued from development. Nearly two thousand dinosaur tracks are now preserved on site; some are on display in the Exhibit Center, while others have been covered again for future inspection. No one knows for certain what creatures made these tracks, but speculation focuses on small, birdlike ornithopods from the early Jurassic period. What was small then was still nearly 20 feet long! A walk through the center will reveal the trackway, truly a wonder to behold.

From I-91, take exit 23 and follow West Street east ½ mile to the park entrance on your right. The Exhibit Center is open Tuesday through Sunday year-round; pets are not allowed on the nature trails.

After a visit to the center, a walk through the grounds will take your mind off dinosaurs—although you may be distracted by what are now considered their close relatives, birds. You can thank your luck to live in an era when 20-foot birds don't exist, let alone get labeled "small." There are few places where humans have to look up the food chain, and Connecticut isn't one of them.

The trails begin just to the left of the center at an information building. You'll hike around a red maple swamp next to a traprock ridge. This small piece of the earth's surface represents 200 million years of landscape changes since the park's dinosaur tracks were made.

Pass the amphitheater to your left and follow the blue-blazed graded path to your right through the gardens, bearing right at the first gravel junction to proceed to the orchard. Pass under a four-stemmed red maple with shaggy bark. The multiple stems indicate that the tree sprouted from a cutover stump. The sprouts develop on the exterior living cambium of the tree stump and eventually grow to encompass the entire original stump, creating a multistemmed tree from a single stump. The shaggy bark, somewhat like a shagbark hickory, indicates maturity: Young red maples have smooth bark that grows shaggy over time. You can put any doubt as to the tree species to rest by an inspection of the leaf—three lobed with toothed edges—or by the early fall foliage display of bright red leaves.

Enter the woods by a bench, cross over a bridge, and pass through eastern redcedar into another field. This field features the mature apple trees of an orchard. Be careful inspecting the apple trees—poison ivy has taken advantage of the unkept orchard to reach upward to the ample sunlight here in the field. This obnoxious plant follows any of three different growth patterns: a low ground-covering plant, a shrub, and (most often) a climbing vine that frequently branches off a tree trunk to gather extra sunlight. It is this form that you should remain conscious of while wandering through the orchard.

You'll pass a bat shelter to your left. Bats are important friends in Connecticut forests—they spend their evenings consuming as many flying insects as they can. With our growing concern about diseases spread by mosquitoes, we should encourage as many mosquito-eating creatures as possible. The shelter provides a warm, safe place for bats to gather while they rest for another night's hunt.

Leave the orchard behind by crossing over a wooden walkway bordered by wetland tree species like spotted alder and red maple. The walkway takes you onto well-drained soils on a hillside on the property's southern edge. Pass through a stone wall and climb up into a forest of oak and black birch, beech and sugar maple, hickory and witch hazel. The view downhill to your left gives you a fine visual illustration of the overstory, or canopy, and the understory within the forest. The tall oaks and birches are the overstory species; the shrubs below constitute the understory, here obviously shade-tolerant species.

Black birch predominates here, with an occasional big 18- to 24-inch-diameter red oak tree. Native Americans used black birch sap as a sweetener, although it isn't nearly as sweet as sugar maple. Fresh twigs have a distinctive wintergreen flavor, identical to that of yellow birch. Don't waste your time tasting white birch twig—the "birch flavor" is limited to black and yellow birches.

You'll pass a shagbark hickory with a trail blaze on it. Compare its appearance to the mature red maple—the hickory's shagginess

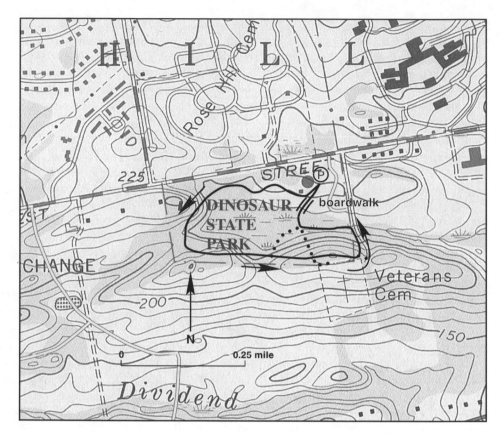

is very pronounced, almost feathery, with long strips of bark hanging off the tree's stem or trunk. Once you've made the connection you'll find yourself drawn to the distinctive appearance of this hickory. Along with oak, the shagbark hickory is a dominant tree in the southern hardwood forest that extends northward into Massachusetts and beyond, onto the southern slopes of northern New England. This contrasts with the northern hardwood forest—dominated by red maple, beech, and yellow birch—whose southernmost reach extends into Massachusetts and the northern slopes of Connecticut and New Jersey. Red maple is a common swamp tree in southern New England, however; hickories require well-drained soils.

Stay straight at a trail junction to follow the yellow-blazed trail along the hillside. A single white birch stands out in a forest of black birches. This white birch is probably a remnant from the successional forest that grew in what was once a field. Since white birch is not a long-lived tree, most of the early white birch stand is long gone, leaving one last survivor among the stand of black birches. Continue straight through a four-way junction descending slightly to a second junction. Here you turn left to follow yellow blazes back toward the swamp.

You'll find sugar maple seedlings—their distinctive five-lobed leaves have smooth edges, in contrast with the toothed edges of red maple leaves. At the junction with the red-blazed trail, bear left by the rootball of a large fallen oak. The falling of a great tree helps mix the soil. The mineral soils held by the large root system are pulled up and thus mixed with the organic soil layer on the surface, which consists of fallen leaves, twigs, and small creatures like worms and insects. This slow but inexorable process develops soils capable of supporting a variety of life-forms—forests, fields, pastures, dinosaurs, and squirrels!

You soon reach the junction with the blue trail; you have indeed reversed your direction and are headed back the way you started. Turn right to stay with the red-blazed trail leading to the boardwalk over the swamp. An early-fall visit is highlighted by the red maples and red foliage of Virginia creeper. This vine is different from the poison ivy you observed in the orchard. The leaves come in clusters of five leaflets; the vines themselves are smooth, not hairy like poison ivy's. If you see a hairy vine, leave it alone—even the bark of poison ivy can cause the characteristic rash.

The boardwalk leads you back to the gardens just outside the visitors center. Notice the odd conifer tree just to your right on your way to the parking lot. Like many of the exotic species planted on the park's grounds to represent species related to those found in the days of the dinosaurs, it's labeled. The dawn redwood, a native tree of China, is a close relative of our coast redwood and sequoia trees. The sidewalk between the Exhibit Center and the parking lot provides one last sense of geologic time with stages in the earth's development labeled from the beginning through the age of dinosaurs through the present day.

4

Mount Tom Tower

Location: *Morris*

Distance: *1.5 miles*

Vertical rise: *360 feet*

Time: *1 hour*

Rating: *C*

Map: *USGS 7.5-minute New Preston*

Though short, this is a rewarding half-day hike. By using the swimming and picnicking facilities, you can profitably spend the whole day here. The tree-topping tower on the crest of the mountain offers a full 360-degree view of the surrounding countryside.

Mount Tom State Park is located just off US 202 southwest of Litchfield, 0.6 mile east of its junction with CT 341. Watch for the state park sign by the access road (Old Town Road). Once inside the 233-acre park (a fee is charged on most summer days), follow the one-way signs to a junction with a sign that directs you to the Tower Trail, just before the main picnic area. Turn right and park here.

Take the yellow-blazed gravel road through a wooden gate and steadily up a gravel road (no vehicles allowed). Mountain laurel and red oaks predominate on this slope. In early spring you will see the white blossoms of the shadbush, or juneberry, so named because it flowers at about the time the shad run up the rivers. This shrub, with its light gray bark, is much less noticeable at other times of the year. The juicy berries that ripen in July are edible and taste not unlike huckleberries. Native Americans used to dry and compress them into great loaves, chunks of which were broken off over the winter for use as a sweetener.

Turn left at the top of the rise and follow the ridge toward the top of the mountain. In about ¾ mile the trail ends at the base of a circular stone tower more than 30 feet high. Wooden stairs inside lead you to a cement roof—watch your head as you emerge. This tower was built in 1921 to re-place the original wooden structure. You may see turkey buzzards soaring on Mount Tom's thermals.

Below is spring-fed Mount Tom Pond, with its bathhouses and trucked-in sand beaches. Beyond Mount Tom Pond to the northwest you see the Riga Plateau with, from left to right, Mounts Bear (see Hike 38), Race, and Everett; the latter pair of mountains are in Massachusetts. To the right of the plateau and beyond Bantam Lake, a popular boating and fishing spot, white church spires mark the historic town of Litchfield. Toward the southwest the rug-ged hills contain New York State's Harriman Park. On clear days, you can see Long Island Sound to the south with the outskirts of New York City at right.

To return by a different route, follow the yellow blazes back down, but at the first level (and frequently wet) spot turn right at the grassy area down a steep, rocky, yellow-blazed trail. Here, in late October, the ever-green mountain laurel provides a colorful contrast with the shades of rust displayed by the oaks and beech trees of the ridge. You should have no problem following the well-worn treadway.

Near the bottom, as you approach a gravel road, you pass a handsome stone chimney and fireplace with nearby cement foundations. This is all that remains ofCamp Sepunkum's assembly hall. The camp housed the Waterbury Boy Scouts, who helped with the development of the park be-tween 1916 and 1934. Follow the gravel road to your left until it turns left, and then take the path that branches to your right downhill. Log steps embedded in the slope reduce the erosion caused by the straight downhill route. Go left at the tar road and in about 0.1 mile you will see the marked Tower Trail that you started on.

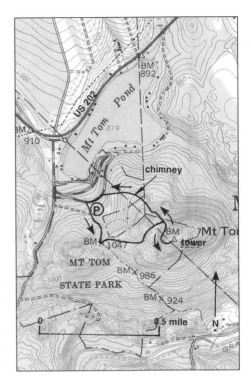

In mid-April we encountered our first blackflies of the season here. Three biting insects are dominant in Connecticut: black-flies, mosquitoes, and deerflies. Blackflies need well-oxygenated, flowing water to breed in, so their season is happily short here; they are a merciless scourge for much of the summer in northern New England. Only repellents that contain high percent-ages of DEET work against them. If the weather isn't too hot, long-sleeved shirts and trousers are often preferable to chemi-cal defenses. Mosquitoes breed in stag-nant water throughoutmost of the summer, but good herbal repellents work on them. In later spring deerflies arrive, hovering around your head and waiting for a chance to land and dig in. Fortunately they rarely occur in great numbers, so by paying atten-tion you can usually kill them as they alight and physically reduce your personal cloud

The view from Mount Tom Tower

of these pests, with great satisfaction.

As we stood by the car discussing the hike, a pileated woodpecker with red crest and white underwings flew overhead. This distinctive bird, as large as a crow, is the drummer that excavates great rectangular holes in unsound trees to reach infestations of carpenter ants.

5

Rocky Neck

Location: East Lyme

Distance: 3 miles

Vertical rise: 150 feet

Time: 1½ hours

Rating: D

Maps: USGS 7.5-minute Old Lyme, Niantic

Families sometimes have difficulty finding a place everyone will enjoy. The outdoor activities at Rocky Neck State Park are varied enough to provide something for everybody. Youngsters can fish off the jetty, teenagers can loll on the beach, and hikers can explore the practically deserted woodland paths.

The park entrance is located off CT 156, 2.7 miles west of CT 161 in Niantic. If you are traveling on the Connecticut Turnpike (I-95), take exit 72 (Rocky Neck) to CT 156 and follow the signs east (left) to the park. In addition to complete day-use facilities— beach, bathhouses, rest rooms, and picnic areas—the park has a separate camping area. The attractive sites scattered amid trees can be reserved in advance. In summer there is a weekend and holiday park entry fee. If you are going only to hike, you may choose to avoid this fee by parking on CT 156 about 0.5 mile west of the park entrance and starting this loop hike at the log gate there.

Within the park, drive into the first grassy parking area on your right, 1.6 miles from the entrance (where park maps are available), just beyond the bridge over Bride Brook. Head for the far northwest corner of the lot and the picnic tables, away from the beach; the trail starts at a red blaze on a post to the right of the outhouses.

The trail passes quickly through a fringe of oaks and maples to a short causeway leading across a marsh. While crossing the causeway and a small bridge, you are threatened by poison ivy, treated to the sight of large pink swamp roses, startled by

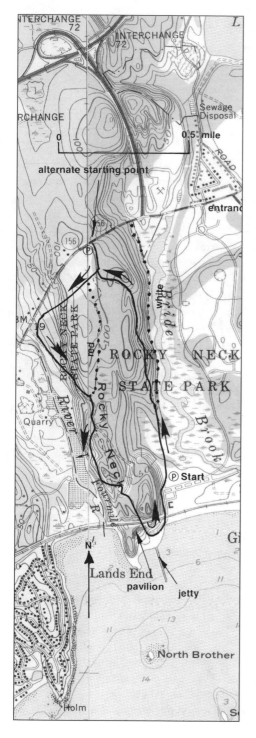

ducks you have inadvertently flushed, and delighted by gracefully circling terns.

As you enter the woods beyond the marsh, mountain laurel, sweet pepperbush, blueberry, huckleberry, greenbrier, and sassafras make up the bulk of the undergrowth. The shade of birch and oak provides relief from the summer sun. Occasional glacial erratics and rounded ledges complete this scene.

Cross a white-blazed trail that circles around the marsh behind you and leads to your right along Bride Brook. Gently climb the ridge above the brook and reach another junction about a mile from the start. Take a short detour straight ahead here. The path leads to a field where Japanese honeysuckle, with its highly perfumed yellow or white blossoms, lines the edge. Just beyond is the wooden gate at the parking lot on CT 156 and this hike's alternate starting point.

Return from the highway and turn right (this is a left if you chose not to take the detour) to follow red and blue blazes west. Bear to your right to continue on the blue-blazed trail where the red-blazed trail turns left, and then take a sharp left onto an old road to parallel the brackish Four Mile River. Cross Shipyard Field. A boatyard lying across the way reminds you of this hike's oceanside location. Follow the woods road over easy terrain, passing a junction with the red-blazed trail to your left.

Continue to the junction with the yellow-blazed trail near the top of the hill. Follow the yellow-blazed trail to your right and ascend a rocky ridge. Follow the ridge toward the ocean. Views of Four Mile River and the open bay await you from a vista called Tony's Nose, partially obscured at first by oak foliage. Clamshells litter the open ledges. Gulls drop clams from on high and then pick out the meat from the shattered shells.

Looking into Long Island Sound from the trail.

At the end of the open ridge the trail drops down to your left to meet a tar road. Proceed to your right through a small parking lot to the paved uphill walkway. Cross the arched bridge over railroad tracks to an imposing pavilion. A public works project of President Franklin Roosevelt's Works Progress Administration (WPA), the pavilion, completed in 1937, has given us more than full value! If the pavilion is open, it is well worth a visit. The walls of this massive building are made of fieldstone, and large fireplaces cheer the inside. The internal woodwork includes pillars made of great tree trunks; at least one trunk was taken from each then-existing state park.

Return to the arched bridge and descend the paved path toward the pavilion's rear garage. Pass through the stone archway under the pavilion and bear left toward the picnic area and the beach. A rocky fishing jetty thrusts into the water before you, and beyond it spreads the graceful curve of the beach. The rocky arms at either side of the bay provide shelter from all but the roughest storms. Turn left through the railroad underpass at the near corner of the beach. Swamp roses adorn the embankment here.

If you follow the road straight past the concession stands, you will find your car in the second parking lot on your right.

6

Larsen Sanctuary

Location: Fairfield

Distance: 3 miles

Vertical rise: 100 feet

Time: 1½ hours

Rating: D

Map: USGS 7.5-minute Westport

Save this walk for a lazy summer day. An oasis in the urban sprawl of Fairfield County, the Connecticut Audubon Society's Roy and Margot Larsen Sanctuary is small, and its 6.5-mile trail network traverses flat, undemanding terrain. While it lacks the rolling hills and sweeping vistas of many Connecticut trails, intriguing names like Cottontail Cutoff, Dirty Swamp Trail, and Old Farm Trail hint at the diverse habitats to be discovered. Because of the predominance of low, marshy land so attractive to birds, the sanctuary makes a particularly fine birding area.

To reach the sanctuary, take exit 44 in Fairfield off the Merritt Parkway (CT 15). If eastbound toward New Haven, at the end of the ramp immediately turn right (west). If westbound toward New York, at the end of the ramp go left, then left again to pass under the parkway, and immediately turn right. Either way, you are on Congress Street, which you follow for 1.2 miles to Burr Street. Turn right and drive 1.1 miles to the sanctuary entrance on your left. A small fee is charged to enter the sanctuary. There is no charge, however, for Fairfield residents or members of the Connecticut Audubon Society. Pets are not allowed in the sanctuary.

A large, gray, contemporary building houses the nature center, which, in addition to the bookstore and exhibit areas, has a large auditorium and library. Both the studious nature lover and the casual browser can spend many a worthwhile hour here. The nature center is closed on Sunday and Monday, but you may still hike the trails.

You approach the trail system through a

small, sheltered gateway to the right of the nature center. Pick up a trail map on the way through. From the multitude of loop opportunities, you'll follow a route that hits several points of interest. Although it was early March when we first explored this sanctuary, it was alive with birds. A trio of ducks flew overhead, and several other species sang from the trees and underbrush. We heard the distinctive flutter and owl-like coo of the mourning dove and the cheerful (though far from melodious) chatter of that faithful harbinger of spring, the red-winged blackbird.

Follow the trail, strewn with wood chips, to your left through scattered overgrown apple trees past their original Trail for the Disabled to your right. Mountain laurel and rhododendron flank that trail, while a pair of open fences guide the way.

Pass the Garden Marsh Trail and turn right onto the Edna Strube Chiboucas Special Use Trail, which is a 1-mile handicapped-accessible trail for wheelchairs prepared with compacted stone dust. Cross a bridge, pass Garden Marsh Pond to your left, and bear right at the fork onto Old Farm Trail. As you pass the pond, almost hidden on your left, note the wood duck nesting boxes set on poles above the water. Sweet-scented honeysuckle vines festoon many trees along the marshy pond's edge, and the heavy growth of sharp, spiny greenbrier vines guards both sides of the trail.

Shortly you pass through a little clearing. Here a trailing vine of the blackberry family, the dewberry, winds around the tall grasses. Its rather sour, edible, black berries can be refreshing on a hot, humid day. You also pass some fenced-in hackberry trees, planted for birds and butterflies. The fence keeps the growing deer population from eating the trees' twigs and buds before they grow out of reach.

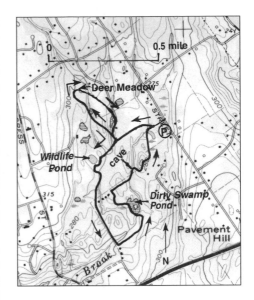

Continue on the Old Farm Trail past the Azalea Trail (left), and bear right onto the Wildlife Pond Trail (right). Right after crossing a large bridge across Sasco Creek, leave the Special Use Trail and turn right onto the Deer Meadow Trail to continue toward Deer Meadow. Continue on this woodland path past Black Pond and follow bog bridges uphill to the meadow, which is maintained by annual mowing. The meadow lived up to its name early one October morning when we saw eight white-tailed deer at once! At the top of the meadow is a raised observation deck. Follow the path through the meadow and reenter the woods by a bench. More bog bridges lead you once again past Black Pond to complete your loop. If the trail beyond the tower is difficult to follow, just turn around and retrace your steps to the Wildlife Pond Trail.

Return to the Special Use Trail, turn right onto the Wildlife Pond Trail, and proceed to Wildlife Pond. Again, interpretive signs inform you about the pond's abundant plant and animal life. Leave the Special Use Trail again and turn left onto the

Early colors in Larsen Sanctuary

Trillium Trail to follow a boardwalk along the western edge of Pin Oak Swamp. This not only keeps your feet dry, but also protects the trail. Were it not so elevated, the thousands of tramping feet would make a quagmire of the trail. Future users would then edge to one side or the other to avoid the swampy mess, widening it further. Cross the Pin Oak Swamp/Special Use Trail and continue away from the swamp on the Trillium Trail.

Bear left onto Country Lane, an old woods road. Continue past Chipmunk Run and cross a gas pipeline clearing along the old road, flanked on both sides by stone walls. In earlier days, the stone fences on either side separated farmers' fields from the roadway, limiting the wandering of their farm animals. A route flanked on both sides by stone walls is almost surely a town road. Originally, the farmers erected wooden fences. Wood eventually became scarce,

however, and was more useful for buildings and fires for heating and cooking, so the farmers piled the ever-plentiful stones from their fields along the fences. Eventually the wooden fences rotted away, leaving the stone fences in their place. Recently we found a box turtle on Country Lane. This slow but sturdy fellow retreated into his shell and waited for us to leave him alone. Box turtles are New England's tortoises, and are usually found far from waterways we usually associate with turtles.

Pass the southern loop of the West Woods Trail to your right, cross over a brook on a bridge, and turn left onto the Dirty Swamp Trail. This trail can be somewhat difficult to follow, but it parallels the brook upstream to Dirty Swamp Pond. At the shore of the pond, you may choose to spend a little time at a park bench before proceeding to your left over the earthen dam. From the dam, follow the Dirty Swamp

Trail north back across the pipeline to Chipmunk Run, another significant woods road.

Turn right. A short distance past the end of the Old Farm Trail (left), the trail forks at the top of a small rise. The Azalea Trail goes to your left; stay to your right on Chipmunk Run. Follow a path down to the stream.

Just before crossing the brook below Wood Pond on a substantial wooden bridge, take a brief detour to your left and explore the cavelike rock ledge above. Little children love this sort of place. Cross the bridge and immediately go to your right onto the Rock Ledge Trail (the Streamside Trail goes left). Bear left at the top of the rise and follow the twists and turns of the Rock Ledge Trail. Shortly after the two paths rejoin, you reach the Special Use Trail and Farm Pond, which has large numbers of tame mallard ducks and Canada geese. All have malformed wings or other problems that keep them from flying.

At the junction, go right and continue past the Garden Marsh Trail (left) to the entrance. Before leaving the sanctuary, visit the compound for injured animals behind the center. Here, with a special permit from the state, the Connecticut Audubon Society treats more than five hundred injured animals each year. Most are eventually returned to the wild.

7

Highland Springs and Lookout Mountain

Location: Manchester

Distance: 2.5 miles

Vertical rise: 350 feet

Time: 1½ hours

Rating: C

Map: USGS 7.5-minute Rockville

Once billed as the "Purest and Best Table Water in the World," bottled mineral water from the springs at Highland Park was distributed throughout southern New England and as far away as New Jersey. However, while the water-bottling business is now flourishing as it did in the 19th century, this particular spring has been sealed off. The pollution that closed it may have come from the numerous housing developments that have cropped up in the area in recent years.

This loop hike begins at the Highland Springs parking lot. From eastbound I-384 in Manchester, take exit 4, Highland Street. From the end of the exit ramp, go right onto Spring Street about 0.2 mile to the small parking lot at the bottom of the hill on your left. From westbound I-384, take exit 4 and go right at the end of the exit ramp to the traffic light. Turn right onto Spring Street, cross over the highway, and proceed as above. The town bought this area under the now defunct Open Space Program.

Before starting out, look for the large, piebald sycamore standing near the trailhead. The mottled effect results from the tree's normal growth; while the bark of most growing trees splits into vertical furrows as new wood forms just inside, the sycamore's thin bark periodically breaks off in plates, leaving a clean white surface that contrasts markedly with the older, darker bark.

From the parking lot, follow the gated, white-blazed carriage road uphill to Lookout Mountain, keeping the chain-link fence on your left. This part of the hike was once

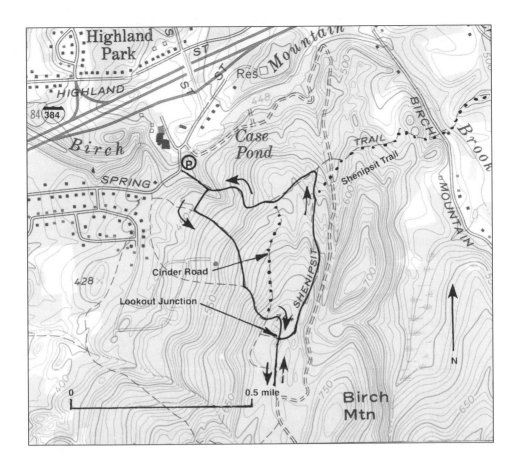

notable for the majestic hemlock grove to the left of the carriage road, which was salvage-logged after succumbing to the woolly adelgid. Soon the road becomes a wide gravel path. Turn right into the woods on the pink-blazed Highland Trail just above the last house to your right. Shortly you reach a fork in the trail; take the pink-blazed, eroded trail to your left and follow it up the hill.

Near the top of the rise bear right onto the pink-blazed trail at a junction with an orange-blazed trail. Your route levels out and then climbs gently, and about ¾ mile from your starting point you reach the gravel carriage road. Follow this to your right; it leads directly to the lookout. The few remaining young hemlocks thin out until they are almost wholly replaced with oak and a scattering of maple, hickory, and black birch. The soil here may look the same to us, but the thirsty roots of the hemlock know the difference.

Shortly you come to a trail crossing at the summit of Lookout Mountain (744 feet), known as Lookout Junction. The view from the lookout depends upon the visibility; too often, especially in summer, Connecticut Valley smog reduces your horizon. A recent winter visit with crisp, cold air afforded a clear view of Manchester in the foreground, but because of its well-treed streets, this city of 65,000 was hard to see. Only the broad, flat-roofed box of the high school and the white spire of Center Congregational Church were readily identifiable. In the middle distance the towers and high-rise office buildings of Hartford stood out. On the clearest of days you can see the white finger of the Heublein Tower rising from Talcott Mountain (see Hike 45) northwest of Hartford.

Today you will follow the pink blazes at the junction only a short distance to your right past a screen of laurel to a 30-foot hemlock on your right. Look to your left—there is a mysterious clearing where only sedges and mosses grow. Surrounding the opening are numerous highbush blueberry plants that are heavily laden in season. Unfortunately, these berries, though beautiful, are extremely sour—perhaps because of very acidic soil. No woody plants grow within the opening; it is possible that the annual spring snowmelt flooding kills them. Such vernal pools provide spring breeding habitat for a host of amphibians and insects.

Retrace your steps to the junction and proceed to your right to follow the yellow-blazed trail relocation that leads to the Shenipsit Trail. Soon you reach its junction with the blue-blazed Shenipsit Trail. To your right it leads to Gay City State Park (see Hike 18) some 6 miles to the south. Bear left to follow the Shenipsit Trail north along a ledge below the summit and walk along the top of a ridge above an old stone quarry. To your right the land drops off quickly in stepped ledges to a flat forest floor. On your left lies a long, narrow depression, which snowmelt floods each spring. This is another vernal pool, a spring breeding ground for the wood frog.

These black-masked, tan-colored frogs are the earliest spring breeders of our native amphibians. Although probably more numerous than the familiar spring peepers, they lack the high-pitched carrying cry of the latter and therefore are not as well known. You often hear their low croaks in this area as early as the fourth week of March. The tadpoles, though safe from most predators, must go through their metamorphosis and become small frogs quickly, since the depression is dry by early summer.

The thin, poor soil along the exposed ledges of the ridge dries out quickly and is largely treed with chestnut oaks, which are more tolerant of these conditions than the moisture-dependent hemlocks. With their deeply furrowed, dark gray bark, these oaks are distinctive at any season. The trail now slopes down toward the flat forest floor. After bearing right downhill, go to your left near the end of the ridge.

The young hemlocks are thick about the trail again—a legacy of the moisture from Highland Springs on the other side of the hill. Watch for the turn where the blue-blazed trail bears right downhill. At this point continue straight ahead on the red-blazed path through mountain laurel. Watch carefully for a junction with a white-blazed trail and follow it uphill to your left.

The blazes lead to a rusted, open-mesh fence near the top of the rise. To your right you'll pass a lightning-riven hemlock. Notice the healed scar slashing down one side of the tree. The extreme temperature induced by the lightning vaporized the tree's sap, causing the wood to explode.

Although there are few blazes here, continue along and bear right onto the old trail that leads to an old tote road. Follow it to rejoin the carriage road you started up on. Go right, downhill, to your car.

8

Wadsworth Falls

Location: Middlefield

Distance: 3 miles

Vertical rise: 200 feet

Time: 1¾ hours

Rating: CD

Map: USGS 7.5-minute Middletown

Moving water holds a special fascination for humanity that is rivaled only by the flickering of fire. The ebb and flow of ocean waves mesmerizes us, boiling rapids and cascades captivate our attention, and waterfalls enchant us wherever they occur. This hike features not one but two of these liquid attractions. Best viewed during spring's heavy runoff, the larger of the pair is worth a visit at any season.

From the junction of CT 66 and CT 157 in Middletown, take CT 157 southwest, following signs to Wadsworth State Park. You will reach the park entrance on your left in 1.6 miles. Since this park has swimming, there is a fee to park here on summer days. In addition to swimming, the park features bathhouses, picnic tables, fireplaces, and hiking trails.

The Rockfall Corporation gave Wadsworth Falls State Park to the state in 1942. The will of Colonel Clarence Wadsworth, a noted linguist and scholar, established this nonprofit group.

A nice routed map of the park's trails has been set up just beyond the entrance. From this spot, pass through the picnic grove to the main trail, which begins by a culverted stream; this trail is blazed with orange paint.

Immediately after crossing a bridge over a small stream that splashes down a series of ledges, the trail forks. Bear right. Cedar, maple, birch, and poplar form the woods backdrop, while sweet fern, yarrow, blackberry, and a large patch of poison ivy line the path. On your left the trail passes one of the largest mountain laurels in the state.

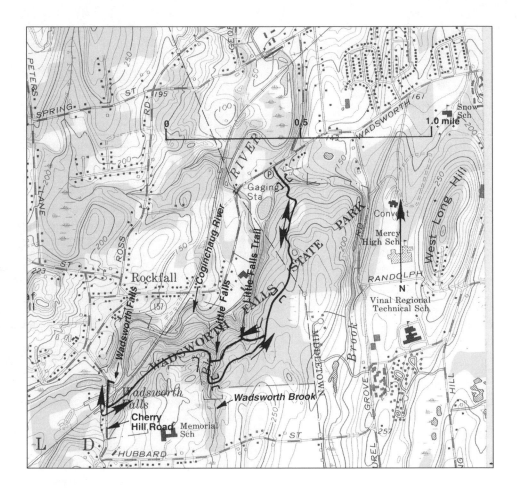

A short distance farther on you come to a second small stream. The stone bridge here is supported by sidewalls of masonry cloaked in mosses and lichens. It is said that Colonel Wadsworth himself used the bridge, and two dates are etched in the rock, 1910 and 1945. Here the woods are composed of tall straight hickory, oak, black birch, and hemlock. Red squirrels chatter loudly from safe perches far above the trail. Every so often, unmarked side trails leave the well-worn main path, inviting exploration.

In ½ mile, when the trail splits, turn right onto the blue-blazed fork toward Little Falls (you will return by the left path). Follow the blue blazes downhill as you wind through beautiful treed ravines and eventually parallel the small stream that glides over the mossy ledges. About ¾ mile from the start you reach Little Falls. Cross Wadsworth Brook below the falls and climb the steep hill on your right. Be careful, because this compacted soil can be slippery when wet. On the hilltop there is a falls overlook to your left.

When you have finished admiring the falls, return to the side trail, which continues to the nearby wide, worn main trail. Turn right. Less than ¼ mile from the falls

Anglers at Wadsworth Falls

and about 1 mile from the start, railroad tracks and power lines appear below on your right. In another ½ mile you'll reach the paved Cherry Hill Road.

Turn right to cross the railroad tracks. A short walk along the tracks in summer will reveal the blue bells of the creeping bell-flower, and in season black raspberries tickle the palate. Great banks of multiflora roses and a few striking Deptford pinks will attract your attention.

Continuing on Cherry Hill Road, cross a new bridge over the Coginchaug River and an old sluiceway. The river provided water-power to drive a textile mill by the falls. Nearby industries included a 19th-century pistol factory and a gunpowder factory that

operated for nearly one hundred years before blowing up in 1892.

On the far side of the bridge, cross a field beyond an established parking lot to your right, and descend a path to your left, which takes you to the river at the base of Wadsworth Falls. You may have to share this spot with anglers trying to entice the elusive brown trout. A fenced-in overlook provides yet another view.

To finish this hike, retrace your steps on Cherry Hill Road and the orange-blazed trail, passing the blue-blazed trail to your left to Little Falls before and after crossing a plank bridge over Wadsworth Brook. Continue along the orange-blazed trail over the stone bridge back to the parking lot.

Wadsworth Falls

9

Audubon Center in Greenwich

Location: Greenwich

Distance: 3 miles

Vertical rise: 300 feet

Time: 1¾ hours

Rating: CD

Map: USGS 7.5-minute Glenville

Mention Greenwich, and you may invoke visions of high-walled estates surrounded by dense urban areas and ribbons of concrete. Long ago, urban New York City engulfed this southwest corner of Connecticut. A visit to this 280-acre sanctuary, established in 1941, is a pleasant surprise; its woodland beauty compares favorably with that of many wilder, less accessible areas of the state. Rolling hills, large hardwoods on rich bottomland soil, swamps, a small river, and a pond attract many kinds of birds, as well as hikers.

To reach the sanctuary, take exit 28 off the Merritt Parkway (CT 15) and turn north (right) onto Round Hill Road. After 1.5 miles turn left onto John Street. Drive for 1.4 miles to Riversville Road; the Audubon Center entrance and parking lot are on your right at the intersection. In addition to maintaining a network of hiking trails, the center, which is open Tuesday through Sunday 9 AM–5 PM, operates an excellent bookstore, an interpretive center with seasonal exhibits, and a variety of natural history programs and demonstrations on weekends. All are worth the nominal entrance fee. There is no charge for National Audubon Society members.

Before you begin walking, pick up a map of the trail system at the center. There are no painted blazes here to help you, but there are signs at all the trail junctions. As you can see from the map, there are many trails to explore here—we describe one loop—and you may want to try some or all of the others.

Starting by a large routed wooden sign

showing the trail system in contrasting colors on the outside wall of the interpretive building, follow the paved trail to your left downhill, through an orchard dotted with birdhouses. After passing the Discovery Trail, continue on the now mulched path, passing a wooden fence and a bench to a row of apple trees to your right, near the second junction with the Discovery Trail. You'll find an apple tree with several rows of evenly spaced holes in the bark. These holes are the work of a provident woodpecker with the unglamorous name of yellow-bellied sapsucker. It drills the neat rows one day and returns on succeeding days to drink the sap that has welled up in the holes and to feast on insects attracted by, and stuck in, the sap. After examining this tree, return a few yards and turn left at that first junction with the Discovery Trail.

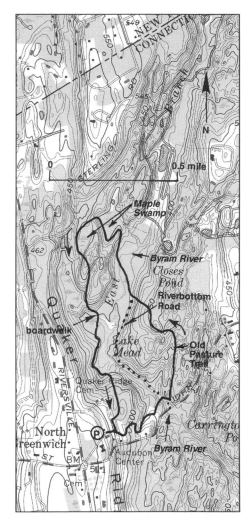

Cross a bridge with handrails and walk along the left side of Indian Spring Pond, following signs to the Old Pasture Trail. You'll soon pass an old stone-and-mortar springhouse. In a short distance the trail becomes surrounded by thick undergrowth, especially blackberry canes with their formidable thorns. The trail tends downhill. Level log steps partially embedded in and perpendicular to the trail retard the erosion that running water causes as it courses down a trail. Without the steps, this well-traveled path would rapidly erode. The wood chips that you find elsewhere on the trail are meant not to ease your way but to protect the trail.

Two giant tulip trees serve as your introduction to the great trees of the preserve. Most of this sanctuary, with its large, mature trees, is made up of rich bottomland hardwoods—beech, ash, tulip tree, oak, and maple. The woods are left to their own natural growth and eventual decay. Dying trees and fallen branches are left to rot where they fall, recycling their nutrients into the surrounding soil and contributing to the diversity of life in the sanctuary.

Turn right onto the Clovis Trail. Follow this trail to the small stream draining Indian Spring Pond, turning sharply left just before leaving the woods and eventually crossing the stream before going downhill to the Byram River. Cross the river as well; you soon reach an old woods road, Riverbottom Road, and turn right. Soon bear left onto the Old Pasture Trail and follow this old woods road past ponds and rock outcroppings. A holly tree, with its evergreen leaves, was very conspicuous on a gray day in February in the leafless hardwood forest. You'll pass through old pastures where evergreen eastern red cedars and various briars thrive in the sunlight. The red cedars' bark appeared gnawed by some hungry animal.

While traversing these trails in well-heeled suburbia, you may ponder the value of the land in this 280-acre oasis. Perhaps think in terms of the Crown Jewels of England. The value of their individual gems and precious metals is far less than their worth as a whole. So it is with this rare oasis—its value, if broken up and sold as lots, would be far less than its value to the present and future generations who will explore these woods.

Descend the hillside to Riverbottom Road. Its overgrown condition, a surprising development in recent years, is another example of nature absorbing our impact on the landscape. One of the conspicuous plants is greenbrier. The stem of this thorny vine is green year-round; its tangled masses are particularly distinctive during the leafless months. Turn right and follow the old road to cross the Byram River upstream of Mead Lake on a bridge.

The muddy floodplain on the far side of the river is liberally dotted with skunk cabbage, a rather unattractive and malodorous plant that blossoms very early in spring. Its shape and smell are specially adapted to attract the only insects available for pollination this early—carrion flies that search out the carcasses of animals that died the previous winter. Attracted by the dark reddish color of the hoodlike spathe and its fetid odor, the flies mistake the skunk cabbage flower for a dead animal. In the process of investigating, the flies pollinate the tiny flowers inside the spathe.

After crossing the river, follow the trail up the slope through a large grove of beech trees. Riverbottom Road terminates at the top of this rise. Proceed to your left on the Hemlock Trail. This route is neither blazed nor well worn, so be careful following it. Be particularly alert near the top of the ridge, because the trail zigzags sharply to your left. The Hemlock Trail skirts part of Maple Swamp on your right, then rises sharply to its junction with the Maple Swamp Loop. Turn right to circle more of the swamp to your left.

The Maple Swamp Loop climbs steadily to the Beech Hill Trail—bear left here. This trail ascends to the ridge and then drops gradually and merges with Dogwood Lane, which you also follow to your left toward Mead Lake. You pass more large beeches here. Unfortunately, defacing initials carved on the smooth, tender bark can still be deciphered after the passage of many years.

At a fork turn left. You are now on the Lake Trail. Soon a right turn takes you out onto a boardwalk built in 1977. The numbers and variety of plant species growing in this swampy area are truly amazing. Pass poison sumacs to your right along the boardwalk—its compound leaves are some of the first to turn color in early autumn. Soon you reach the west side of Mead Lake. Elaborate bird blinds hug the far shore. Turn left beyond the boardwalk and continue on the Lake Trail to its junction, just before the dam, with the Discovery Trail leading to the center. Stay on the Lake Trail for a short distance to your left to visit the dam, rebuilt in 1998. Early-fall views across the pond highlight the foliage surrounding you. Return to the Discovery Trail and follow it back to the center.

Climb out of the hollow, passing an old root cellar in the apple orchard on your right. You may have noticed a straggly vine

The view from Lake Mead's dam.

clinging to many trees and shrubs along the path. This vine, the Asiatic or Oriental bittersweet, depends on its coiling ability to work skyward, unlike poison ivy and Virginia creeper, which hold themselves up with the aid of aerial roots. Because its coils do not yield to tree growth, the host tree tries to grow around the vine, which cuts deep spiral ridges in its trunk, often girdling–and killing–the tree. This alien is considered a pest in the sanctuary. Bear right beyond Indian Spring Pond and ascend the paved walk back to your car.

10

Hurd State Park

Location: East Hampton

Distance: 3½ miles

Vertical rise: 600 feet

Time: 2 hours

Rating: C

Map: USGS 7.5-minute Middle Haddam

Serendipity. It's a lovely-sounding word with a beautiful meaning: "the faculty of making fortunate and unexpected discoveries by accident." Perhaps the most important example of serendipity was Sir Alexander Fleming's discovery of penicillin while investigating the noxious green mold that was killing his bacterial cultures. For a hiker, *serendipity* should be a familiar byword. In this book we point out what we have seen, but you should always be prepared for serendipitous happenings. Remember that "adventure is not in the guidebook and beauty is not on the map."

With this thought in mind, pay a visit to Hurd State Park, perched atop the east bank of the Connecticut River. From the junction of CT 151 and CT 66 in Cobalt, drive south on CT 151 for 2.4 miles to a traffic light at a four-way junction. The road to your right leads to the park entrance. Park in the lot to the right of this road at the junction. This cross-country skiers' lot, with a large routed wooden sign showing the trails of the park, will be your starting point.

As we entered the park on a recent visit, we saw a bluebird, the first we'd spotted in a few years. Bluebirds are the same shade as the most breathtaking patch of sky you've ever seen. Unfortunately, their numbers have dropped because of competition from a pair of drab aliens—the English sparrow and the starling. A few people are trying to redress the imbalance by constructing bluebird trails with series of specially built birdhouses along forest margins. With luck and the effort of these dedicated

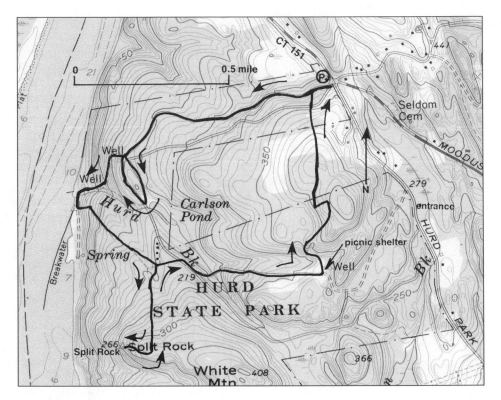

people, this rare bird might once again become common.

Pass the yellow metal gate and follow the right-hand road through the woods. The macadam surface is slowly breaking up after years of disuse. You'll soon pass a trail to your left; stay on the road and gently descend, following occasional green paint blazes. The hemlocks along this road look very unhealthy, and many have died, victims of the hemlock looper and the hemlock woolly adelgid. These pests feed on hemlock needles and twigs, respectively, and southern Connecticut hemlock stands, particularly along the Connecticut River, are the most noticeably affected. Salvage-logging began in 2000 to remove some of the trees; we hope new ones are planted in their place to reduce the soil erosion that could result from the loss of these stands.

Follow the road to the paved circular loop road and another routed trail map. Take a side trip to your left, following the road to the dam by picturesque Carlson Pond, and inspect the 60-year-old stonework left behind by the Civilian Conservation Corps. A small quarrying operation left a cleft in a ledge along the road. Circle back to the trail sign, pass the yellow gate, and descend to your right on the red-blazed River Trail. Follow the road down the steep hillside treed with black birches, beeches, tulip trees, and more unhealthy hemlocks.

Emerge at the bottom of the descent into the clearing along the Connecticut River. Follow the river downstream to your left. This grassy area is used mostly by boaters plying the river. Across the river to the right is the United Technologies jet engine facility. In addition to private craft, tugs pushing rusty barges

The Connecticut River from Split Rock

occasionally chug by. Spend a while exploring the riverside. Wandering off to the right, we saw two young black ducks in a quiet spot. The trees here are different from those on the surrounding hillsides: sycamores, dying elms, tall sassafras, cottonwoods, silver maples, and willows form this canopy. Podded milkweeds fringe the open areas, which are covered with coarse grass that glistens with dew on clear summer mornings. Across the river to your left is Bear Hill (see Hike 44). Only power lines (progress) mar this view of the hills along the river. Retrace your steps and continue left along the riverbank, crossing the small stream over a stone slab.

After enjoying the riverside, climb the red-blazed trail to your left away from the river. Before reaching the paved park road, you'll turn right at a three-way trail junction. Gently climb along the hillside, following the yellow blazes. At the top of your climb, turn right at a T-junction to Split Rock. Head downhill past a great white glacial boulder. Continue downhill to Split Rock, a ledge bearing a narrow crevasse 25 feet deep. The U.S. Geological Survey benchmark confirms your location on the map at elevation 266 feet. This is a fine, sunny spot for lunch, with a good view of the Connecticut River 200 feet below.

After the respite, retrace your steps and climb back uphill, parallel to the ledge. Rejoin the trail and retrace your steps to the junction near the paved park road. Walking along this trail early one morning, we froze at a movement farther down the trail. A spotted fawn tottered to an uncertain stop, eyed us a bit, snorted to absorb our smell better, and—deciding that we were dubious characters—bounded away down the trail. Serendipity!

At the junction, turn right and follow the woods road to the paved road. Bear right and follow this road toward the park entrance. Shortly you'll see a gated road to your left. Take this road down to a stream crossing and then ascend on deteriorating macadam, following sporadic yellow blazes to the picnic area. Pass to the left of a large picnic shelter and follow the stone wall beyond it. Turn left toward an impressive white oak with great, gnarled, extended branches. This is a perfect example of white oak growth in an open field, complete with said field! Many hikes in Connecticut pass similar trees growing in the forest. These trees matured in open fields, and the forest has grown around them. Foresters know these trees as "wolf" trees. A white oak growing with other trees around it will grow straight and tall. To compete for sunlight, it will channel all its energy into growing tall, rather than broad.

Passing the white oak, take the leftmost, faded-red-blazed trail, and follow a woods road past some intriguing stone ravines. A close inspection reveals a series of these ravines that must have been carved from the hillside. What these quarries yielded is open to speculation. The rock walls seem to have a fair amount of mica in them, so mica, used for early lanterns, might have been the miners' goal.

Bear right beyond the quarries to climb uphill, following red and orange blazes. You cross many stone walls while ascending the hill, which is covered with young hardwood trees sprinkled with occasional evergreen eastern red cedars. Pass just west of the hilltop and descend gently to cross through more old fields with abundant briars. Cross a woods road and soon reach a T-junction with another woods road. This is the road you started your hike on. Turn right to return to your car.

11

Sunny Valley

Location: Bridgewater

Distance: 3 miles

Vertical rise: 700 feet

Time: 2 hours

Rating: C

Map: USGS 7.5-minute New Milford

A hike can be far more than just a bit of exercise in the woods or a chance to chin with a variety of like-minded folks. The woods are a wonderland where your depth of understanding can have no limit. The trees, the low-slung plants, the animals of chance encounter, the geologic clues, and our impact on the landscape are all there for us to see. The nicest thing about reading from nature is that, for the ever-curious amateur naturalist, there are no tests, no one to satisfy—except you! Some things are seasonal, some are around for decades, some date to colonial times, and still others go back to the Ice Age and beyond. An encyclopedia would be needed to detail each hike you take, especially if you take the time to look closely and return each season. We will touch briefly in this hike description on three of these categories of wonder—the Ice Age, trees, and traces left by the original colonists.

The Nature Conservancy's Sunny Valley Preserve provides trails as one facet of its multiple-use land management plan. The preserve's properties encompass nearly 1,500 acres; trails are maintained on about 480 acres, with more than 1,000 acres managed as natural areas, woodlands, and farmlands.

From the junction of CT 67 and 133 in Bridgewater, go south on CT 133 about 0.7 mile, then turn right at a stop sign to follow Hat Shop Hill Road. After 0.6 mile, turn left onto Christian Street, then right onto Hemlock Road, which you follow for 1.7 miles to the gated Stony Brook Farm entrance. Park on your left just before the gate, where there is room for three cars.

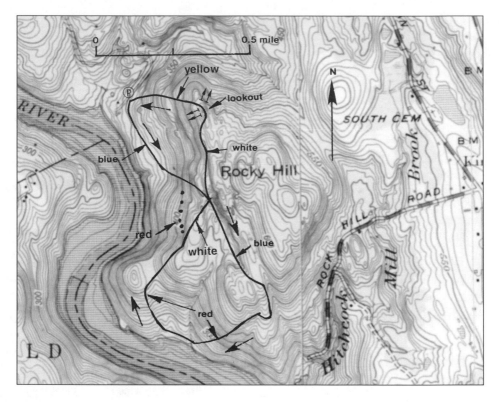

Follow the Silica Mine Trail, which proceeds south, uphill, from the parking area. Climb the gently graded woods road, following blue blazes. Shortly your path levels and proceeds along an old tote road before climbing again. Gradually the grade steepens before reaching a white-blazed trail on your left. This is the trail to the Lookout, which will be part of your return route. Continue along the blue-blazed trail, passing numerous chips of quartz from the nearby silica mines along the path. You'll soon pass an old stone foundation to your left and descend through hemlocks. Cross a small swamp over puncheon bridging made of local logs and pass over a small ridge. Pass another swamp to your left and then follow a ridge with a deep ravine to your left.

The glaciers that covered our area more than ten thousand years ago left many traces. There are thousands of these geologic reminders in Connecticut—glacial erratics, old kettle holes, and dying ponds. The swamp, once a long narrow pond here on the side of the mountain, is such a remnant. The ice sheet gouged this depression in the ledge, the bottom of which is relatively impervious to water. The natural demise of all ponds comes sooner or later, depending on their original depth. Aquatic vegetative growth and wind- and water-borne debris have all contributed to the filling in of the pond. The scum on its surface and the trail wending through its former outlet are signs of its return to dry land.

As you begin to descend toward Lake Lillinonah, you'll reach a junction. Take the red-blazed trail to your right through a clearing. Follow this trail up through a little ravine and then down an old tote road to Lake

Looking west from the Lookout

Lillinonah below. Turn right at the river and cross a small brook. We spotted a mink at the edge of the brook on a recent hike here! Climb away from the water's edge over a stone wall and parallel the shoreline northward. You'll turn right and ascend a series of ridges through thick hemlock woods.

Hemlock forests tell an interesting story. Look beneath this dense stand of hemlocks. The thick, acid bed of fallen needles and twigs and the tightly interwoven, light-intercepting foliage have banished all other plants from the forest floor, until only young hemlocks can grow. Connecticut's climax forest will then be maintained until fire, ax, or disease (see Hike 10, Hurd State Park) allows another cycle to start.

Just as the ascent eases, turn right onto a white-blazed trail to climb again to the crest of a ridge, where you'll descend briefly to a woods road, which is the blue-blazed trail you started on. Across from you are the old silica (quartz) mines that the colonists carved in the hillside. These abandoned silica mines are indicative of the lack of mineral wealth in New England. When our state was first settled, dreams of mineral wealth led to much part-time prospecting in Connecticut. Limited amounts of cobalt, iron ore, garnets, silica, and even traces of gold lured these early prospectors. Most of the holes they dug have since filled in. In a few places some small successes caused larger diggings, where activity faded after the discovery of richer lodes elsewhere. This silica mine is a case in point. Like other local mines, it's just a relic from the past to stimulate our curiosity.

Bear left and soon arrive at the junction with the white-blazed trail now leaving to your right to the Lookout. Follow it and climb steadily but gradually past large stone slabs to the Lookout just to the left of the trail, with good views to the west.

As you leave the Lookout, go to your left downhill steeply on the yellow-blazed trail through mountain laurel and oak. Soon you come to an old woods road, which you follow left, continuing on the yellow-blazed trail through another hemlock forest. When you reach the paved road, bear left to return to your car.

12

Bluff Point

Location: Groton

Distance: 4.5 miles

Vertical rise: 100 feet

Time: 2¼ hours

Rating: D

Map: USGS 7.5-minute New London

A combination of historical circumstances and heavy demand for shoreline property has kept most of Connecticut's short coastline inaccessible to the public. One of the very few state parks on this shore, Bluff Point State Park's undeveloped 800-plus-acre peninsula is a special place for the walker. The only such sizable acreage on the Connecticut coast, Bluff Point is free of concessions, cottages, and campsites.

There are signs to direct you to Bluff Point. From the intersection of CT 117 and US 1 in Groton, drive west for 0.3 mile on US 1 to Depot Road. Turn left, following this street past Industrial Road and under the railroad tracks (where the paved surface ends) until you reach a large parking lot and closed gate about 0.7 mile from US 1. You know that you have arrived when you spy a sign listing park regulations. There is an ample picnic area to the right of the gate.

Proceed on foot down the gated dirt road. Owing to the park's proximity to civilization, you'll share the roads with joggers and bicyclists. Fishing boats ply the bay to your right, and windrows of dead eelgrass, one of the few flowering plants that grow in salt water, line the rocky shore. The brant, a smaller relative of the Canada goose, feeds almost exclusively on this plant. When a mysterious blight in the 1930s all but exterminated the eelgrass, the brant nearly went, too. The emaciated flocks subsisted on a diet of sea lettuce until the grass came back. If you walk this way in the colder months, you may see a few of the hundreds of brant that winter along the shore of Long Island Sound.

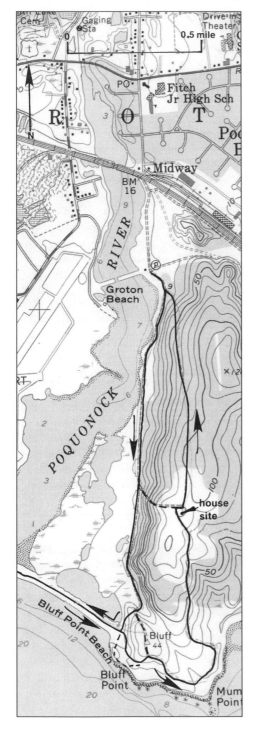

Numerous side paths cut off from the main road. Due to the pervasive influence of the sea, the woods of Bluff Point are more varied than most inland forests. The tangle of vines and brambles—grape, red-fruited barberry, rose, blackberry, black raspberry, honeysuckle, Oriental bittersweet, and greenbrier—is thick enough to make Br'er Rabbit feel at home. Various oaks, cherries, long-thorned hawthorns, tight-barked hickories, shagbark hickories, sumacs, and blueberries represent the deciduous trees, and an occasional cedar represents the evergreen trees.

You will probably see one or more swans gracing the bay on this hike. They will almost certainly be European mute swans. These birds descended from captives that escaped from various estates, mostly on Long Island. They are now spreading rapidly throughout the waterways of the Northeast.

During an April visit you may hear the mating chorus of the male peepers and toads. These dryland dwellers congregate, upon breaking hibernation, in various temporary waters to breed. The peeper has a high-pitched, two-note call, hence its name. The toad produces a long trill. If these amphibians mistakenly choose a permanent body of water in which to lay their eggs, various water-dwelling enemies will devour the tadpoles; if the pools they select dry up too soon, the tadpoles will die before completing metamorphosis. As with many things in nature, a very delicate balance exists.

The most common tree in this narrow strip of woodland is probably sassafras, usually recognized by its mitten-shaped leaves and greenish-barked twigs. Sassafras leaves usually come in three shapes—like a mitten with no thumb, one thumb, or two thumbs—often on the same branch. As a rule, those leaves nearest the end of a twig have the fewest thumbs. Henry David

Bluff Point

Thoreau found the fragrant leaves to be reminiscent of the Orient.

About 1.5 miles from your start, you reach the low bluffs on a point of land. Over the water to your right lies Groton Heights, and to your left Groton Long Point. Fishers Island, part of New York State, lies to the right of center, while Watch Hill in Rhode Island is at left of center.

A bit before the bluff, a boardwalk on your right detours you onto Bluff Point Beach. Wander down this beach a bit before continuing your exploration of Bluff Point itself. Castoff treasures from the sea await your curious gaze: rope, great blocks of wood, blue mussel shells, great whorled whelk shells, marble-sized periwinkle shells, scallop shells, rectangular shells from razor clams, flat wide strands of kelp, bladder-floated algae (seaweed), crab husks, and the everlasting, ever-present plastics—the bane of all the world's oceans.

When you have satisfied your yen for beach walking or have reached the end of this beach, retrace your steps, following sprawling masses of delicate beach peas back to the bluff. Before you start around this point, pause for a moment among the wild primrose and beach plum. You are standing on a terminal moraine. This hasty-pudding mix of rocks and sand was dumped here some 10,000 years ago, when the glacier that completely covered present-day New England retreated.

Follow the road around to the east. Soon after leaving the shore, take the better-worn path inland to your left, and at the fork 50 yards farther on, bear right. The trail to your left soon connects with the outward-bound leg of your hike. Rounding the point, you look over a cattail swamp. These are being taken over throughout the state by the giant reed phragmites (pronounced frag-MI-tez). Here, their waving plumes stand sentinel by the sound. Across the bay, a seemingly solid wall of cottages stands in stark contrast with this wild oasis.

The trail moves inland to follow the center ridge of the peninsula. Stone walls stand in mute evidence of colonial cultivation. The trail forks after about 0.5 mile. Near this fork is the foundation at the site of the Winthrop house. Built around 1700 by Governor Fitz-John Winthrop, grandson of the famous Massachusetts Bay governor, it had a 300-foot tunnel to the barn and a room-sized brick chimney in the basement for protection from Native American raids.

Leaving this area, take the right fork (the left joins the bayside road you followed earlier). The path tends left until it joins the outbound trail near the parking lot. Go to your right to reach your car.

13

Day Pond Loop

Location: Colchester

Distance: 4 miles

Vertical rise: 500 feet

Time: 2½ hours

Rating: C

Map: USGS 7.5-minute Moodus

New England's forests, rock formations, and hills make a very nice setting for our hikes. We even have one feature that is world famous and almost unique—our glorious fall colors! Westerners may rave about their yellow aspen—we have not only yellows (including aspen) but also a riot of other colors that are beautiful in themselves and glorious together. What a grand and pleasant surprise it must have been for the Pilgrims to be greeted their first New England fall in 1621 by our magnificent colors!

Around Labor Day, the sumac and the red maple turn red and scarlet. Then the yellow of popple (Yankee for aspen) and birch appears, followed by seemingly translucent ash (perhaps our favorite), with deep purple on top of the leaf and yellow beneath; the wind ripples this two-toned effect beautifully. Our crown jewels, the sugar maples, with their fantastic range of hues from yellow through orange to brilliant reds, burst into brilliance, and finally the various oaks, with their deep, long-lasting rusts, complete the tapestry.

The only area in the world with colors to rival ours is eastern China, but our far greater number of trees makes New England's show unsurpassed. You may wonder why only these two areas, half a world apart, are so blessed. One reasonable theory is that many millions of years ago, between ice ages, at a time when our present trees were developing, Greenland was a warm, forested island that served as a bridge over the pole between northern Asia and North America. The return of the ice pushed the forest south into both areas. The color genes were thus derived

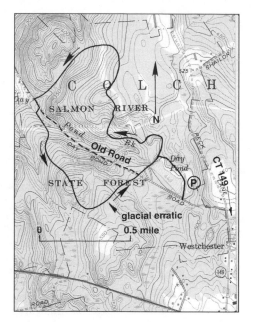

glacial erratic
0.5 mile

from a single source and spread into both eastern China and eastern North America.

To get to Day Pond, take exit 16 off CT 2 in North Westchester and go south on CT 149. In 3 miles turn right onto Peck Lane at the sign for Day Pond State Park. After 0.4 mile take your first left onto Day Pond Road, then turn right at the gate for Day Pond State Park. The park is 1.1 miles north of CT 149. There is ample angle parking along the road around the pond.

Several water-loving swamp maples surround the entrance. Various oaks and the yellow-leafed tulip trees are also found here. Follow the dirt entrance road around the pond on your left past a large picnic shelter, also on your left.

There are a few outhouses scattered about, but the next building (again on your left) is an elaborate bathhouse complete with water fountain. Such development is necessary to protect the park's resources, but is costly in terms of the state's budget, and may cut into funds necessary for public land acquisition. We believe the priority should be land acquisition to protect land for wildlife habitat and to provide space for recreational opportunities for our ever-increasing population. But we also understand there is a need to manage the natural resources and our use of them. Striking a balance between these priorities will continue to be a challenge for professional land managers, conservationists, recreationists, politicians, and the public.

After curving around the beach and adjacent dressing rooms, turn right by a pair of outhouses just before the dam. The blue-blazed trail heads downhill on an old tote road. If you choose the latter part of October for this hike, you will find that the shorter hours of daylight, rather than frost, as is commonly believed, have painted the foliage lavishly with a spectrum of reds and orange.

In a few yards the trail turns sharply left off the tote road; you are still following the blue blazes. Jog slightly to your left and cross the gas pipeline easement; continue downhill toward the stream.

The outlet stream from Day Pond lends a cheery background to the first part of this hike. The stream moves quickly downhill, matching the trail and forming a series of small falls and rapids on its way to the Salmon River. Less than ½ mile from the pond, turn sharply right uphill away from the stream on the blue-blazed trail. Here, an un-blazed trail also goes left to cross the brook and continues to the road that bisects the Day Pond Loop.

It is interesting to note the young beech at this turn in your path. Depending upon how late in the autumn you are walking, many of the trees may have lost their foliage. The red maple leaves are often off before the other colors have fully developed. The various oaks will usually hold their leaves until well into winter. However, young beeches

A new bridge aided an icy stream crossing.

will often hold their leaves into early spring. By then the leaves are bleached almost white, but they are still holding on.

Cross under the power lines and climb until you reach a rocky knoll nearly a mile from the start. The rock-strewn area (these are glacial erratics) culminates in a small, circular, almost flat top. The path starts down the other side, where a few cedars still reach the sun.

After several minor ups and downs, the trail changes its mostly northerly direction and heads west downhill, crossing a stone wall. Upon reaching a woodland valley, you go along the left side, following the blue blazes. You'll pass a number of stone walls and foundations in this valley. As the valley cuts deeper into the local water table, a stream becomes visible, growing as you proceed downhill, deeper into the valley. Soon you cross the stream.

The valley and its stream end at a deeper valley carved by a larger stream that origi-nates at Day Pond. At the bottom of a hill the rough tote road you have been following hits a well-defined old road, where you turn left uphill. After again crossing the smaller stream that you followed down the valley and starting up a gentle grade, turn right onto another woods road to continue along the blue-blazed trail.

Follow the blue-blazed trail into the woods and cross the larger stream from Day Pond; this once challenging crossing has been tamed by a bridge utilizing the old stone abutments. You are now better than halfway around the circuit. Go left along the bank of this stream beside a stone wall. Soon go right uphill away from the brook. Cross under the power line and wind slow-ly upward through what, at first glance, appears to be an almost featureless wood-land. However, our woodlands are never featureless! Along here we saw a large ex-panse of white pine and eastern hemlock, a young deciduous woodland, and acres of club mosses, many carrying their spore stalks like banners.

After almost a mile of gentle upgrade, you crest the hilltop and bear left to immediately cross a linear clearing carrying a buried transcontinental cable. After crossing a small, mostly dry-bottomed valley, the blue-blazed trail resumes its gentle upward slope.

Pass on your right a 400-ton glacial erratic. Besides a patina of algae and lichen, this great rock supports a young black birch on its top and a clump of polypody fern clinging to a foothold on its side. You can estimate such things as the weight of this boulder, the grains of sand on a beach, or the number of leaves on a large tree quite handily by taking a small section and multiplying by the whole—you will definitely not be exact, but you will have a good idea of the actual number. For this boulder we estimated its weight at about 200 pounds per cubic foot (water weighs about 64 pounds per cubic foot) and its size as 20 feet square by 10 feet high. A simple calculation produces a volume of 4,000 cubic feet and a weight of 800,000 pounds, or 400 tons.

As you reach the end of the loop, the path meets, parallels, and then crosses a stone wall. You soon cross an old tote road whose dirt surface is below much of the surrounding land—erosion from past heavy use. Shortly you reach the park road just south of the dam.

You then cross the pond's outlet stream and dam on two bridges; pass the two outhouses (to your left) where you started the loop hike, and retrace your steps to your car.

The two consecutive bridges over the pond's outlets are particularly interesting and show that the dam's designer knew what he was doing. The smaller stream's outlet in the dam is lower so that it will always carry some of the pond's overflow with its cheery burble. The second outlet is higher, but much wider than the first. In case of heavy floods, this can drain off a large amount of water, while the smaller dam is more limited. The two outlets prevent an unacceptable water buildup against the dam, which could result in overflow and increased erosion if the smaller outlet were unable to drain off the accumulating water. This pond, then, has the best of both worlds—it has the advantage of a small, compact outlet, with a safety valve that comes into play in case of heavy floods.

14

Hartman Park

Location: Lyme

Distance: 4 miles

Vertical rise: 600 feet

Time: 2½ hours

Rating: C

Map: USGS 7.5-minute Hamburg

This delightful woods ramble takes the hiker through three centuries of our history and is a result of the generous donation of 300 acres to the town of Lyme by John and Kelly Hartman. The nearly 10 miles of trails are the work of local volunteer hikers. Come and enjoy the fruits of their labors; maybe this example will inspire others!

Find Hartman Park from Hadlyme by taking CT 156 for 1.8 miles south from its junction with CT 82. Turn left onto Beaverbrook Road, just past Lyme School. After 2.7 miles turn left again onto Gungy Road. The park entrance is 1 mile down this road on your right. There is ample parking near the gated road into the park. Take care not to block the road, which may be needed for emergency access.

The trails are marked with painted aluminum disks. You'll follow the orange-blazed Heritage Trail into the woods just before the metal gate. Soon you'll reach a junction with the Nature Trail, marked with green disks. Follow it to your right. This trail follows along the base of a hill and features painted stones, wooden mobiles, and hidden curios intended to surprise children. The open hardwood forest includes some prominent American hornbeam, once called blue beech. The gnarled trunks and thin gray bark give the tree its common name, musclewood. However, this tree's wood does not hold up well to the elements and rots quickly in contact with the ground.

Pass a junction with the yellow-blazed Lee Farm Road and continue on the Nature Trail to return to the Heritage Trail. Turn right

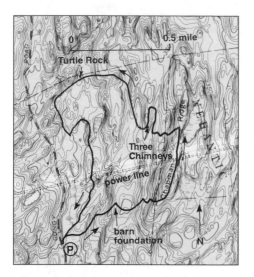

to follow the orange disks up the hill to the impressive stone foundation of a barn to your right. On the way up the hill, check out the variably lobed leaves of sassafras. Its leaves resemble both right- and left-hand mittens, as well as double-thumbed mitts. A tea made from the roots of this plant was credited with keeping the Native Americans healthy. Hence, sassafras was the colonists' first export home from New England and matched tobacco as the largest export crop. The active ingredient in sassafras, safrole, has been found to be carcinogenic, so we do not use it in today's beverages.

The red oak in front of the barn foundation was struck by lightning a couple of years ago. Although only one branch initially showed signs of the strike, the next year the tree was dead and had no new leaves.

Follow the park road briefly past the foundation, and turn right up an old tote road opposite the foundation of the farmhouse. The 100-year-old white ash growing out of its cellar supports a large poison ivy vine. This house was probably built in the early 17th century and burned after the Civil War.

Climb over the hill and descend into a wetland. Cross it and ascend Chapman Ridge via switchbacks through mountain laurel. Following the ridgeline north, you'll pass the remains of the Chapman Farm of two centuries past. Continue past the blue-blazed Chapman Path and cross a power line. The trail is marked with wooden stakes painted orange. After following the ridge a bit farther, drop to the valley to the west past a stone fireplace and turn right onto the worn park road. Follow the road until the orange-blazed trail turns left to climb to the top of Three Chimneys Ridge.

On this ridge the small, pointed evergreen leaves of the striped wintergreen stood out among the brown leaves of late March. These leaves have prominent white veins, making the plant striking regardless of the season.

The orange-blazed Heritage Trail links up with the red-blazed Nubble and Ridges Trails, and all three stay together to the Three Chimneys to your left. Perhaps the most intriguing feature of the park, the chimneys may, it is speculated, be the remains of one of a series of forts Lyonel Gardiner was contracted to build for the original Puritan settlers of Saybrook Colony. In 1634 Gardiner was sent to build the forts in case the political and religious problems in England worsened. Oliver Cromwell's success made the forts unnecessary, and this fort possibly reverted to a farmstead. The arrangement of the chimneys resembles medieval forts of that period, and is similar to structures found at Plimoth Plantation. The Three Chimneys may be one of Gardiner's lost forts.

Follow the orange-blazed trail to your right soon after leaving the fort and descend to a woods road at the base of the hill, where you'll turn right to follow the yel-

"The Snout" in Hartman Park

low blazed road through a wetland. Bear left onto the red-blazed trail at a fork and eventually climb up to Jumble Ridge. The trail passes a number of rock formations, including Laughing Rock, Turtle Rock, and the aptly named Snout.

After passing below Coyote and Cave Cliffs, the red-blazed trail turns south toward Hartman Field. Turn left onto a yellow-blazed connector trail that follows a woods road. Cross over a bridge, turn right onto the orange-blazed Heritage Trail, and pass a charcoal kiln to your right, marked with a white disk. The kiln is nothing more than a large, circular, level spot in the forest with no large trees growing in it. The local farmers would pile up wood and cover it with soil to permit a slow-burning fire, thereby creating hot-burning charcoal for future use in blast furnaces.

Cross the power-line clearing, bearing uphill and passing the Flume, a cas-

cade over moss-covered rock. Soon a yellow-blazed connector comes in from your left and then leaves the trail to the right. Follow it to your right and turn right again to a small cemetery on a rise. The unmarked stones probably indicate the graves of the less wealthy and those of lower social standing, such as slaves and itinerant workers. The only pertinent documentation in the Lyme records is of a penniless man of partial Native American descent who was buried by a white landowner, who then sought reimbursement from the town.

Turn left onto the red-blazed trail and follow it to the School Room, an open-air gathering site on the park road with an informative bulletin board and visitor's register. Please sign in and let the park manager and volunteers know about your visit. From the School Room, take the orange-and-green-blazed trail south to the mill site just below an earth and stone dam. It was probably an old sawmill; however, there is no positive identification in the records. It is only known that 50 years after the settling of Saybrook Colony, there were complaints from Lyme of overcutting of timber in the uplands. Much of this was exported as wood products to lumber-starved England.

Below the mill, come out onto the gravel park road and turn right to pass through the gate and return to your car.

15

Soapstone Mountain

Location: Somers

Distance: 4 miles

Vertical rise: 700 feet

Time: 2½ hours

Rating: C

Map: USGS 7.5-minute Ellington

Soapstone—an intriguing name for a mountain—sits in the midst of the 6,000-acre Shenipsit State Forest. A quarry on the east slope used by Native Americans and early settlers once yielded the soft, talclike, greasy, lustered stone from which the mountain derives its name. In colonial times this stone was valued for its high heat retention; flannel-wrapped hot soapstones lessened the shock of icy bedclothes.

Soapstone Mountain is located east of the Connecticut River in Somers. From the junction of CT 140 and CT 83, drive north on CT 83 for 4 miles to Parker Road and turn right. After 1.3 miles (the last 0.4 mile is a rough, three-season dirt road), at a four-way junction with Soapstone Road and Sykes Road, park across the way to your left.

Follow the gravel Soapstone Road east toward the mountain.

Pass some logging yards to your left and reach an old woods road flanked by car-sized boulders blazed with yellow and blue paint, also to your left. (If you miss this turn, follow the road to the summit of the mountain and then pick up these directions again from the tower.) Turn left onto the woods road and descend to where the blue-blazed Shenipsit Trail bears right uphill, away from the descending yellow-blazed trail.

The Shenipsit Trail heads to the right up the main peak of Soapstone Mountain—a good steady climb. Climbing, you reach the top (1,075 feet) ½ mile after leaving the road.

This summit is a good example of the sometimes rapid effects rendered by the hand of humanity. When we first wrote about this summit in 1977, the old fire tower that

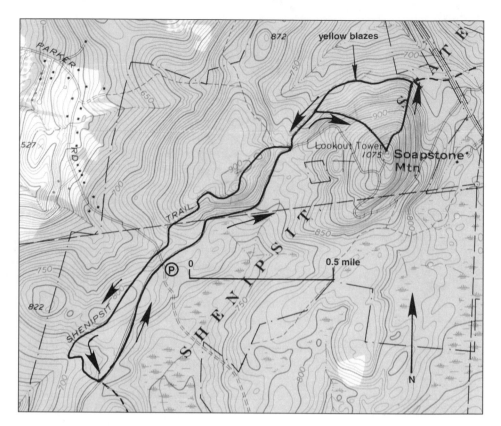

we had used so many times had been removed because it was unsafe, but the following year an observation tower was erected in its place. Now covered with graffiti, the structure nonetheless offers wonderful views.

An easy climb of the observation tower presents a bird's-eye view of the surrounding country. Off to the west is the flat valley land. To the northwest are the high-rise buildings of Springfield, and Mount Tom and the Holyoke Range in Massachusetts. To the north and south is the well-wooded mountain ridge of which Soapstone is a prominent part.

The trail down from the summit is a bit obscure due to removal of trees, a handy marking medium. You enter the woods just to the left of the telephone line. Your route threads down a rocky path through an attractive field of glacial erratics. After 0.3 mile turn left onto the yellow-blazed tote road. (The blue-blazed Shenipsit Trail continues to your right to the Massachusetts border about 6 miles farther on.)

Gently ascend on the yellow-blazed tote road around the north side of Soapstone Mountain. Continue climbing toward Soapstone Mountain Road and bear right onto the blue-blazed trail to climb the steep hill to the west. Eventually you'll stand on the rocky summit of West Soapstone Mountain (930 feet). Near the top in spring you may find an atypical species of violet, the northern downy violet. The leaves are long, oval, and fuzzy rather than the more familiar heart-shaped, smooth leaves, but the familiar violet-blue flowers are unmistakable. There are dozens of species of violets, and with hybridization even the experts have trouble with some identifications. So we have a ready-made excuse if we cannot identify a violet—it must be a hybrid!

On a leafless day, the microwave tower on the summit of the main peak of Soapstone Mountain appears across the valley. The trail works downhill and passes another rocky outcropping over upward-tipped ledges. This is gneiss, the basic bedrock of much of Connecticut, which was laid down in flat layers hundreds of millions of years ago. These protruding ledges were tilted by subsequent crystal deformations.

Near a road crossing, you'll pass a swamp to your right. In spring the swamp resonates with the high-pitched chorus of peepers. We have all heard countless thousands of these diminutive tree frogs with the big voices, but have you ever seen one in song? Cautious creeping in the evening with the subtle use of a flashlight may reward you with the sight of one of these small, tan frogs, whose throat swells into a great, white, bubblelike sound box from a body less than an inch long. Summer sightings are more a matter of quick eyes, quicker hands, and luck. Most of the woodland hoppers you find are the black-masked wood frogs, but occasionally you will find a tiny frog without the mask and a faint contrasting X on its back—this is the spring peeper.

In spring fern fiddleheads pop up everywhere. Instead of growing gradually like most annuals, the fern uncoils like a New Year's Eve party favor from a tightly curled mass into a fully grown plant. In northern New England the fiddleheads of the ostrich fern are considered a delicacy. We are told that our common cinnamon fern fiddlehead is also good to eat, but you have to remove all the light brown fuzz before you can eat it—seeing what a job that is, we have never tried it, nor have we found anyone who has!

Cross gravel Parker Road and continue east, following the blue-blazed trail. Carefully follow the blazes through here. There are many paths and old tote roads in this forest. If you are daydreaming or taking the path of least resistance, it is very easy to miss a turn or two and find that the worn path you are traveling is devoid of blue blazes. In that event, retrace your steps to the last blaze and try again.

In late spring there are at least two aspects of vegetation that you may have noticed and wondered about. One is the plentiful clusters of starflowers. Spreading mostly by means of underground rhizomes, they are usually found in large stands or not at all. There seem to be more multiblossom plants here than usual. Second, you may think the compact masses of moss have grown hair. Actually, in late spring moss sends up flowering stalks that allow the resulting spores to spread farther after they ripen.

The forest you're hiking through has a lovely, soothing sameness. An understory of maple and black birch struggles for sunlight in the gaps among large red oak. The leaf-littered floor is carpeted with masses of ground pine and wild lily of the valley. Many of Connecticut's forests are, like this one, all of a size. The last great timber harvests were in the early years of the 20th century, and since then cutting has been sporadic—far less than the annual growth—resulting in many trees across the state being about the same age. The logging that does occur, some of which you pass by on this hike, appears to leave the trails virtually untouched.

Soon you bear left to cross Sykes Road. Turn left here to follow the road less than ½ mile back to your car.

16

Penwood

Location: Bloomfield

Distance: 4¾ miles

Vertical rise: 600 feet

Time: 2½ hours

Rating: C

Map: USGS 7.5-minute Avon

The traprock ridges flanking the Connecticut River Valley offer secluded hiking on the outskirts of the central cities. Penwood State Park sits atop one such ridge. Only a few minutes' drive from Hartford, the trails of Penwood carry you beyond the sights and sounds of our workaday world to a place where the most blatant intrusions are the blue blazes marking your route on the Metacomet Trail and the broken macadam of the closed access road.

The park entrance is on the north side of CT 185, 1 mile west of the CT 185 and CT 178 junction in Bloomfield. There is a large paved parking lot just to the right of the entrance. This park's proximity to Hartford, along with its paved circular loop road, makes it very popular with joggers, fitness walkers, and dog owners year round.

Pass a plaque honoring Curtis H. Veeder, an industrialist, inventor, and outdoorsman who, in 1944, gave the state the nearly 800 acres that is now a state park. Pick up the blue blazes of the Metacomet Trail and follow them a short distance down the right-hand road (east). Just past a blocked tote road, bear left into the woods, climbing quickly onto the hemlock-shrouded traprock ridge. Once on the top, the trail undulates gently within the forest, passing a number of little-used side trails that lead north and south to the park's loop road. The forest dampens the sights and sounds of our harried world. Even the park road is invisible. Recent salvage-logging to remove the dead and dying hemlocks has opened up the forest floor to sunlight where once few shrubs could survive. The next few years' growth will see the development of a new primary succession forest under the scattered oak trees.

In 1.8 miles the trail crosses the tar end of the loop road. Take a break from the hike to explore the little ridgetop pond. Head across the pavement onto a short board-walk leading through the thicket and onto the edge of the pond, grandiosely named Lake Louise, for Mr. Veeder's wife. The teeming fecundity of life here makes the dry, forested ridge look like a desert.

Discounting the usual forest birds that are drawn to this cornucopia, we saw or heard more varieties of living things in just a few minutes of standing by the pond than in our total time spent on the ridge—dragonflies with outstretched wings, damselflies with folded wings, water striders miraculously skimming the pond's surface, circling whirligig beetles setting a dizzying circular pace when disturbed, and water boatmen riding just under the water's surface. Gaily colored butterflies displayed marked contrast with the mud perches on which they sat, ab-sorbing moisture from their surroundings. Tadpoles were flitting into sight along the pond's edges when they came up for an oc-casional gulp of air. Through the water flicked aquatic green newts, the adult form of the red efts found on the springtime forest floor after a night of gentle rain. Here and there small frogs sat propped up, half in and half out of the water, still exhibiting the rounded softness of their recent tadpole stage, and we saw two small water snakes sunbathing near the boardwalk.

Even the vegetation here is varied and lush. Lily pads dot the surface. Marsh fern, swamp loosestrife, and buttonbush edge the pond, and a sour gum tree grows on your right. The white blossoms of swamp azaleas perfume the air. Look for the few

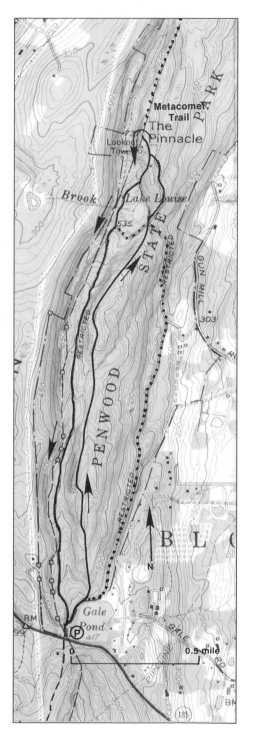

The view south from the Pinnacle

clumps of swamp Juneberry amid the numerous smooth alders. Their lustrous black berries, which resemble huge huckleberries, make a nice snack. If such a place fascinates you as it does us, read the book *Watchers at the Pond* by Francis Russell.

When ready, return to the loop road. Just beyond the boardwalk bear left onto the blue-blazed trail and climb steeply toward a fine scenic lookout called the Pinnacle. Cross a paved circle where Mr. Veeder's cabin of chestnut logs once stood, and pick up the blue-blazed Metacomet Trail again for the final ascent to the Pinnacle. The ridge traversed by the Tunxis

Trail lies to the west across the valley. To the south rises Heublein Tower on Talcott Mountain (see Hike 45), and farther left the great tilted volcanic slabs of Mount Higby (see Hike 28).

Return to the cabin clearing and stay to its right to follow a white-blazed trail down the steep slope back to Lake Louise. Turn right to follow the old woods road around its north side. Cross the lake's outlet on a plank bridge and follow a boardwalk through the swamp to the broken pavement of the loop road. Bear right onto this road and follow it back through the woods on the west side of the ridge to your car.

17

Northern Metacomet

Location: Granby

Distance: 4.0 miles

Vertical rise: 500 feet

Time: 2½ hours

Rating: C

Map: USGS 7.5-minute Windsor Locks

Choose a cool, clear day for this hike. It begins with a pleasant walk along a traprock ridge of north-central Connecticut, offering sunny vistas, and then a visit to the forbidding environs of the infamous Newgate Prison. The blue-blazed Metacomet Trail will take you along Peak Mountain's volcanic cliffs. After the hike, Newgate Road will lead to the prison site, which was also America's first copper smelter.

To reach the hike's start, follow CT 20 west 0.7 mile from its junction with CT 187 in Granby to Newgate Road on your right. Go north on Newgate Road a little way until you see the blue-blazed Metacomet Trail enter the woods on your right. The trail ascends from the first prominent pulloff to your right. There is room to park on the road.

The path climbs steeply onto the traprock ridge and then bears left along the top. In leafless season the views here are particularly nice, but even in summer you catch glimpses of the countryside below through occasional breaks in the trees. The utility line you soon pass beneath services a string of beacons for planes approaching Bradley International Airport, which is just east of the ridge. The airplane buff will appreciate the procession of jet airliners and the myriad smaller, private aircraft that come and go over-head. The exhilarating cliff edges and views offset the aircraft noise for the rest of us.

In a little under a mile you'll scramble up to a lookout about 300 feet above the

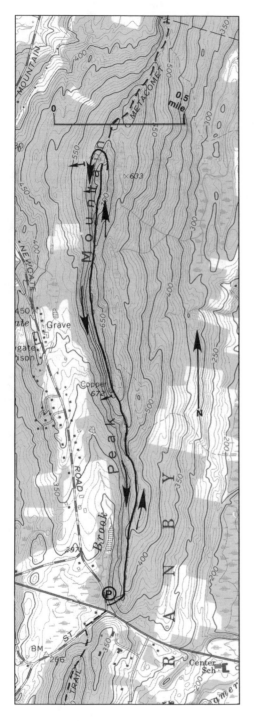

valley floor. The USGS benchmark reads COPPER MOUNTAIN. The Tunxis Trail follows the traprock ridge across the road directly west opposite you; to the south stretches the sinuous ridge curve that the Metacomet Trail follows. Penwood State Park (see Hike 16) straddles the nearest hump; Heublein Tower on Talcott Mountain (see Hike 45) stands out prominently behind it; and beyond the tower the tilted slabs of Mount Higby (see Hike 28) rise on the horizon.

Staying on the ridge, you'll reenter the woods and descend slowly but steadily and then climb again. Nearly 2 miles from the start, just beyond the third beacon tower, you reach an excellent lookout ledge with fine views to the west. Below you and to the south, there is a fine view of another traprock ridge framing the valley below. Continue on the trail, soon coming to a grassy spot that overlooks the scree slope.

Retrace your steps to your car, and then drive north on Newgate Road for 1.1 miles. Before long you come to the impressive ruins of Newgate Prison on your right. Originally a copper mine (circa 1705), it was pressed into service as a prison just before the Revolutionary War. It became most famous as a prison for Tories during the war. The prison is open daily from Memorial Day through October. There is a small entry fee.

For a short excursion into the seamier side of our nation's past, join the line of waiting visitors. After descending 50 feet in a narrow shaft, you enter the mine proper. Water seeps down the walls. A motley crew of Tories, thieves, and debtors were forced to live and labor in this cavernous prison while fettered with leg irons, handcuffs, and iron collars. Marks worn on the floor by pacing prisoners are still visible two centuries later, and tales of barbarity seem to echo in the hollow chambers.

After exploring the prison, return to Newgate Road. The fresh air will be especially welcome after the dank dungeon. Above, the traprock ridges beckon to you for a return trip, perhaps a good idea after a visit to the prison.

18

Gay City

Location: Hebron

Distance: 5 miles

Vertical rise: 250 feet

Time: 2¾ hours

Rating: CD

Map: USGS 7.5-minute Marlborough

A religious group led by Elijah Andrus founded Gay City in 1796. Andrus left town for reasons unknown and in 1800 John Gay, for whom the park is named, was appointed president of the remaining 25 families. They were known as an unsociable group; an itinerant peddler was robbed, murdered, and thrown into a town charcoal pit, and a blacksmith's assistant was slain by his employer for failing to show up for work.

The two most prominent families were the Gays and the Sumners, whose rivalry outlasted the town. The Gays called the settlement Gay City, and the Sumners called it Sumner, although it seems the settlement was known locally as Factory Hollow. Ironically, when the Foster sisters, descendants of the Sumners, deeded the 1,500-acre area to the state in the 1940s, they stipulated that it be called Gay City!

The town's decline, well under way before the Civil War, followed the usual pattern of hardscrabble areas: The old died and the young left. A paper mill outlasted all the houses; when it burned in 1879 the town was gone. Come hike along the now empty dirt roads of this New England ghost town.

Gay City State Park is located off CT 85 just south of the Bolton-Hebron town line. In addition to the hiking trails, the park offers swimming and picnicking; facilities include outhouses, bathhouses, picnic tables, outdoor fireplaces, and, in summer, an open refreshment stand. There is a fee for parking inside the gates on summer weekends.

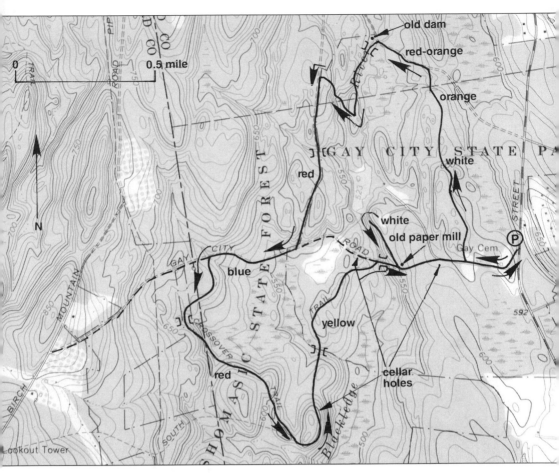

Emulating the thrifty Yankees, your hike avoids the toll by parking in a hiker's lot just north of the park entrance on CT 85. Pick up a park trail map at a bulletin board just above the parking lot. Walking in on the paved road, you pick up a few features that you might otherwise miss. Fields separated by stone walls grace both sides of the entrance road, and picnic tables are scattered throughout the area.

You will soon pass an old graveyard on your right—save it for your return. Leave the paved park road not far from the cemetery and enter the woods on an old tote road to your right, the white-blazed Pond Loop Trail.

After ¾ mile the Pond Loop Trail veers left. Stay straight on the woods road, now blazed with orange paint. Bear left at a fork and continue to a T-junction with the red-blazed Outer Loop Trail. Turn left to follow the red and orange blazes.

After about another 0.25 mile you reach a place where the old road continues past a signpost; your route continues straight (the old road turns right to cross an old dam and leaves the park) and crosses the Blackledge River on a small but impressive stone footbridge at the site of an old dam.

After crossing the river, continue straight through an intersection and follow red

A sunny January morning along one of Connecticut's many forgotten woods roads.

blazes uphill away from the river. Continue along the red-blazed trail as it gently ascends the hill. At the top of the rise, you reach a T-junction. Turn left here along an old woods road to continue following the red blazes. Pass two white-blazed trails leading left to the pond, and then bear left, following the red blazes over a rise and then down to the blue-blazed Gay City Trail. Go to your right, following red and blue blazes. This was the old Gay City Road, which was the main route to Glastonbury and the Connecticut River.

The old road climbs gradually. Alert ears may hear noises in the brush: the dash and chirp of the chipmunk, the heavy-bodied bouncing of the gray squirrel, the drink-your-tea call of the towhee, a common woodland bird with a black back, rufous sides, and a white belly.

Just after crossing a small brook with no bridge, turn left onto the red-blazed Outer Loop Trail. Along this section in spring you may hear the low-pitched drumming of the male ruffed grouse. It perches on a log that gives its wings freedom to move and then beats them faster and faster until they become a blur. The resulting thumping attracts females and warns away other males. The first time you hear this sound you may think it is a distant motor running, or even wonder if you are really hearing anything at all. We like to think of this soft buffeting as the heartbeat of the New England woods.

In just under a mile you reach the junction with the yellow-blazed South Connector Trail. Bear left and begin the final leg of your circuit. Continue following the yellow blazes to the spot where a boardwalk crosses a swampy area and a brook. The trail then climbs gently to overlook a beaver pond below and to your left. The familiar stick-and-mud lodge is on the near bank of the pond.

Proceed downhill until you reach the blue-blazed Gay City Trail. Just before this junction, note the old cellar hole to your left; it is one of many in the park. Turn right and cross the bridge over the Blackledge River; detour left on a white-blazed trail briefly to view the remnants of the old paper mill and the pond beyond it. A bit past the old cut-stone foundation on your right is a ditch separated from the river by an artificial ridge. The small, now dry canal diverted water from the pond to power the mill downstream. The pond and the canal assured an even flow; the system dumped out the high water and accumulated water for controlled periods of operation during droughts. Just under ¾ mile from the dam, the trail drops to your right off the canal and crosses a bridge over the mill's sluiceway. The squared blocks of the building's foundation and the square hole that diverted flow from the canal over the waterwheel to the sluiceway are very prominent. The canal was reputed to be 10 feet deep in its heyday. A bit farther on along the canal is the pond.

Retrace your steps and proceed to your left uphill, following the blue blazes, passing another old cellar hole on your right fronted by four decaying sugar maples. Pass the red-blazed Outer Loop Trail coming in to your right, and then bear right onto the paved park road.

Stop now at the graveyard to your left before returning to CT 85 and your car. It tells a poignant story of the dour little settlement. It is a small plot—a mere dumping ground for the dead. The rival Gays and Sumners are buried at opposite ends of the cemetery. The outlook and character of this vanished town may be reflected in the harsh epitaph on a seven-year-old girl's grave:

Com pritty youth behold and see
The place where you must shortly be.

19

Mount Misery

Location: Voluntown

Distance: 5.25 miles

Vertical rise: 380 feet

Time: 2¾ hours

Rating: CD

Maps: USGS 7.5-minute Voluntown, Jewett City

The delightful little summit of Mount Misery belies its name. Set amid the flat pinelands of Connecticut's largest state forest, this prominent rocky mass adds a nice, short climb to an otherwise level hike. Your route to the top, where there are nice views across wooded terrain, follows the Nehantic Trail. This hike picks up the blue-blazed Nehantic Trail on CT 49 in Voluntown. From the intersection of CT 49, CT 165, and CT 138, head east on CT 165 to CT 49 north and turn left. The blue blazes of the trail run along the road. Continue 0.6 mile to the Beachdale Pond boat-launching area parking lot on your right, opposite the forest access road to the west. There is a ramped wharf supplying fishing access for the handicapped here on the Pachaug River. The Nehantic Trail crosses CT 49 and goes off the Pachaug State Forest access road into the woods at the picnic area, about 100 yards beyond the parking lot.

As you enter the woods, even rows of white pines stretch away on either side. These conifers begin to thin out and are replaced by short, scrubby, head-high bushes of bear oak. These trees flourish (if that word may be used for these scraggly specimens) in dry, barren soil. Less tolerant but more vigorous trees prevent them from gaining a foothold in richer, deeper soil.

Eventually you cross the paved access road and follow an old forest road softened by a carpet of pine needles. Next you walk under and then along utility lines before bearing right off this forest road into the woods. The blue-blazed trail here is well

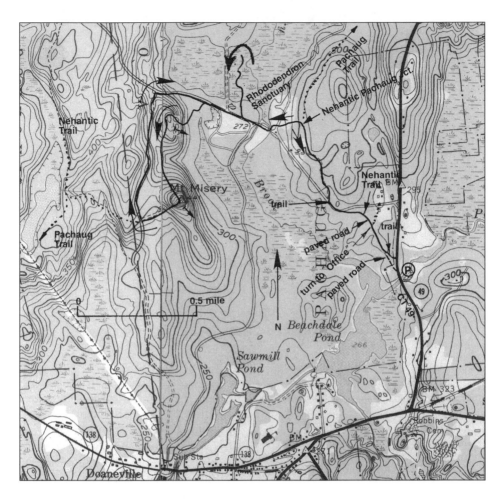

worn and not difficult to follow.

About ½ mile from the start, the Pachaug Trail enters from the right and, bearing to the left, the two trails continue as one over Mount Misery. From the trail junction, proceed downhill, bearing left; go under the utility line and continue through the open campground field to the stone-gated campground road. Cross this paved road and go through a picnic site, shortly crossing Mount Misery Brook on Cut-Off Road. Follow the blue-blazed gravel road to the Rhododendron Sanctuary, first passing a playing field.

A handicapped-accessible trail to your right opposite the field makes a fine side trip into the cedar and rhododendron swamp. You immediately appreciate the dry, raised, crushed-stone pathway through the swamp. Along this stretch of the swamp, junglelike rhododendrons flank the trail. This native evergreen can grow surprisingly tall—to 40 feet—and its leathery leaf can reach 8 inches in length. The combined effect of all that green is most impressive. In July these huge shrubs are dotted with white or pink bell-shaped flowers, creating a spectacular display. Here and there the straight, even boles of tall

---

Mount Misery

Mount Misery's summit lodge.

white cedars thrust through the mass. Their bark is soft and flaky; the greenish tint you see is algae growing on the tree's damp surfaces. The durability of its wood was so highly valued that cedars were once "mined" from beneath swamps and put to use. Follow the path to an observation platform in the middle of the swamp. When ready, retrace your steps to the campground road.

Before you return, stop and listen. On one mid-March hike here the sun beating down on the swamp to the right had aroused the resident wood frogs, despite the light coating of snow from a recent flurry. Their full, guttural chorus was broken only by the plaintive peep of a solitary spring peeper too groggy to give the second half of his familiar call.

Return to the gravel road, which you follow past the campground road to your left before turning left into the woods again. The level trail passes through oaks, hemlocks, and large white pines. A dead white cedar with a split down the center large enough to see through stands just to the left of the trail. What caused this hole? Did two trees once grow together? One of the pleasures of hiking is trying to figure out the reason for such strange phenomena.

Climb to the top of the ridge. Switchbacks make the slope easier to surmount. Such trail design features not only make hiking uphill easier but also reduce the trail's susceptibility to erosion by avoiding the fall line of the slope. Turn left and soon emerge on open rock. Here, go to your right to the vista of the open fields below. A singularly misshapen, wind-twisted pitch pine grows on the ledge lookout. This distinctive old friend is one of our favorite trees in Connecticut, as well as a common sight on the dry, rocky ridgetops we frequent. Often twisted by the prevailing winds, it is easy to identify, because it is our only three-needled pine. Its wood contains so much resin, or pitch, that it is easily lit and was often used as a torch (before our modern flashlights)—resulting in its common name, candlewood.

The trail soon drops a bit and crosses a small brook before making its final assault on Mount Misery. The bolts you see in the ledges at the top used to support an abandoned fire tower. The more efficient but far less romantic small spotter planes have now replaced the picturesque fire towers dotting the woods of old. Although Mount Misery, at 441 feet, is not very high, the summit provides a fine view of Voluntown, which lies to your far right, while Beachdale Pond is dead center.

On a calm day the open summit ledges also make a fine picnic spot. Be sure to carry out your garbage with you; even fruit scraps such as peels and cores should be carried out. The forest's animals should not be exposed to such popular throwaway items lest they become dependent on them.

Keep following the blue blazes down the backside of Mount Misery, soon joining a woods road cul-de-sac. Follow the blue-blazed road until the trail reenters the woods. Here bear right to follow another gravel road north. Continue on this road to a T-junction with Cut-Off Road and turn right again, toward the Rhododendron Sanctuary.

On this part of your return journey, as the day grows warm and your legs grow weary, you may shorten your hike and avoid the swamp by staying on Cut-Off Road. Continue past the playing field to your right. After crossing the brook, bear left onto the paved road to the campground field. Turn right into the field and reenter the woods at the near corner across the field. At the junction of the Nehantic and Pachaug Trails, be careful to follow the Nehantic Trail to your right back to your car.

20

Wolf Den

Location: Pomfret

Distance: 5 miles

Vertical rise: 600 feet

Time: 2¾ hours

Rating: CD

Map: USGS 7.5-minute Danielson

Some words roll off the tongue with melodious grace. Although Mashamoquet (mash-muk-it; "stream of good fishing") is definitely not one of those, this state park has a special beauty and grace due to its botanical and zoological diversity. Among the almost infinite attractions of this hike, you will find nestled within the park's 781 acres the legendary wolf den where Israel Putnam, of Revolutionary War fame, reputedly shot the last wolf in Connecticut.

From CT 101 just east of its junction with US 44 in Pomfret, head south on Wolf Den Drive (shown on the topographic map as Botham Road) for 0.7 mile. Turn left into the Wolf Den camping area, where there is ample parking by the campground office.

The NO PETS sign applies to the campground; pets are allowed on the trail if under control. Taking the family dog on a hike seems only natural to many owners. However, dogs do reduce your chances of seeing wildlife, can spread disease by tracking animal feces into streams and ponds, can dig up fragile vegetation, and can frighten other hikers, especially children. Pet owners can ensure that hiking trails remain open to their dogs by controlling their pets, especially by burying or packing out their pets' feces and by leashing their dogs around open water and around people. An important consideration for pet owners is that sometimes dogs decide there's something more exciting in the woods than their human companions and take off on a trail of their own. This can lead to serious situations, including losing a treasured family pet or

dealing with porcupine quills. It's also a good idea to carry food and water for Fido, especially on a hot day.

Start your hike by walking back up the gravel road and crossing Wolf Den Drive. The trail begins by going though an opening in a stone wall where MASHAMOQUET has been painted in yellow on a rock. The blue blazes lead you across an old field before the path turns left into a large stand of smooth alder. Here skunk cabbage spreads its large, aromatic leaves across the swampy, shaded ground. Within this thicket the hulk of a great black willow matches its vigor against the dissolution of age.

When you reach the edge of an over-grown field, turn left by a large shagbark hickory, go through a stone wall, and enter the woods. These first few hundred yards provide a wonderful illustration of the suc-cessive stages in the development of a ma-ture forest. You pass first the open field,

Wolf Den

next the swamp-nurtured invading alder grove, and then cleared wasteland with red cedar. These trees are among the first to colonize open spaces. The forest is further advanced in the woods you just entered; here large red cedars are losing the battle for sunlight to the taller, faster-growing birches. In time the oaks that comprise the climax forest here will crowd out the birches. Then fire or lumbering will remove the oaks, and succession will start all over again.

Beyond a stream, several large, plate-barked black birches guard the trail, which soon runs parallel to a stone wall. Where the stone wall turns a corner the trail joins a tote road. A red-blazed path goes left, cutting across the blue-blazed loop trail, but you turn right with the level, blue-and-red-blazed tote road through maturing oak and maple woods. Stay on the blue-and-red-blazed trail until the red blazes fork left. Follow the blue blazes—shortly a yellow-blazed trail veers right to both the campground and the picnic and swimming area.

Continue on the blue-blazed trail. Your route curves left through the woods, crosses a stream over a bridge, moves up a gentle slope through large hardwoods, and continues left along an open cornfield. It is easy to let your mind wander as your feet take you down worn old roads such as this one; we still miss marked turns off such an obvious path after thousands of miles of hiking experience.

The trail levels and then meets a gravel road. Turn right and then left almost immediately onto another gravel road, passing between a pair of well-built stone cairns. Each cairn contains a large stone with WOLF DEN ENTRANCE chiseled and highlighted with yellow paint.

Follow the dirt road back past thick clumps of laurel to a parking area with a few picnic tables nearby. Continue through the lot to the back of a small, circular drive and proceed downhill on a wide, eroded path. Soon the red-blazed trail comes in from your left. Directional arrows to Table Rock (left) and Wolf Den (right) are chiseled into a nearby rock. The red-and-blue-blazed trails now drop together steeply into the valley below on stone stairs. Less than halfway down you reach the fabled Wolf Den.

According to legend, it was here in 1742 that Israel Putnam slew the last wolf in Connecticut. In fact, the last wolf in the state was probably killed near Bridgeport about 1840. Putnam's wolf had preyed on local sheep for some years. Finally, after tracking it for several days from the Connecticut River some 35 miles to the west, the intrepid Putnam crawled into the den with a lantern, saw the burning eyes of the trapped beast, backed out, grabbed his musket, crawled in again, and fired. Temporarily deafened, he backed out of the smoke-filled hole, paused, went in a third time, and hauled out the carcass.

As you peek inside, note the weathered initials on the sides of the den entrance. In the last century such graffiti were etched on rocks. Today's vandals are lazier—they use paint cans.

When you finish examining the den, continue down the slope on the red-and-blue-blazed trail. Cross the brook and climb the sloping ledges on the other side. Just over the crest of the next rounded hill, the red-blazed trail breaks off to your left. A short distance beyond, the trail bears left on the slope; here you go right a few feet to a ledge overlook and the Indian Chair. An appropriately shaped boulder, the chair commands a fine late-fall-to-early-spring view of the countryside.

Return to the trail and bear left, gently downhill, keeping the stone wall on your

The Indian Chair

right. Shining club mosses perch on some of the fern-framed boulders; wood, polypody, and Christmas ferns thrive in these shady woods.

Now climb the boulder-strewn hill ahead. The slope is softened near the top by a carpet of white pine needles. After dipping and hesitating slightly, the trail curves to your right up a rocky draw, turns right again, and descends, passing a black birch and a hemlock embraced in slow-motion mortal combat for the same piece of sunlight. To your right the sterile evergreen fronds of the maidenhair spleenwort are lodged in the cracks of a large, seamed boulder. The fertile fronds unfold in spring and die with the first frost.

The trail bends right and then zigzags down the hillside, passing through a stone wall before reaching the field that borders the camping area where you started. Pause to admire the vegetation around the borders of the forest. Nature, with all her diversity, loves edges. Edges provide habitat for plants that can stand neither full sun nor full shade. Wild animals use the woods for cover and feed on the nearby field plants and border shrubs.

In the nearby woods is a backed-up pond where we flushed a great blue heron. This long-necked bird with a 6-foot wingspan uses its long legs to keep its plumage dry while wading in the shallow water. The sharp, pointed beak unerringly spears small fish, frogs, and other aquatic creatures that make up the heron's diet. Finally, cross the field to your waiting car.

21

Collis P. Huntington State Park

Location: Redding

Distance: 5.5 miles

Vertical rise: 350 feet

Time: 3 hours

Rating: CD

Map: USGS 7.5-minute Botsford

The casual searcher easily finds many of Connecticut's trails. However, Collis P. Huntington State Park in Redding is off the beaten path and frequented primarily by locals. The trails within this park of more than 800 acres, opened to the public in 1973, are on old woods roads that meander through this secluded area. The land was a gift from Archer M. Huntington, the stepson of the railroad magnate and philanthropist for whom the area was named. Archer was a noted poet and Spanish scholar in his own right. Two striking sculptures by the world-renowned Anna Hyatt Huntington (Archer's second wife) adorn this park. She is best known for her equestrian statues, including one of General Israel Putnam in nearby Putnam Memorial State Park. It is appropriate that representatives of her wild animal tableaux decorate this park.

To get to this delightful out-of-the-way spot from the junction of CT 302 and CT 58 in Bethel, go south on CT 58 (Putnam Park Road) for 1.3 miles and bear left and then right on Sunset Hill Road. After 2.2 miles on Sunset Hill Road, turn left into Collis P. Huntington State Park. The entrance road is flanked by the wildlife sculptures by Anna Hyatt Huntington: wolves baying at the moon at left and a mother bear with cubs at right. There is a parking lot just inside the gate.

Colored plastic markers indicate the various trails in the park, although the well-trodden paths and woods roads make it relatively easy to follow your route. Go downhill on a woods road on the right side of an open

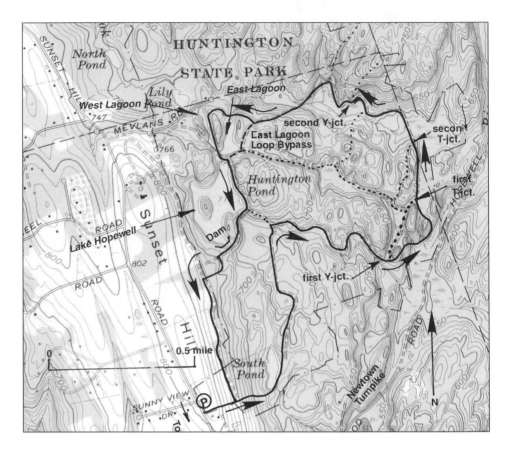

field. Turn right onto the well-defined trail through an open area plagued with a too-common choking alien—Oriental bittersweet. The animal and bird sounds you often hear in this area are reminiscent of the background noises of an old jungle movie! Surrounded by vines, the eroded trail continues downhill, bearing left around South Pond. Pass an old foundation and bear left at the fork to briefly skirt the edge of this pond. Continue straight past a low dam on your left and cross the bridge over the pond's outlet stream. Stay on the well-trodden trail, marked with intermittent blue plastic blazes, as it curves left around the pond.

After passing a trail on your right, walk through a well-managed woodlot. Selective harvesting has been used to eliminate junk species such as black oak, to remove wolf trees (oddly shaped trees that have grown in ungainly configurations, do not produce good timber, and shade out potentially valuable trees), and to create optimum conditions for the growth of usable trees.

Proceed past a trail at right by a huge split rock. Stay straight on a wide trail, soon passing another trail at your right. Pass several scarred beech trees. The beech's smooth, gray bark grows with the tree—it doesn't flake off with time, so marks or initials decades old still retain their shape. Legend has it that Daniel Boone carved his name into a beech tree when he once "cilled a bar" in Tennessee. The carving lasted for more than 150 years before the tree finally toppled.

Bear right over a small rise, cross the bridge that spans Lake Hopewell's outlet, and immediately go right at the junction about 1¾ miles from the start, staying with the blue markers. A stream comes in and soon parallels the trail on your right.

Shortly you reach your first Y-junction (see map) below a large rock face—follow the blue markers to your right. A short side trail here leads left to the top of the rock. Your route goes downhill and then bears left, reaching a small stream below still more rocks. Cross the stream on a bridge, and soon you will cross yet another stream running under a wooden plank bridge. Pass through an area of old blowdowns within a narrow stream valley. You can see Newtown Turnpike to your right through the trees in the distance.

Parallel the turnpike, climb uphill, bear left, and cross a stream on a small footbridge with a large boulder on your right. The boulder's source, a ledge, is on your left. At your first T-junction (see map), stay with the blue markers and go right—there is now a swamp to your right.

Follow the trail to your left and reach the second T-junction (see map) with a generic park trail sign. Again, stay with the blue markers and turn right. After crossing a stream, curve left and then right before reaching another junction with a trail leading to your left about 2½ miles from the start—stay straight on the worn woods road. This route will quickly crest a rise and bear to the right. In about ¼ mile bear left onto the lower woods road blazed with white markers at your second Y-junction (see map). Your way curves right and then left uphill to a junction in another 250 yards—go left here, following green markers along the base of an outcropping on your right. Cross

Wolves baying at the moon

a stream. This area has a large number of tulip trees, a more southern species that is dominant in the Great Smoky Mountains National Park.

You climb, then level out, passing a stone wall on your right about halfway up the hill. Continue through a rusted gate. Immediately go right onto a less used white-blazed path, away from the wide old woods road. (If you wish, you may eliminate the loop around East Lagoon by staying on the main trail, which shortly crosses the lagoon's outlet on a wooden bridge and then rejoins your path at the bridge between East Lagoon and Lake Hopewell.)

Parallel a rusted fence, and then bear right and uphill around East Lagoon. A parking area soon appears downhill to your right. Turn left onto a narrow path through the laurel before descending toward the lot.

Descend steeply over ledges to the shore of West Lagoon and follow the trail to the bridge over its outlet. Cross between East and West Lagoons on the footbridge. Immediately at the junction, go left over still another bridge with East Lagoon to your left and Lake Hopewell to your right.

At the junction just past this bridge, go to your right uphill on an orange-marked gravel road that goes along and above Lake Hopewell. At the junction at the lake's end, turn right onto the white-marked path and walk across an earthen dam. At the end of the dam the road curves left to follow above the outlet stream's valley. You will shortly see a lightning-struck tulip tree. The tree was struck very high up, and the ribbon of blasted bark can be traced all the way to its base. Such bark removal is caused by the instantaneous conversion of the sap to steam, which in its violent escape blasts off the bark. An extra-tall tree such as this one gets the lion's share of life-giving sunlight, but because it is the highest point around it is also a magnet for lightning bolts.

You parallel a fence, and then reach a T-junction—turn left to follow blue markers. Shortly you will pass through a gateless, pole-flanked opening in the wire fence. Continue on the old road through seemingly impenetrable vine and brush thickets. In about ½ mile you reach the trail that leads uphill through the field to your car. Ascend along the edge of the field to the parking lot.

22

Green Fall Pond

Location: Voluntown

Distance: 5.7 miles

Vertical rise: 540 feet

Time: 3 hours

Rating: CD

Map: USGS 7.5-minute Voluntown

Far eastern Connecticut seems to have been forgotten by the 20th century—let alone the 21st. Roads change from tar to dirt, and stone walls are strikingly square and straight, evidence that they are not the trappings of gentlemen farmers but carefully maintained, functional components of working farms. Except for occasional fields and farmhouses, this untenanted, overgrown area is much as the westward-bound pioneers left it. Your hike on the Narragansett Trail to Green Fall Pond in Pachaug State Forest takes you through this secluded region.

From the junction of CT 49, CT 138, and CT 165 in Voluntown, drive south on CT 49 for 4 miles, and then turn left onto Sand Hill Road. In about a mile turn right onto Wheeler Road and go 0.5 mile, where you will see the blue blazes of the Narragansett Trail. Park near the blazes, pulling off the road as far as possible; the traffic is minimal. In May the flowering dogwoods punctuate the springtime greens with their white bracts. Their flowers are actually green clusters in the center of the white-colored, specialized leaves.

Enter the woods on the east side of the road (to your left as you drove down Wheeler Road from Sand Hill Road). The Blue Trail System marks trail changes with double blazes, usually offsetting the upper blaze in the direction of the turn. Follow the trail gently downward, with several seasonal streams interrupting the path and soothing the soul with their melodious chatter. This thin-soiled, rock-ribbed land is largely clothed in oak.

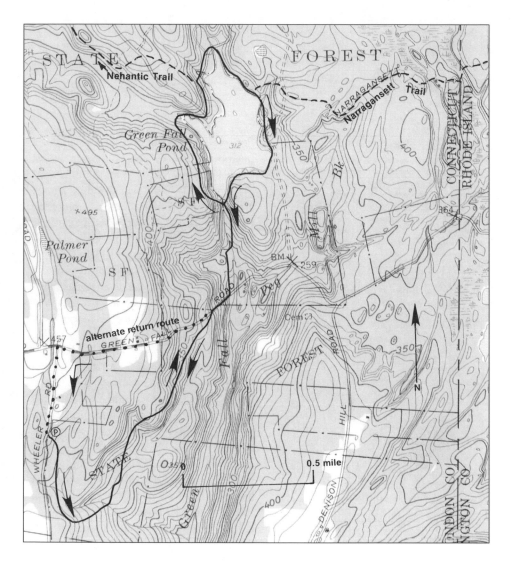

After 0.4 mile you'll descend a steep, rocky slope toward the valley. Parallel and then cross a stream. On your left you soon pass a 25-foot rock face graced with lichens, mosses, ferns, and even a few struggling trees. Just beyond is an even more impressive rock face, with larger trees growing from its sides. At its base lies a jumble of large rock slabs that were once part of the cliff but have split off since the glaciers bulldozed their way through here. Perhaps these slabs were forced off in years past by trees, since vanished, whose incessant growth slowly but surely split the rock.

After crossing another stream, you soon find yourself on the edge of Green Fall River Valley by a large, crumbling boulder. Look closely at this rock mass; its shade, moisture retention, and slant toward the sun create miniature ecosystems. While the stark, drier sides are gray with lichens, the shaded areas with pockets of soil hold a soft cushion of mosses. In wet times the surface of a moist, crumbly hollow is colored with light green algae. The thin soil of its horizontal surfaces supports clumps of polypody fern. Large birches buttress the sides of the boulder, which is crowned with an unexpected juniper; the rock's sunny, well-drained top provides the conditions that the juniper needs. An early settler of untended, tired fields, this prickly evergreen is ordinarily shaded out by the forest canopy as taller trees eventually grow in above it.

Bear left, crossing two rocky seasonal streams. Step carefully; the smooth rocks become very slippery when their covering of mosses and lichens swells with moisture. After the second stream, proceed gradually uphill and along the valley rim to Green Fall Road, a dirt road 1.4 miles from your start. This road is an eastern extension of Sand Hill Road.

Turn right and follow the road downhill for 0.1 mile. Turn left off the road, just before crossing the bridge, and follow the blue-blazed trail along the river, which is now on your right. The path climbs a rocky ridge and passes a large cairn before descending to follow the bottom of a narrow ravine that speeds the river over boulders and ledges. About midway to the pond you cross the river at a shallow, rocky spot.

The trail clambers over boulders where root-hung hemlocks cling to a steep, eroding slope. The inward-pressing rock walls are thickly covered with mosses and lichens. Soon the trail climbs steadily up the side of the ravine to avoid a sharp drop into the river. Be careful not to trip on the exposed roots along the top.

You reach the base of Green Fall Pond Dam 1.9 miles from the start. Climb up the embankment to the right of the dam, and turn left to cross over the top of the dam on a wooden footbridge with handrails. Follow the route, now marked by blue blazes with orange spots (called orange blazes for simplicity), around the west side of Green Fall Pond. The Narragansett Trail goes around the east side of the pond—you will return that way.

Follow the orange blazes, first on a gravel road, then onto a footpath, keeping Green Fall Pond always on your right. This trout-stocked pond is one of Connecticut's nicest—it has lovely ledges dropping into the water, small islands, fully wooded shores, and no cottages.

The trail hugs a shore thickly grown with laurel, oak, birch, and hemlock. About 0.2 mile from the dam, the path crosses a feeder stream and continues rounding the pond. If you lose the trail here, head toward the pond—in most places the trail edges the shore. A ledge-tipped point across the bay to your right comes into view.

After ascending a wide, wooden-stepped path, you reach the paved road that services the campground; turn right. Continue following the orange blazes along the road. You'll pass the blue blazes of the Nehantic Trail to your left. Shortly after passing the campground and crossing the major inlet to the pond, the trail turns right at a sign for the Green Fall Trail. Many of the large outcroppings on your left bear patches of a large, thick-fleshed, curling lichen called rock tripe, which is considered nourishing in case of a dire emergency. Canadian voyageurs reputedly used it to thicken their soups.

The trail is now in sight of the pond. The orange-blazed trail ends at the blue-blazed Narragansett Trail 1.2 miles from the dam; turn right to follow the blue blazes along the edge of the pond. Cross a small brook on

Green Fall Pond

stepping-stones; at times of high water, an upstream detour will let you cross dry-shod.

The trail climbs a rocky ridge for the view of nearby rolling hills, drops down, and visits a rocky point. Enjoy these meanderings—a well-laid-out trail lets you explore all points of interest. Go right on an earth-filled auxiliary dam. The underwater face of the dam to your right is covered with rock riprap to minimize erosion.

The trail enters the woods just beyond the auxiliary dam. Follow the ridge overlooking the pond before descending diagonally down to the shore. Pass the dam to your right and descend the embankment. Retrace your steps down the ravine and back to your starting point. For variety, instead of reentering the woods on the other side of Green Fall Road, you may choose to continue along the gravel road, passing a farm, to the junction with Wheeler Road. Turn left onto Wheeler Road; your car will be ½ mile down the quiet road.

23

Northern Nipmuck

Location: Ashford

Distance: 5¼ miles

Vertical rise: 550 feet

Time: 3 hours

Rating: C

Map: USGS 7.5-minute Westford

The entire 14-mile section of the northern Nipmuck Trail, opened in 1976, offers delightful woods walking. This particular hike loops through the private Yale Forest and returns to your point of origin along two little-used gravel roads with the unusual names of Boston Hollow Road and Axe Factory Road.

The start of this hike is located in northern Connecticut, where the crisscross roads are as independent as the area's people. Follow CT 89 north for 4 miles from the junction of US 44 and CT 89 in Warrenville. Bear right at the Westford blinking traffic light. In 0.3 mile, where the tar road bends right, stay straight on gravel Boston Hollow Road. The blue-blazed trail crosses the road in another 1.3 miles. There is enough room for three cars to park on your left.

Follow the blazes north (left) into the woods. In late summer the flat forest floor is liberally decorated with Virginia creeper, wild sarsaparilla, and fruiting blue cohosh, as well as interrupted and rattlesnake ferns. The latter is the largest and most common of the succulent grape ferns; the simple, large, triangular leaf and its early-season spore stalk are unmistakable.

Shortly the trail climbs steeply onto a hemlock- and oak-covered ridge and bears left. Boston Hollow Road, parallel to the trail, is visible below through the trees. Then, winding west through thickets of mountain laurel, the path gently climbs the side of a hemlock-covered hillside. Although the hiker finds mountain laurel lovely—in

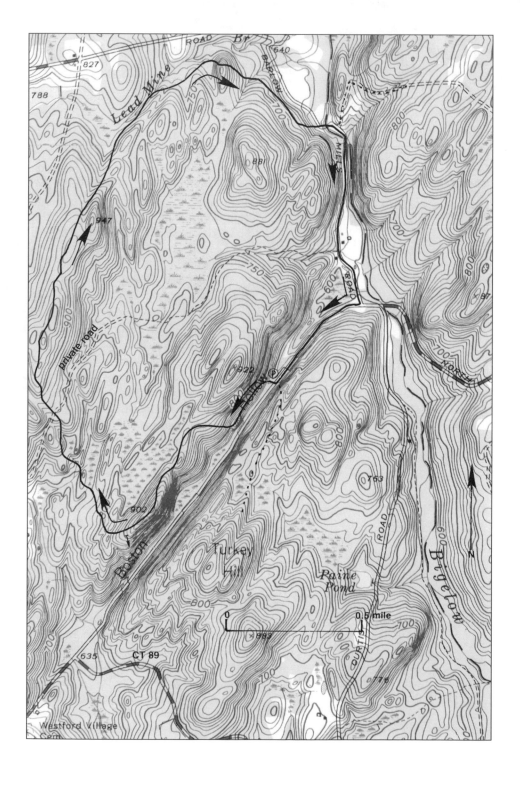

Black-eyed Susans at a field's edge

winter the evergreen leaves add color to the woods, and in late spring there is no more beautiful blossom—its tangled growth is the bane of the trail maintainer; it is a tough, stubborn bush whose stubs must be cut off lest they impale the stumbling hiker!

Jouncing up and down several small, rocky ridges, you pass scattered patches of striped maple. Lovely views of the woodlands to the north, west, and south greet you as you reach the top of the ridge before bearing right downhill, away from Boston Hollow Road.

If you walk this way in mid-August, you can catch the first signs of the tipping of the year's seasonal hourglass. The lush vegetation looks slightly shopworn. Evergreen plants, previously overshadowed, sparkle with the fresh sheen of their new leaves, which will carry them through fall, winter, and into the start of yet another spring. Goldenrod and aster—fall's premier flow-ers—are prominent. The autumn spate of mushrooms has started: white and yellow puffballs, white *Amanita* that only the real experts dare to sort and eat (the deadliest is appropriately called the destroying angel—it is said to taste good going down, but with the passage of a few hours the fully absorbed nerve poison is 100 percent fatal), and the red-capped emetic *Rusula* (also poisonous, but fortunately it can't be kept down when eaten). Moss-bedded, dry, rocky rills recall spring's long-gone moisture. The ghostly Indian pipes have become blackened skeletons, although they are just erupting through the forest litter in the mountains to your north. An admirer of a particular flower can often prolong the viewing season by moving north with the blooms.

In about 2 miles you cross a private dirt road. After a little way the trail follows the remnants of an old tote road north, soon joining another tote road coming in from the southeast. There has been some recent logging on this ridge, but the trail remains easy to follow and well blazed. Connecticut's forests have been spared the ax (or the chain saw) compared to other New England woods, but its highly valued oaks appear to have reached a size suitable for harvesting. We hope that trails and logging can coexist; remember that a productive forest is one worth keeping and that interesting hiking trails need forests.

The trail then swings right (northwest) off this road to descend from the ridge and enter a small ravine. Finally, you ascend a hemlock-covered escarpment; below is one of Bigelow Brook's small, noisy tributaries.

In another ½ mile or so, after bearing left downhill, you emerge on gravel Axe Factory Road by a stream-threaded meadow. Although the woods vegetation has faded, late summer brings a riotous flowering in open fields and meadows. Great purple-crowned stalks of joe-pye weed, white-flowering boneset (an herbal fever remedy), goldenrod, Saint-John's-wort, the three-leafed hog peanut vine, and pealike clusters of groundnuts are everywhere. Blackberries invite you to snack, bumblebees engage in a final orgy of nectar gathering, and the sweet smell of pepperbush pervades the air. Here the marshy stream trickles through metal culverts; minnows and pickerel play a deadly game of hide-and-seek amid the waterweeds.

You are just less than 1.25 miles from your car as you come out onto the road. Leaving the trail behind, return to your car by following Axe Factory Road to your right and then Boston Hollow Road, also to your right. Both these gravel roads are little used and a delight to walk. Cement and stone remnants of a mill wall are visible from the next bridge. Pasturing cows and a farm pond farther on compose a peaceful scene—a fitting conclusion to this relaxing hike through the countryside.

24

Chatfield Hollow

Location: Killingworth

Distance: 5.5 miles

Vertical rise: 500 feet

Time: 3 hours

Rating: C

Maps: USGS 7.5-minute Clinton, Haddam

Hikers may complain about the overuse of a few select areas, yet Connecticut's trails are for the most part underutilized. As throughout the East, Connecticut's portion of the Appalachian Trail is heavily traveled, while most other trails are often practically deserted. If you feel that one of the joys of hiking is temporarily leaving behind the clamor of fellow human beings, consider Chatfield Hollow State Park. Despite several hundred carloads of people in the park on a summer weekend, on our visits we've met very few folks on this park's well-maintained trails.

Chatfield Hollow lies within that wide band of woodland separating the overdeveloped shore from the inland tier of cities. From the junction of CT 80 and CT 81 in Killingworth, drive west 1 mile on CT 80. The park entrance is on your right. Park at the hikers' lot just to the right of the park gate.

Follow the tar road, keeping to your left to pass over the dam for Schreeder Pond. The pond, which offers fishing, swimming, and picnicking, is the focus of park activity. Turn left down the park exit road. A short detour to your right just beyond the dam leads to Oak Lodge, built, along with the dam, by the Civilian Conservation Corps in the 1930s. A marker honors CCC Camp Roosevelt, Company No. 171. Backtrack to follow the park exit road south. Beyond the maintenance buildings (the winter home of the Old Mill Pond waterwheel), turn right into the woods opposite a small grove of white pine trees on the orange-blazed Deep Woods Trail.

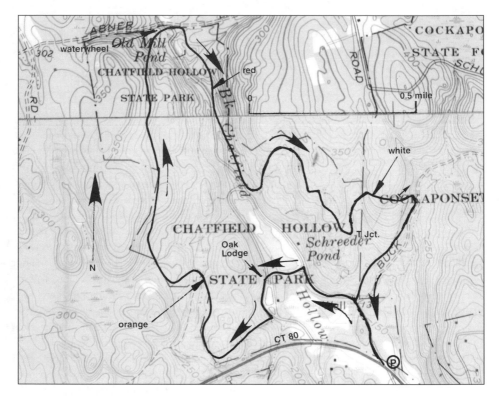

Climb up a rocky slope, atop which are open rock ledges decorated with mountain laurel. Whenever we mention mountain laurel to people, they often exclaim that they will have to go there in June to catch the display of gorgeous flowers. However, any one twig of mountain laurel blooms at best every other year, so you could conceivably have half the flowers in bloom each year. Most areas have a great year followed by a so-so year, when most twigs are busily putting their energy into new growth instead of flowers. Once you know an area's pattern, you can usually depend upon hitting the great flowering every other year; mid- to late June is the best time.

One-half mile from the start you curve left off the ledges, then pass beneath them. The ledges' rock faces are stained with mosses and lichens, and trees sprout from great cracks. You can use lichens as an indicator of air quality; an abundance of lichens signifies clean air, whereas pollution inhibits their growth and can even kill them.

Near a small brook crossing, a park naturalist once attached signs to many trees—among them yellow birch, black birch, chestnut oak, white oak, American beech, sugar maple, pignut hickory, and tulip tree. Most of the signs are in this area, but we saw a few signs scattered throughout the park.

Not very far from here Gerry once caught and released a hognose snake. This snake is so safe to handle that it makes the common garter snake look dangerous. When accosted, this slow-moving species will stop, flatten its head and throat, hiss, and otherwise threaten you. Unfortunately, this fearsome display has gotten the hognose snake killed on occasion.

If this ploy doesn't work, then it will writhe, turn over, and play dead, lolling its tongue. To all appearances it is dead, but if you turn it onto its stomach, it will promptly roll over onto its back—a "dead" snake must be belly-up! It will only play dead for a while before it will once again try to flee. The most annoying thing about these snakes, which we've never known to bite, is the foul-smelling fluid they leave on your skin when handled—it can take some time before this smell wears off or washes away. All things considered, snakes should be observed, but not picked up—it's safer for both the human and the snake.

After passing a blue-blazed trail and descending the slope gently, you turn sharply right, pass an old foundation, and drop to the park road, passing a second blue-blazed trail, well beyond Schreeder Pond. Proceed to your left along the road, across the bridge, and around the east side of dammed Old Mill Pond to pick up the red-blazed Ridge Trail. Initially this footpath parallels the stream and passes abreast a waterwheel (an undershot wheel, wherein the water strikes the middle of the wheel and its falling weight turns the wheel). Bear left uphill just before reaching a covered bridge.

Follow the red-blazed Ridge Trail generally uphill, passing beside and over several ledges. Finally turn left steadily uphill. After a few yards the trail curves back on itself. The park's trail system does a marvelous job of twisting and winding through and along the most interesting areas. You'll level off a bit, climb steeply again, and emerge on top of a ledge after passing around the left end of a large, almost perpendicular rock wall.

At a T-junction turn left, following an un-blazed trail that leads to the White Trail, leaving the red blazes. Follow it a short distance to the white-blazed Look Out Trail. Bear left (north) onto this trail. (If you go right, you'll soon reach Buck Road and then the paved entrance road, having completed about 4.5 miles.)

In another ¼ mile along the Look Out Trail you'll reach an open ledge with a cameo view down the valley. Eventually you come out onto a ledge with a nice view south that encompasses Foster Ponds south of CT 80. Then curve around to your right and zigzag steeply down the slope. Briefly join the blue-blazed East Woods Trail, then bear right to remain on the white-blazed trail.

Several times, on your left, you will glimpse a gravel road (Buck Road) below you as you tend downhill. Descend through pines and sugar maples to the paved park road, and turn left. Follow that road to CT 80 and your car.

25

Great Hill

Location: East Hampton

Distance: 5.5 miles

Vertical rise: 800 feet

Time: 3 hours

Rating: C

Map: USGS 7.5-minute Middle Haddam

This hike begins on the Shenipsit Trail near a long-abandoned cobalt mine in the obscure town of Cobalt. From there you climb a rocky ridge to Great Hill, which rewards you with a panoramic view over the Connecticut River. A short hike along the ridge brings you to a beautiful secluded cascade at the foot of Bald Hill.

From the junction of CT 66 and CT 151 in Cobalt, drive north on Depot Hill Road. At the first fork, keep right up a steep hill. After almost 0.9 mile, turn right onto Gadpouch Road, the first right after Stage Coach Run. The blue-blazed trail starts on your left in 0.5 mile, soon after the road becomes dirt. Park on your right nearly opposite the trailhead.

Before you start the hike, walk over to the large hemlock grove near your car. The entrance to the cobalt mine (sealed up at the time we visited) was down the hill in the shaded ravine. Deep pits on top of the hill, farther up the road to your right, tell of the cave-in of the mine roof. Originally opened by Connecticut Governor John Winthrop (son of colonial Massachusetts's John Winthrop) in 1661, the mine was active until the mid-1800s. The cobalt extracted was shipped as far away as England and China for use in the manufacture of a deep blue paint and porcelain glaze.

Return to the trailhead across the road and follow the blazes through ash-dominated hardwoods. These trees range from mature specimens 2 feet in diameter to fast-growing, strong, lightweight sprouts the size of baseball bats—in fact, ash sprouts are used to make most wooden baseball bats!

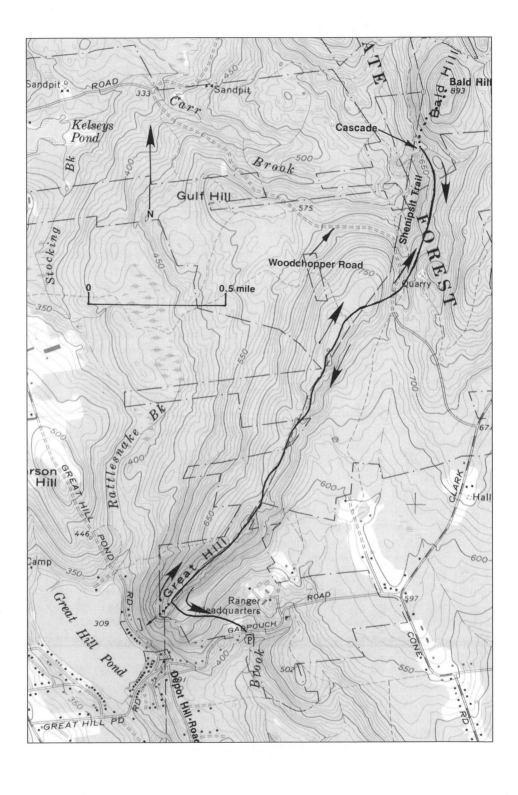

This section of the trail, always wet and muddy, is at its worst during the spring thaw.

The trail starts climbing gradually. Look to your left for the round-leafed shoots of the wild onion. The leaves and bulb can provide a sharp-tasting treat. In spring the skunk cabbage raises its hooded head above the soggy ground. Soon the trail climbs steeply before leveling off briefly. When you resume climbing, look to your right for a patch of a creeping evergreen: partridgeberry. The tiny, heart-shaped leaves set off any of the bright red berries that may have been overlooked by ruffed grouse and white-footed wood mice. Oddly enough, this relative of the dainty bluet thrives in Mexico and Japan, as well as in most of eastern North America.

The trail zigzags steeply up the rocky side of Great Hill. At the crest, take the white-blazed trail left a short distance to a rocky lookout treed with oak and pitch pine. Follow the Connecticut River with your eyes. Directly below you is cottage-rimmed Great Hill Pond. In the middle distance are the smokestacks of the Middletown power plant. To your left, next to a girder-framed dock, the Pratt and Whitney Middletown jet engine facility sprawls over the countryside. At the dock, barges and small tankers offload their cargoes of jet fuel. Continuing southward, the river's wanderings become lost to your eye amid the horizon's low rolling hills. The Mattabesett Trail follows the western horizon ridge. Northwest of the power plant, the bare slopes of the Powder Ridge Ski Area punctuate the hillside. The old colonial seaport of Middletown lies on the west side of the river.

Retrace your steps to the blue blazes. The trail continues north-northeast along the straight, narrow ridge for almost 2 miles before descending.

About a mile into the hike you'll see several deep holes in a live black oak just to the right of the trail. The pileated woodpecker cut these in its eternal quest for black carpenter ants. If you look closely, you will see the remains of the ant galleries at the bottom of some of the holes. By sound and/or smell the birds detect the insects in the rotten heartwood through several inches of living wood and use their great chisel beaks to reach them.

About 1½ miles into the hike look for an attractive rock jumble on your right. Several of the larger, flatter rocks have masses of the evergreen polypody fern on them. The deep green leaves of this shade-loving fern arise from creeping rootstocks. It grows on rocks, cliff edges, and even downed trees where acidic humus has accumulated. In midsummer the undersides of the upper leaflets are decorated with double rows of red-brown spore bodies—the next generation.

The trail descends the ridge gradually and joins a tote road 1¾ miles from the start. Used mostly before World War I, tote roads were cut to "tote" logs from the woods. The soil became so compacted from this use that many of these old lanes are still virtually free of vegetation.

After another 0.2 mile of branching onto several tote roads, the trail crosses a gravel forest road (Woodchopper Road). As you cross to the west-facing slope along this gravel road, notice the scattered, straight, tall tulip trees that were absent from the east-facing slope. Here, near the northern limit of the tulip trees, minor differences of soil or exposure can create distinct demarcation lines. The large, tuliplike orange and green flowers and distinctive, four-pointed leaves with notched tips are unmistakable in summer. The numerous flower husks clinging to the upper branches make for certain winter identification.

Continue on the blue-blazed trail and you'll soon pass the remains of a small quarry and join a relatively recent lumbering road. Continue to follow the blue blazes along this road for about ¼ mile. Leave the road and follow the trail to your left downhill, soon crossing a small brook. After crossing a second, larger brook, you'll reach a cascade, which is at its best during the early-spring runoff. However, crossing the brook can also be problematic during runoff.

This is a favorite place. In spring the sheet of water flowing evenly down the steep face of the moss-covered rock ledge creates a soothing sound. Bubbles formed in the turbulence glide merrily across the pool at the base of the cascade, accumulating in windrows of pollution-free foam. This is a fine place for a quiet picnic, a good book, or simply a restful interlude.

When you are ready, retrace your steps, taking care to follow the blazes through the maze of tote roads back to Woodchopper Road. Pause for a final view from the Great Hill lookout before returning to your car.

McLean Game Refuge

Location: Granby

Distance: 5 miles

Vertical rise: 600 feet

Time: 3 hours

Rating: C

Map: USGS 7.5-minute Tariffville

Tucked away in north-central Connecticut, the privately endowed McLean Game Refuge was established in 1932 by George P. McLean, a former governor of Connecticut and U.S. senator who wanted "the game refuge to be a place where trees can grow . . . and animal life can exist unmolested . . . a place where some of the things God made may be seen by those who love them as I loved them." Comprised of nearly 3,500 acres, the refuge is open to the public daily from 8 AM to dusk.

Today, be you hiker or cross-country skier, the refuge's excellent trail network provides access to acres of woodlands teeming with wildlife, as McLean had hoped. Although it is hard to predict what you will see on any given hike, on a mid-February day we watched a fairly common, but rarely seen, brown creeper moving in fits and starts up a shagbark hickory; a flock of bustling chickadees; and a chipmunk breaking its hibernation in the above-freezing temperatures. A small quick noise proved to be a ruffed grouse taking a few short steps before launching into flight with a thunderous roar.

The main entrance to this refuge is located on US 202/CT 10 in Granby, 1 mile south of its junction with CT 20. Year-round parking is available just off the highway in a gravel lot.

Cross the field on the macadam road surface to the edge of the woods. To your left is a beautiful trail map giving a sense of the trail system ahead of you. Walk along the road a short distance to an old shelter on your left. Cross the bridge over Bissell

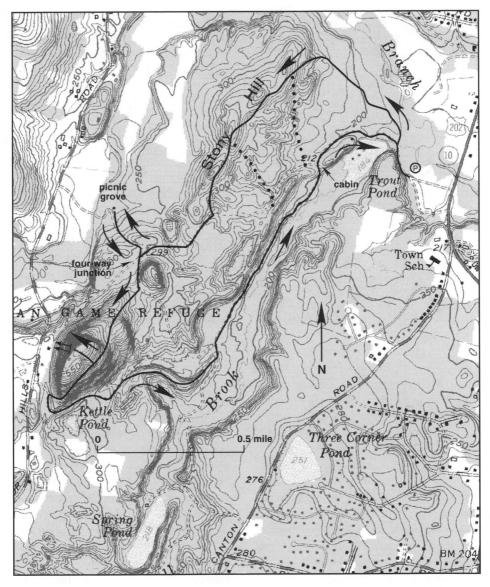

Brook, which flows from the trout pond just beyond the shelter. The loop trail starts just beyond the bridge on your right. Follow its blue, orange, and red blazes to ascend a small knoll. Look carefully down the slope to your right for two decaying butternut trees. The early settlers used a short-lived member of the walnut family, the butternut tree, as a source of yellow, water-soluble dye. Butternut dye was famous for coloring Confederate uniforms during the Civil War. The nuts have an excellent flavor, but their iron-hard shells beneath the sticky green covering are difficult to crack.

The trail, which has been paralleling Salmon Brook just out of sight to your right,

Pond view in McLean Game Refuge

bends away from the brook to the left. About ½ mile from the start, at the top of a small rise, the red-marked loop trail leaves to the left to return to the woods road west of the trout pond. Continue following the blue and orange blazes. However, first look back to the left of the trail and note what remains of the large, dead red pine with several narrow, 6-inch-long, vertical holes in its trunk. Only the jackhammer bill of the pileated woodpecker can make such an opening. Although this tree is now dead, newer growth around the hole indicates that the cavities were made while the pine was still living. The decayed, honeycombed interior indicates that the tree's center was infested with the fungus-eating, large, black carpenter ants that are the woodpecker's favorite food.

After a level stretch, the blue-and-orange-blazed trail tends gently upward. In another ½ mile or so you will reach an over-grown clearing atop Stony Hill with the Barndoor Hills visible to the south through leafless trees. Shortly, the orange-blazed trail diverges left toward the valley below. Keep following the blue-blazed trail over a rise to a worn woods road. Here you would turn left to complete the loop. Another blue-blazed path goes straight into the woods. Turn right to follow the unblazed woods road over a rise to a woods road junction.

Turn left at this junction, following signs to the summit. After a short ascent, pass a woods road to your left and resume climbing. As you ascend, the forest changes from the moisture-loving hemlocks to the oaks of well-drained hillsides. The woods road is more appropriately called a rock road as it hugs the steep western slope of Barndoor Hill. Near the top of the rise turn right and follow a blue-blazed trail on a short, steep climb to the summit. This is an ideal lunch spot, with grand views to the north and

50 Hikes in Connecticut

west. The viewpoints along the cliff have fairly well-trodden paths between them. Try not to wander off the path; the vegetation here is already stressed by the lack of moisture on this hilltop. Stepping on the plants can easily kill many years of slow growth.

When ready, retrace your steps to the woods road and turn right, descending steeply southwest toward Barndoor Hills Road and Kettle Pond. Turn left 50 yards in front of a wooden gate and follow the worn path northeast toward the pond. You'll soon pass the depression of Kettle Pond to your right. Continue along the main path, passing a side trail to your right, through a mature pine forest with plenty of partridgeberry, a trailing shrub, on the forest floor. Bear right at a Y-junction to stay on level ground and start following blue blazes along a narrow ridge. Turn left at a T-junction to leave the ridge. Descend to another junction and turn right onto a wide woods road. Continue along the unblazed woods road to a T-junction (see map). Signs here tell you the road to your left leads to Trout Pond; to your right is Spring Lake. Turn left and follow this unblazed woods road north, keeping a ridge to your left and Bissell Brook to your right.

Near the trout pond you'll reach another signed woods road junction. This time the road you were on leads back to Spring Pond; to your left is Picnic Grove, and to your right is Route 10 Cabin. Bear right and soon you will pass a locked cabin to your right, and then the trout pond. Spend a few minutes at the pond's edge. This is an ideal place to identify fish swimming in the water. Tossing some small pieces of bread into the pond may attract some fish. Since fishing in the refuge is prohibited, they are quite tame. Watch for the flat ovals of the sunfish and bluegills, the former distinguished by sharper coloration and a sunburst of yellow on their breasts. The vertical-barred yellow perch, constantly cruising black bass with horizontal side stripes, and swarming shiners complete the list of the pond's bread-eating fish. Lurking in the weeds you may see a long, thin pickerel sliding in for a quick meal of one of the bread eaters.

This fecund pond is also the annual breeding ground for Canada geese. If you look sharply to your right toward the pond's shallow end, you may notice a large brush pile—a beaver lodge. The beavers occasionally create trouble by damming up the pond's outlet. Leave the pond and follow the woods road to your right, passing the start of the loop trail you began on, and hike back to your car.

27

Northwest Park

Location: Windsor

Distance: 6 miles

Vertical rise: 200 feet

Time: 3¼ hours

Rating: CD

Map: USGS 7.5-minute Windsor Locks

A major feature of the Connecticut River Valley is fading fast. Our world-famous crop of shade-grown tobacco, once the most valuable agricultural crop in the country, is about gone. In the late 1930s Windsor alone had 3,000 acres of shade-grown tobacco. More than 1,600 square miles of tobacco, under its head-high cover of shade-cloth, were found in the Connecticut River Valley and dominated the landscape long after World War II. Cheaper tobacco from other countries, a reduction in the number of smokers, and the astronomical increase in the value of the land for housing have all contributed to the near extinction of our shade-grown tobacco.

Most of the state's thousands of imposing tobacco barns, where the crop was dried for use as top-quality cigar wrappers, were torn down for their weathered lumber, which, ironically, was extensively used in the same houses that contributed to the decline of this valuable crop. One of the special features of this hike is the still-looming presence of tobacco barns. A generation ago these barns were everywhere. These days they are about gone, but here you will pass several of these reminders of bygone days on this 465-acre property now owned by the town of Windsor.

This park includes 8.2 miles of trail, and the hike we have chosen is about 6 miles long. Pick up a trail map on your visit to the park and invent your own loops to create shorter or longer hikes if you wish. To get to Northwest Park, take exit 38 off I-91 (about 7 miles north of Hartford). Go north on CT

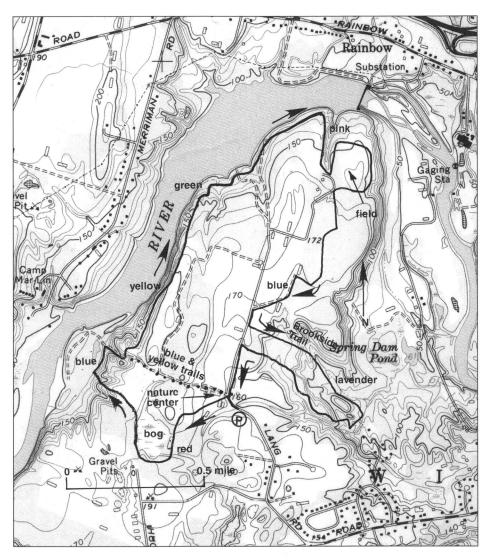

75 (Poquonock Avenue) for 1.6 miles, and then turn left onto Prospect Hill Road. After 1.2 miles, at the traffic circle, go right onto Lang Road. Continue 0.4 mile to the parking lot at the entrance to Northwest Park.

Walk past the small pond to the interpretive nature center (call for hours; 860-285-1886). You may want to wait until after your hike to visit the center, but do go in before you leave. Trail maps are available near the door to the center. Go down the dirt road to the left of the nature center (playground at left) past the old tobacco barns. Cross the field, keeping the nature center to your right and the picnic pavilion to your left. Enter the woods and follow the signs straight ahead to the Bog, Hemlock, and Pond Trails—there is a picnic area on your right. Shortly the Pond (and Wetland Forest) Trail goes straight, but you go left toward the

Bog Trail on a red-blazed old road. At another junction, stay straight to follow the red-blazed Bog Trail.

The Bog Trail is a 0.6-mile Braille trail, dedicated to the memory of Merlin W. Sargent in appreciation of his many years of service to the American Youth Hostels Yankee Council. The guide rope will conduct you around the bog and return you to the starting point. Once we had scouted this hike on a day that was warm and humid (ideal mosquito weather), we decided to continue straight ahead to the Hemlock Trail. Our decision was reinforced when a solitary hiker came by, telling us, "I just tripped over a mosquito in the bog!" In cooler weather, however, this is a delightful trail. A few interpretive signs provide some good forest and bog information.

Pass through a chain-link fence associated with the landfill to your left, and about halfway around the bog, pass a junction with the white-blazed Hemlock Trail. Bear left onto the blue-and-white-blazed Pond Trail and descend to the swampy pond.

Turn right at the junction, and follow the blue-blazed Pond Trail. You soon loop to your right uphill and then down again. Cross an old log bridge, which may be slippery. Look out at the pond ahead, then bear right onto another wooden bridge before turning sharply right uphill on an eroded trail just before reaching a gravel road.

At the top of the hill, go left on the yellow-blazed Wetland Forest Trail. (If you go straight, the blue- and yellow-blazed trails run together until you reach a dirt road that leads back to the nature center in less than ½ mile.) Continue downhill on the yellow-blazed trail, soon crossing an old road as the trail levels out. Shortly after passing a large boulder on your right, you catch glimpses of the Farmington River below at

left. You soon parallel the edge of a field to your right.

When you reach the next junction, leave the Wetland Forest Trail and continue straight on the green-blazed Connector Trail A. To your left there are intermittent views of the river as you drop down to the riverbank. Soon the trail goes right and you cross a wooden footbridge before meeting the red-blazed Rainbow Reservoir Trail. Continue straight, following the red blazes. Pass picnic tables and then a bench at a vista over the reservoir, and bear right away from the river. Parallel the shoreline for a way before reaching a significant feeder stream. Here you'll turn right and follow its ravine upstream to cross. During one March visit we observed a small flock of turkeys in this hollow. Near the U-turn in the trail, pass the green-blazed Connector Trail B to your right.

Stay on the Rainbow Reservoir Trail and head back toward the reservoir. After passing through a wet section of trail, you'll enter a field and bear right away from the reservoir again. Follow the road clockwise around the edge of the field. The route is sporadically blazed with posts, but the tobacco road is easy enough to follow. After traveling south along the eastern edge of the field, turn right to follow its southern edge.

Leave the field as the road enters the woods, passing the remains of an old gate. Soon you turn left at a woods road junction to follow the blue blazes of the Open Forest Trail. Turn right off the road and follow a path through the woods just west of a housing development that was visible through March's leafless forest.

Reenter the clearing that once boasted tobacco fields. Turn left on another farm road, passing the barns that were once full of curing tobacco leaves. Bear right onto a gravel road that leads back to the nature center. Within sight of the center, turn left to follow the lavender-blazed Brookside Trail. This path takes you down and back through a hollow filled with impressive trees: hemlock, white pine, American beech, and red oak. It is well worth the 1.1-mile walk. Upon returning to the gravel road, turn left back to the center and your car.

28

Mount Higby

Location: Middlefield

Distance: 5.0 miles

Vertical rise: 1,100 feet

Time: 3¼ hours

Rating: B

Map: USGS 7.5-minute Middletown

This is a hike that ancient volcanism built; Mount Higby is a traprock ridge. The rough footing is counterbalanced by sweeping views of the woods and pastoral settings, or superhighways and development, depending upon where you look.

You start this hike west of the junction of CT 66 and CT 147, west of Middletown. Pull off the westbound lane of CT 66, ⅓ mile west of Guida's Drive-In. A short, red-blazed woods road leads north 100 yards to the blue-blazed Mattabesett Trail. The side trail to Guida's still exists, but parking is no longer permitted in its lot. Still, a short walk east after the hike for refreshments is always a good reward for family and friends.

Follow the blue-blazed Mattabesett Trail uphill away from the road. You may want to take a botany detour left to the ditch next to the paved road, where you can see some small, pinelike plants. These are horsetails, diminutive descendants of ancient forests. Eons ago they dominated the land, along with club mosses and ferns, towering more than 100 feet high. The silica content of their cells not only betrays their origin at a time when carbon compounds in the soil were far less common than they are now, but also suggests their colonial use and name—scouring rush.

Heading back toward Mount Higby, the trail threads through hemlocks and chestnut oaks parallel to a tote road off to your right, but you soon cross the tote road and begin to climb the cobbled traprock slopes. After several switchbacks, you finally come out of the stony woods at the open rock Pinnacle, a great viewpoint about a mile from your start. Across CT 66 to the south is Mount Beseck, with Black Pond at its base. Continuing, you hike close to the cliffs, with excellent views to the west in a panorama that unfolds as you advance. West Peak and Castle Crag (see Hike 37) are visible in the middle distance; on your right is a traprock quarry. The fields below provide excellent examples of the stages of forest succession: In one field, immature evergreen cedars are just rearing up above the field's pioneer weeds; in another, mature cedars completely obscure the former pastures; and in still others, the succeeding hardwoods are shading out the cedars. Forest succession silently continues.

At your feet along the ridge are large mats of a creeping evergreen shrub: bearberry. The white or pink bell-shaped flowers and tasteless, seedy berries are borne in terminal clusters. Native Americans smoked the foliage in a mixture with tobacco called by the Algonquian word *kinnikinnik* (reputed to be the longest single-word palindrome in the English language).

At 1.7 miles the trail drops down into Preston Notch. After crossing a brook and passing a tote road descending to your left, climb alongside a cliff with additional superb views. Near the top of the ascent look for a natural bridge formation with a faded NB painted on it. Soon you'll reach the summit of Mount Higby. Scanning the horizon on a clear day, you will see to your left Long Island Sound and the New Haven skyline. To their left is the long traprock ridge traversed by the vandal-plagued Regicides Trail and the lumpy mass of the Sleeping Giant (see Hike 49). In front of you is an I-91 interchange; the large building on your right is the University of Connecticut Medical Center in Farmington.

This is also an excellent spot from which

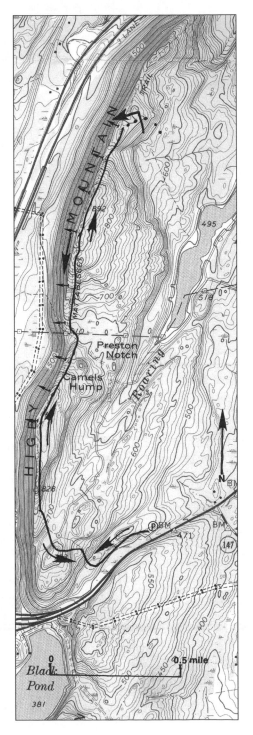

Looking north along the cliffs of Mount Higby

to review visually the northern Mattabesett and southern Metacomet Trails. Ahead, at the end of the ridge you are hiking, the Mattabesett follows Country Club Road (tar) over I-91, enters the woods, and climbs Chauncey Peak (see Hike 32) to the left of the traprock quarry. It continues back along that ridge over Mount Lamentation (partially hidden from view), ending on the Berlin Turnpike (CT 15/US 5).

The Metacomet picks up where the Mattabesett ends, heading west from the Berlin Turnpike over Castle Crag and West Peak. It then proceeds north over Talcott Mountain (see Hike 45) past the Heublein Tower, and eventually reaches its terminus on the Massachusetts border at Rising Corners.

Leaving this cliff edge, your trail drops down and then climbs to another viewpoint. On a clear day you can see the Hartford skyline on your right, with Mount Tom, north of Springfield, Massachusetts, to the east. To the right of Mount Tom, the Holyoke Range stretches like a roller coaster. The gap between the two is threaded by the Connecticut River. The Massachusetts extension of the Metacomet Trail, the Metacomet-Monadnock Trail, traverses these two ridges. At this point, take the time to review what you have seen and implant it firmly in your mind; with time these mountains and ridges will become old friends.

The trail soon bears right and descends away from the ridgeline to the east; here you can choose to hike farther, but this is the turnaround point of this hike. Retrace your steps to your car on CT 66.

29

Devils Den

Location: Weston

Distance: 6½ miles

Vertical rise: 750 feet

Time: 3½ hours

Rating: C

Maps: USGS 7.5-minute Norwalk North and Bethel

The devil was busy in old Connecticut. It may be hard to envision the English colonists' awe and fear of the deep, dark forests of 17th- and 18th-century New England, but this Nature Conservancy (TNC) preserve combines enough acreage, rugged terrain, and an impressive spider-web of roads and trails that you can begin to comprehend folks' trepidation about wandering these woods when hostile Natives, wolves, and mountain lions roamed the hills. Nestled in the heavily populated New York–New Haven corridor, Devils Den's 1,746 acres provide sanctuary from the bustle of urban life as well as a home for birds, mammals, trees, and plants that require large, unbroken tracts of forest.

The Nature Conservancy preserves natural communities and so restricts human activity to passive recreational hiking. TNC prohibits walking the trails with pets or using mechanized vehicles and bicycles. The Den is open sunrise to sunset, and you are asked to register at the map shelter, where a good map is available showing 21 miles of trails. This map is a necessity unless you want to rekindle the feelings our ancestors had for the place more than three hundred years ago!

Take the Merritt Parkway (CT 15) to exit 42. Follow CT 57 north for about 5 miles, turn right onto Godfrey Road, and after ½ mile turn left onto Pent Road. The Den's parking lot is at the end of the road and features the trailhead kiosk and a public phone. A small donation is requested. Numbered junctions primarily mark the trails in the

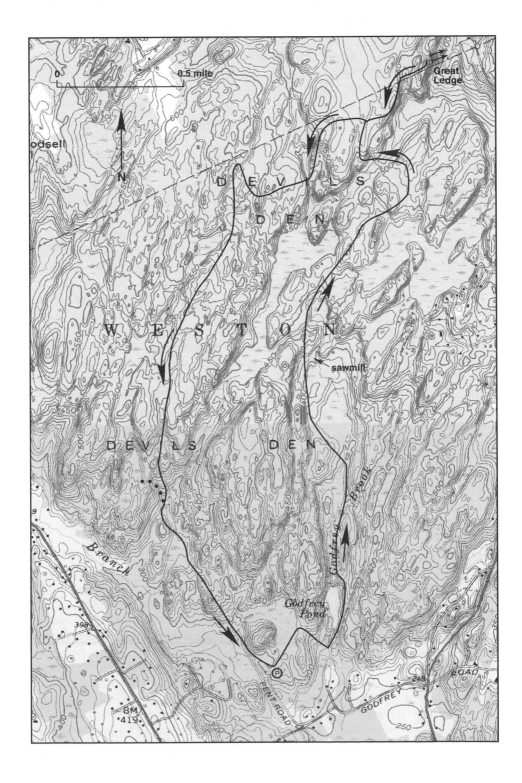

Great
Ledge

odsell

N

D E V ILS

D E N

W E S T O N

sawmill

DEV LS   DEN

Godfrey Brook

Branch

398

350

Godfrey
Pond

PENT ROAD

BM
419

GODFREY

ROAD

248

250

0   0.5 mile

preserve, and the map is critical to understanding the directions to follow at each site.

Follow the Laurel Trail past the public phone uphill on a mulched path. When snow conditions allow, this is also a cross-country ski trail that leads to Godfrey Pond. You soon pass a replica of a charcoal mound. Immense piles such as this one, containing as many as 30 cords of wood, would be covered with soil and ignited by a charcoal collier. He would tend the fire to ensure that it burned slowly enough (a month!) to yield the charcoal required for a variety of uses in 18th- and 19th-century America, most notably for firing the blast furnaces to make iron right up through the Civil War, before coal mined in Pennsylvania moved our iron works west.

Bear right at junction 22 and then left at junction 23 following the trail downhill, passing boulders to Godfrey Pond. Cross a bridge and stay right at junction 24 to cross a dam and pass a mill foundation. Millponds were common in the early days of the industrial revolution, requiring only a stone-and-earth dam that forced water through a sluiceway to turn the wheel that powered the mill. Waterpower is still in use today creating the more portable electricity we all use in daily life.

After crossing the dam, turn left at junction 33 to follow a rocky tote road along the east shore of the pond. Bear right at junction 34 and then left at junction 35, staying on the tote road past junction 36 to remain on the route that takes you north away from the pond and its profusion of trails. You are now on the Godfrey Trail leading into the heart of the Den.

The alternately rocky and swampy ground likely protected this land from the development that surrounds it. The hardwood forest around you has regenerated numerous times after supplying charcoal

and lumber for the nearby towns. The road is periodically hardened with corduroys, a road- and trail-building technique in which logs are laid on wet ground perpendicular to the route to provide a solid if not slip-proof surface. In fact, if the corduroy remains damp year-round, it is likely to last for years: The moist ground retards the rotting process by preventing oxygen from accelerating the growth of molds and fungi.

The road winds through a forest of oaks and tulip trees, and you may see the evergreen pipsissiwa growing close to the ground along the way. You'll pass a portable sawmill to your right—all that remains is the old boiler and flywheel. The steam-powered mill allowed the sawyer to take the saw to the logs, since it was easier to take boards out of the forest than logs.

Continue along the road to your right at junction 39, passing the Saw Mill Trail on your right, and follow the road downhill to cross a stone bridge. At junction 64 hike straight through a four-way intersection to stay on the Godfrey Trail. You'll cross the preserve's yellow-painted boundary to briefly cross on to private property, and then turn left at junction 63 and reenter the preserve on the Dayton Trail.

Ascend alongside a great outcropping of rock and enter an overgrown pasture at junction 58. Turn right and then immediately right again at junction 56 to descend to Great Ledge. Here you'll have a vista over the forest treetops after a couple of hours' walk through the green tunnel. Retrace your steps to junction 58 and turn right onto the Deer Run Trail. We found a leopard frog on this highland route. This frog is frequently confused with the similarly marked pickerel frog. The leopard frog, which is the rarer of the two species, has round spots, while the pickerel frog has square or blocky spots.

Turn left at T-junction 54 and then right at

junction 54 onto the Bedford Trail. Stay to your left uphill at junction 78 to follow the long downhill on the Bedford Trail back to the Den's entrance. This main tote road has side trails to the right at junctions 52 and 49 as well as a loop through Ambler Gorge at junction 44. Cross a bridge over Ambler Brook, then turn left at junction 10 to cross another bridge over Sap Brook. At junction 9, remain on the main road, following signs to the parking lot.

Join the Pent Trail by staying straight at junctions 8, 7, and 6, passing stony hillsides covered with the ubiquitous mountain laurel. Follow this woods road to Pent Road just below the trailhead parking lot. We were following a large woodpecker down the last couple of hundred yards. From a distance its size hinted that it was a pileated woodpecker, and as we slowly drew closer the red crest and white wing flashes confirmed our sighting. No doubt the maturing forest of Devils Den will provide an island of habitat for this bird as well as many others that require a large, unbroken forested landscape.

30

White Memorial Foundation

Location: Litchfield

Distance: 6.7 miles

Vertical rise: 100 feet

Time: 3½ hours

Rating: D

Map: USGS 7.5-minute Litchfield

The 4,000-acre White Memorial Foundation wildlife sanctuary in Litchfield was established in the true spirit of multiple use. Within its boundaries lie more than 35 miles of crisscrossing trails, two family campgrounds, a marina, and the Nature Museum. To balance the more unusual sanctuary uses, over 200 acres have been set aside in four untouched natural preserves. These areas provide bases against which environmental changes on adjacent tracts can be judged. The hike described here explores only a small part of this special sanctuary.

Follow US 202 west 2.2 miles past its junction with CT 118 in Litchfield and turn left by the signs for White Memorial Foundation. The gravel entrance road leads 0.5 mile to a parking area just beyond the carriage house to your right, which is used for staff housing. The foundation's property contains a maze of hiking trails, including the blue-blazed Mattatuck Trail, one of Connecticut's Blue Trails; 6.2 miles of this nearly 35-mile-long trail are within the property.

The hike begins by following the gravel road east from the parking area past the Nature Museum. While there is a small fee, a rewarding half hour can be spent looking over the museum's attractive wildlife, geology, and Native American artifact exhibits. Especially interesting are old photos of the once open expanses of grassy fields, now completely forested.

A bookstore specializing in natural history sells pamphlets and maps relevant to the area. Since the numerous trails through the foundation's land twist, turn, and cross

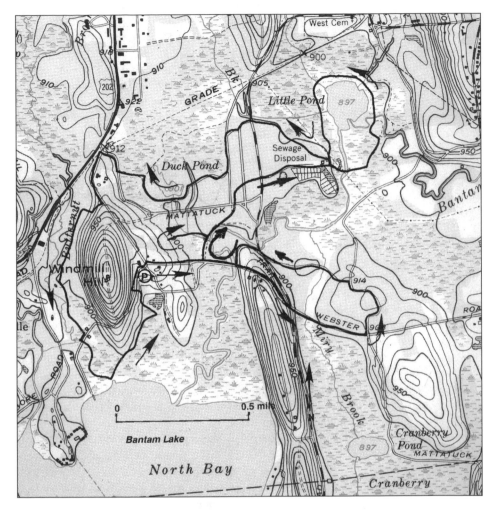

each other with bewildering abandon, a map is a good investment. We have seen even expert hikers have trouble following a particular route. However, if you visit this area several times and familiarize yourself with its lovely intricacies, it becomes relatively easy, and very rewarding, to follow the route we have outlined here.

Continue past the museum on the road. Large sugar maple and white ash grace the road to your left. White ash trees are a special fall treat, with leaves turning a purplish red to contrast with the yellows, reds, and oranges of New England's birches and maples. Cross a gravel road when you reach a gated entrance blocked by a boulder and flanked by two large cement-and-stone posts. Follow this road, now the blue-blazed Mattatuck Trail, east to the edge of the Bantam River and cross the slow-moving river over an old truss bridge. You many see a canoe or two here. Darting dragonflies skim over the water catching small insects like mosquitoes for lunch—never hurt a dragonfly! On the other side the Mattatuck turns left. Stay straight following a woods road uphill to a small circular drive, which you cross to follow another woods road downhill. This woods road crosses busy Whites Woods Road and becomes gravel Webster Road. Follow Webster Road for about ¼ mile to the blue-blazed woods road leading north into Catlin Woods.

Catlin Woods includes 200-year-old hemlocks and white pines on land that was never cultivated, as indicated by the ancient pillows and cradles, or mounds and depressions, formed by the uprooting and decomposition of trees. Follow the blue-blazed Mattatuck Trail again by turning left at a fork, leaving the woods to cross a brook and pass through the marshy clearing. Near the road, pass through a stand of great bull pines. These great white pines gained their early growth in an open field, with little or no competition for the sunlight; the numerous large branches create the wood known as knotty pine. Reach paved Whites Woods Road and cross it again, following the blue-blazed tote road along the river. To your left is a meadow where a few horses are often seen grazing happily. You may see late-summer flowers such as joe-pye weed, boneset, various asters, hawkweed, and purple loosestrife, and hear the strident songs of grasshoppers and crickets. The volume from these singers will build up until the first frost: Light frost will slow them, and a heavy frost will stop them. The round-leafed cornea species of dogwood with light blue berries is common here.

The trail takes you back across the truss bridge and then through the gated entrance toward the museum. Turn right and continue to follow the Mattatuck Trail north on a gravel road. Soon you reach an interpretive nature trail to your left. Take a short detour and follow it into the woods. You'll soon enter a stand of old-growth pines—trees more than 200 years old—at a junction with a closed trail. These majestic giants tower 100 feet above the forest floor and are well worth the visit. Return to the gravel road by retracing your steps and then turn left to continue along the Mattatuck north.

Cross Bissell Road and continue north to the Little Pond Trail. Turn right to follow the black-on-white-blazed Little Pond Trail along another tote road. Hike along the edge of a clearing to the swampy edge of the pond and bear right onto the loop trail, which soon passes through phragmites and crosses the arched Frances Howe Sutton Bridge. Follow the boardwalk around the pond. A late-August visit featured the bright red berries of honeysuckles along the way, as well as an occasional tasty blackberry.

A boardwalk gives you a fascinating look at one of nature's most interesting but least accessible areas—too wet to walk, too dry to canoe! Jumping frogs, innumerable buttonbushes, purple loosestrife, royal fern, meadowsweet, lily pads, pickerelweed—in terms of annual vegetation per acre, a swamp is one of the most productive areas of all.

After passing around the pond, the trail follows a woods road and reaches a junction with the red-triangle-blazed Pine Island Trail. Turn sharply right to follow it through hemlock woods to Whites Woods Road. Cross the road and continue on a woods road, staying right at the first junction, and then turning left down another woods road at the next junction. Where the red triangles bear to your right off the road, continue straight to where the blue-blazed Mattatuck Trail bears right. Follow the Mattatuck Trail west, and follow the blazes to Duck Pond. Continue on the blue-blazed trail around the pond to Bissell Road, which you take to your right nearly to US 202. Bear left down the foundation entrance's White Hall Road to the Pine Grove I camping area, and turn right onto the green-blazed Windmill Hill Trail.

Descend on an old woods road past the campsites and walk around the thickly wooded base of Windmill Hill. The trail reaches a tote road T-junction with the yellow-blazed Lake Trail; turn right and then left to follow the Lake Trail down to the observation deck on the shore of Bantam Lake. White Memorial Foundation owns nearly 60 percent of the property bordering the lake, including nearly all of the visible shoreline.

Return north on the Lake Trail and bear right onto the Windmill Hill Trail past several large oaks. Bear left onto the orange-blazed Ongley Pond Trail, which skirts the western shore of the alga-choked pond, before returning to the Lake Trail near a stone wall. Follow the trail's yellow blazes back to the carriage house and your car.

31

Bullet and High Ledges

Location: North Stonington

Distance: 6 miles

Vertical rise: 600 feet

Time: 3½ hours

Rating: C

Maps: USGS 7.5-minute Voluntown,
Ashaway

People talk of the megalopolis extending from north of Boston to south of Washington, D.C., but there has been a gap in this urban sprawl. This hike, in Pachaug State Forest, is in the middle of this precious undeveloped area. There will always be pressure to develop here, but preserving woodlands is a legacy for the future. Visit and judge the true value of this area for yourself!

The Narragansett Trail to Bullet and High Ledges leads west on Johnson Road from CT 49, 4.8 miles south of its junction with CT 138 in Voluntown. Coming from Voluntown, pass Sand Hill Road on your left and then take a sharp right onto the second paved road. You can park just beyond the stop sign near a formidably spined honey locust tree.

Here, follow the Narragansett Trail along the road away from CT 49 and shortly leave the pavement on a dirt road, flanked by stone walls, to your left.

On your right stands a large sycamore with a massive poison ivy vine climbing on one side. A thick mat of fibrous aerial roots holds it in place. The "shiny leaves three" make this vine easy to recognize in summer, but you should become familiar with it in all seasons. The dormant winter vine is equally poisonous, especially when the sap courses up the stalks in preparation for spring growth.

Follow the woods road generally downhill and then along level ground. In 0.3 mile turn right off the road, just before a gravel pit, and cross a stone wall. Here the forest

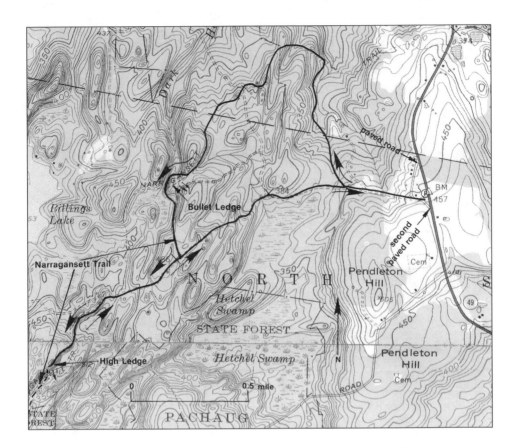

floor is carpeted with club mosses: first ground cedar alone (many capped with candelabrum-shaped spore stalks), then mixed with ground pine, until finally the ground pine predominates. Beyond the club mosses, you may find rounded masses of gray-green reindeer moss. The winter mainstay of the caribou herds of the North, this "moss" is in fact lichen.

Roll with the terrain, crossing and paralleling several stone walls before heading to your right along a seasonal stream and over another stone wall to Myron Kinney Brook—a river in microcosm. Nature's immutable laws are more easily observed when the familiar is seen on a different scale. Spring runoff forms the seasonal headwaters of this small brook. Within a few tenths of a mile, small tributaries entering from both sides swell the brook many times. The water volume increases further from hidden springs where the stream cuts into the permanent water table.

Walk slowly along the stream with an alert eye—the forms darting across gravel riffles and through deep pools are native brook trout. Since these char need an unending supply of ice-cold water, you will see them in abundance only when you have passed the point where the brook has cut into the permanent water table.

While you are looking for trout, notice how the current rushes around the outer curves of the stream, undermining its banks.

A stone wall flanking the Narragansett Trail

Sediment carved from these areas is carried downstream and deposited as sandbars on inside curves, where the current is slower.

You leave the brook in about ¼ mile and turn left uphill. The trail then dips to cross a small stream. Fleshy green ribbons cling with numerous short, hairlike roots to the sphagnum moss along the banks. This is liverwort; an evergreen closely related to the mosses, it is one of the most primitive living plants.

Across the stream, the trail hugs a stone wall going up the hillside. With posted land on your right and Pachaug State Forest land on your left, follow the blue blazes carefully through a network of interlocking stone walls and tote roads.

In an area of prominent ledges, bear left

at a fork. After 0.25 mile merge with an old, eroded road. Follow the blue blazes as the undulating footpath passes through cozy-cornered stone walls and a partially cutover area with mountain laurel stems as thick as a man's arm.

At one point stay straight through a woods road junction. (If you do detour right a bit on this second road, you will see at least two alien flowers—daylily and gill-over-the-ground—a sure sign that an old homestead existed here.) Bear right at another woods road junction and continue generally upward with a rocky ridge to your right. Pass through a compacted dirt clearing in the woods. Just beyond this clearing, when the trail takes a steep right turn downward, continue instead straight ahead to the Bullet Ledge Lookout.

Return to the trail and descend steeply to the rocky valley floor. When you reach the tote road set between a rock ridge and a swamp, turn left. Following the blue blazes at succeeding junctions, you finally emerge on a well-defined old town road flanked by stone walls. To your left, this road leads back to CT 49. Generally when you find an abandoned road with stone walls on either side, it means that this was an old main town road leading from one place to another, rather than a wood-gathering tote road that goes nowhere.

Turn right on this old road, now the Narragansett Trail, for the climb to High Ledge. Fork left off the road, following the blue blazes up onto an oak- and hemlock-covered ridge. After about 0.5 mile it dips slightly into the valley before quickly rising

to the edge of a steep hill. You wind through ledges before dropping into a narrow, rocky valley, which in summer is full of stinging nettles. Unlike poison ivy, its "sting" is short lived. Cross the stream and climb steeply, bearing left toward High Ledge.

A rocky point perched above the valley, High Ledge affords a bird's-eye view of nearby treetops. Island-dotted Wyassup Lake sparkles in the middle distance. On a clear day the faint line of Long Island Sound can be seen beyond the lake against the horizon. On your right you can pick out the fire tower on Wyassup Lake Road.

If you wish to hike an extra mile, just retrace your steps to your car. The 6-mile route described here leaves the Narragansett Trail to follow the old town road, mentioned earlier, and continues directly to Johnson Road at CT 49.

32

Chauncey Peak and Mount Lamentation

Location: Meriden

Distance: 6 miles

Vertical rise: 800 feet

Time: 3½ hours

Rating: B

Map: USGS 7.5-minute Meriden

The traprock ridges within the Connecticut River Valley are a hiker's paradise. Ascents are steep and rugged, but the views from the cliff edges are superb. This hike along a section of the Mattabesett Trail has some of our best traprock cliffs and offers a panoramic view within its first 0.5 mile. Climb Chauncey Peak and Mount Lamentation on a cool clear day and you won't be disappointed.

From I-91 near Meriden, take exit 20 to Country Club Road. Follow this road west 2.7 miles. Where the road takes a sharp left turn, turn right into Giuffrida Park.

Follow the blue-blazed Mattabesett Trail as it leads just below the dam to the right of the parking lot. Ascend through the woods on the far side of the dam, following an unmarked trail steeply to your right. As you turn right at a junction, following blue arrows to climb a gentler slope and rejoin the old trail ascending Chauncey Peak, you pass a large bed of gill-over-the-ground, a small member of the mint family with tiny blue tubular flowers. This alien was once used to ferment beer. Shortly you come across patches of wild onion—a spring favorite that provides a strong flavor for your sandwiches—and silverweed. Gerry first identified silverweed, which looks like a many-leafed strawberry plant, in Newfoundland, and we've since spotted it several times in Connecticut. This illustrates one of the values of recognition: Once you've identified a plant, you will notice it where you never realized it existed.

Your route passes another trail junction and follows the blue-blazed Mattabesett

Trail, soon beginning to climb and becoming steadily steeper and rockier. Many flowering dogwoods light the forest's middle story along the way. After hiking about ½ mile, you finally pass through almost sheer traprock ramparts and emerge on the level summit of Chauncey Peak (688 feet). The southern panorama you see features a number of prominent ridges between you and Long Island Sound.

New Haven and the faint blue line of the Sound lie straight ahead to the south. The lumpy mass to your right is the Sleeping Giant (see Hike 49), and then West Rock ridge. Directly to your right stretch the Hanging Hills of Meriden. South Mountain partially blocks your view of Castle Crag and West Peak (see Hike 37). To your left across the highway rise the cliffs of Mount Higby (see Hike 28).

All of these ridges and related formations are composed of traprock formed some 200 million years ago when this land was volcanically active and the great crack that eventually became the Atlantic Ocean was expanding. Most are remnants of vast upended lava sheets, but a few, like West Rock Ridge, are exposed lava dikes.

The trail tacks east along the southern cliff edge and then turns left to meander across the top to the western cliffs. The trees you pass on top are predominantly chestnut oak and staghorn sumac—two species that can tolerate this thin, dry soil. As you reach the edge, the view south looks down on a traprock quarry (this hard stone is, when crushed, an ideal highway base). Unfortunately, a little farther on the quarry has expanded to eat away the mountain.

The vistas from these cliffs are among the finest in the state; as you work your way along the edge, rocky outcroppings provide unobstructed views of Crescent Lake (Bradley Hubbard Reservoir) 400 feet

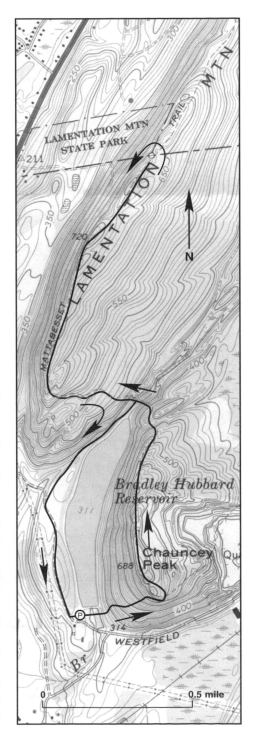

The view from Chauncey Peak cliffs

directly beneath you. From the final outcrop, the vista sweeps from New Haven west past the Hanging Hills and north past the Hartford skyline to the hills crossed by the northern section of the Shenipsit Trail (see Hike 15).

The trail drops off Chauncey Peak, after following along the western cliffs with views across the reservoir to the gentle wooded slopes of Mount Lamentation, and crosses a bridge over an old canal. Turn right to follow the blue blazes uphill on a wide, rocky path. Continue to follow the blazes, bearing left at a fork and left again when you reach a tote road. Climbing steadily uphill, you curve around the southern end of Mount Lamentation and emerge on the western cliffs of this ridge 1.8 miles from your car. The trail passes a U.S. Geological Survey benchmark at 2.1 miles.

While taking an unmarked detour through the woods here we came across a fearless black rat snake. This one was 4½ feet long—average for this species, which grows to 6 feet. Unfortunately, vandals too easily kill these beneficial, rodent-eating snakes. This one let Gerry gently lift it off the ground so we could see the underside checkerboard pattern that distinguishes it from the similar but more common black racer. How easily a misguided person could have killed it!

The trail parallels the cliffs for another mile and ends with a particularly fine view that extends from New Haven to Hartford and beyond. On a clear day you can identify the traprock ridges north of Springfield, Massachusetts. From left to right, the east-facing cliffs of Mount Tom are followed by the gap cut by the Connecticut River, the multisummited Holyoke Range, and finally Mount Norwottuck. This last peak marks the spot where the emergent traprock disappears into the valley's older red sandstone.

You can simply retrace your steps to your car if you wish. Or you can follow the alternate route we recommend: Retrace your steps to the bridge over the canal and, instead of crossing the bridge, stay straight on the tote road south to follow the western shore of Bradley Hubbard Reservoir. Continue on the unmarked trail that hugs the shore. Across the lake above you are the western cliffs of Chauncey Peak, which you traversed earlier in your hike. Soon the path hits an old road—continue on this road along the forested lake edge. Pass a gate and enter the parking lot where you started.

33

Westwoods

Location: Guilford

Distance: 6 miles

Vertical rise: 700 feet

Time: 3½ hours

Rating: B

Map: USGS 7.5-minute Guilford

This 1,000-acre open space in Guilford, consisting of state forest, Guilford Land Conservation Trust, a private tree farm, and town land, is an attractive woodland with a touch of salt. The lake at the south end is brackish, and as you hike the labyrinth of trails, gulls wheel overhead. Because it is so near to Connecticut's overdeveloped coast, Westwoods is especially prized.

From the junction of CT 77 and CT 146 in Guilford, follow CT 146 west 1.3 miles to Sam Hill Road to your right. Parking for the Westwoods trail entrance 3 is at this corner. The white-circle trail starts here.

Westwoods, like Sleeping Giant (see Hike 49), has an extensive trail system of more than 40 miles. The hike described here tries to cover many points of interest. You'll follow the white-circle, yellow-circle, green-rectangle, green-circle, and orange-circle trails in a big loop. In the interest of clarity and brevity, we won't mention most of the numerous other trails you cross; directions to other routes in Westwoods are available in the *Connecticut Walk Book,* as well as in a locally produced Guilford Land Trust Trails Map, both available at the Guilford Town Hall and the local bookstore. We will try to provide the numbers of trail junctions, which should match the map provided in the *Walk Book.* In general, however, the trails blazed with painted circles run north to south, and those with painted squares run east to west.

Mosquito repellent is a must on this hike in summer; we recommend this trip for early-spring and late-fall days to avoid these

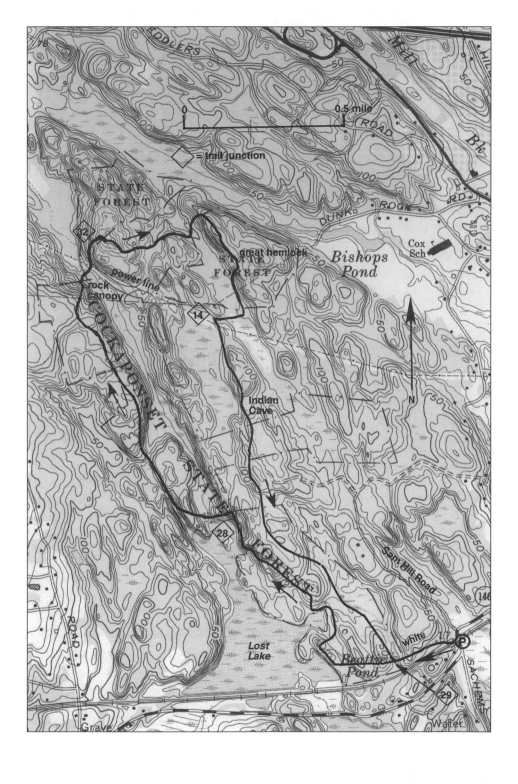

pests. Along the shore, because of extensive marshy breeding grounds, these bloodsuckers always seem bigger, bolder, and more numerous than elsewhere.

Follow the white-circle trail west from the parking lot along an old woods road paralleling the railroad tracks. Pass trail junction 29 (see map) and continue to follow the white circles past an old quarry bearing the drill marks where feather wedges split the rocks. You'll soon head north away from the tracks and rise into a dry, thin-soiled area covered with laurel and hemlock. In general, the trails flirt with a multitude of rocks, ledges, and glacially rounded outcroppings; they were laid out with much thought and care. The terrain that made Westwoods a farmer's wasteland has given birth to a hiker's wonderland.

After crossing a stream, you'll climb an open ledge affording a good view south over Lost Lake. Near the top of the ledge, turn left at trail junction 28 (see map) to follow the yellow-circle trail. Follow this trail carefully; fallen hemlock debris has made route finding difficult. Descend by another quarry site, passing a junction with an orange-square-blazed trail. Follow the yellow circles north over a hill, along a stream, and under a broken-up ledge before climbing through boulders and ascending to junction 36 with the violet-circle trail. Hike uphill through a dying hemlock stand (see Hike 10, Hurd State Park) above the great fallen cliff to your right. Huge blocks from the cliff lie on the valley floor below you.

Your route leads you along the top of the ledges. Often you climb in and out of nooks and crannies that keep the hike interesting; you also pass between two cottage-sized boulders. After regaining the top of the ledge, follow a path down the hillside and cross a brook above a small waterfall. Cross over three rock slabs whose wide expanse makes following the worn pathway difficult. Follow the yellow circles carefully through here—they tend to lead to the right each time. Soon you will see a huge slab of rock that has broken off the ledge to your right (the marks of the drill indicate this was not a natural occurrence). This is the rock canopy. From this point on you'll descend through the woods, enjoying a lowlander's view of the ledge and canopy above.

At trail junction 34 continue to your right on the yellow-circle trail along an old woods road. Cross a bridge and bear left to enter a power-line clearing. Pink lady's slippers grace the trailside and are scattered throughout the undergrowth. We have even heard that the elusive yellow lady's slipper grows in Westwoods. If you listen carefully you may pick out the *szweet-szweet-chur-chur-chur* of the cardinal. In wintertime the brilliant red of this bird against the snow is especially striking. The cardinal has become common in Connecticut only in the last few decades. Possible explanations for this northward expansion of its range include climatic change, extensive artificial winter feeding, and agricultural change.

Cross the clearing and climb yet another ledge along the long root system of a white pine. One enormous root is nearly as long as the tree is tall. You pass through the narrow openings in the ledges and boulders on top of this rise, leaving the power lines that were once above you far below, before reaching trail junction 32 (see map). Bear right on a green-rectangle-blazed woods road and enjoy its easy tread past junctions with the white-circle and orange-circle trails. Turn right off this woods road onto the green-circle trail and follow it over a hill to a sheltered stand of once majestic hemlock trees. The great hemlock is now dead, but its 6-foot-diameter trunk still stands, and half a dozen of the big trees are visible from the trail in a stand of smaller, unhealthy hemlocks. Before their recent demise, the hemlocks' combination of dense shade and tannin-rich needles nearly excluded understory shrubs. Now we'll watch for the beginnings of forest succession with the newly available sunlight.

Turn right onto the green-triangle trail and descend away from the great hemlock grove and the ledges cluttered with fallen branches. Enter a forest thick with birch saplings—potentially the same forest that will succeed the fallen giants above. Turn right onto a well-worn, blue-rectangle-blazed woods road and continue your descent. Proceed on this road to trail junction 14 (see map) and the orange-circle trail. Turn left and soon cross the power line. Then follow along a series of ledges, one of which contains an overhang called Indian Cave—one of at least a thousand so named in the state!

Cross a yellow-triangle-blazed horse trail. Stay on the orange-circle trail over and around ledges, and catch another glimpse of Lost Lake near a white-marked crossover trail. Join a woods road leading to trail junction 29, where you turn left onto the white-circle trail to return to the parking lot.

34

Cathedral Pines and Mohawk Mountain

Location: Cornwall

Distance: 6 miles

Vertical rise: 1,200 feet

Time: 3¾ hours

Rating: BC

Map: USGS 7.5-minute Cornwall

Cathedral Pines, once the premier stand of white pines in New England, is still an impressive array of pines and hemlocks, even though a tornado knocked down much of the stand in July 1989. A recent relocation of the Mohawk Trail makes for an awe-inspiring beginning to a hike to one of western Connecticut's most familiar landmarks.

Mohawk Mountain rises 1,683 feet above its surroundings, offering a nearly 360-degree view from its summit tower. Mohawk State Forest boasts sections of the Blue Trail System's Mohawk (formerly Appalachian) and Mattatuck Trails within its boundaries. These trails, coming from divergent directions, meet near the summit and provide delightful alternatives to the summit road.

The hike begins at the base of the hillside that is home to the great pines. Take CT 4 west 0.5 mile from its junction with CT 125 in Cornwall. Turn sharply left onto Bolton Hill Road and bear right immediately onto Jewell Street. After 0.5 mile go left at the fork up Essex Hill Road 0.2 mile to a pullout on your left. A great scarred pine stands alone across the street. The blue-blazed Mohawk Trail enters the woods at the south end of the pullout by a Nature Conservancy sign. The drive to the trail prepares you for the damaged pines, as the sad condition of many nearby trees bears witness to the devastation of the 1989 storm.

Start the hike by climbing steeply up the hillside, aided by wooden stairs that keep the soil from washing away. The giant pines and hemlocks that survived the blow sur-

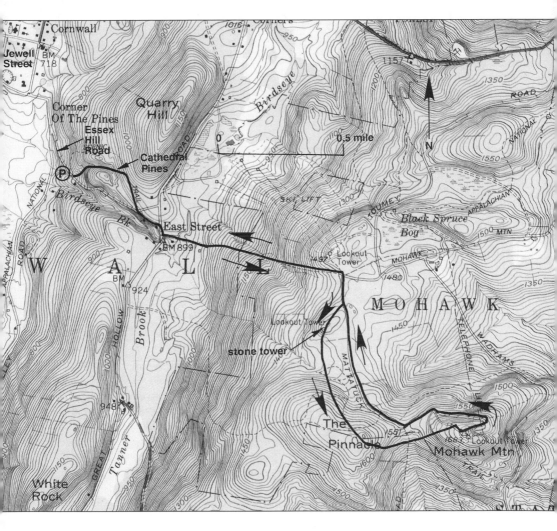

round you immediately, and you pass over and around some that did not. Views through the trees to your left reveal the main path of the wind; few remain standing. Those trees that are still upright lost most of their tops to the windstorm.

Tornadoes are not thought of as a common New England phenomenon and occur much more frequently in the Midwest. However, we do get a few catastrophic storms (two such storms occurred in different locations in New England in 1995) that,

together with fire (another fairly rare occurrence), create natural clearings that nature soon fills in with a variety of early-forest-succession plant species. The 1938 hurricane spared Cathedral Pines but knocked down comparable stands in New Hampshire's Harvard tract, now in Pisgah State Park.

The white pine is not a climax forest species, although its long life span and great height allow it to thrive above a climax forest. A pioneer species that grows quickly in fields, white pines filled untended fields when many of New England's farms and pastures were abandoned for the allure of the midwestern prairies. The white pine is now a common tree in Connecticut, and its abundance and great size make it one of the wonders of the hikes in this book.

Turn right onto an old tote road and descend gently out of the pines. Turn left onto paved Essex Hill Road. Take care to hug the shoulder of the road; while this is not a busy street, drivers have little warning of pedestrians due to the many curves in the road. Bear right again, following the blue blazes, to take Great Hollow Road downhill to a driveway on your left at the base of the hill. In front of you, the effects of the storm on the west side of Mohawk Mountain are visible to the right of the ski area. On a warm July day we flushed out a group of wild turkeys in the woods on the east side of the road; such sights make a summer hike memorable when the haze reduces the bracing effects of the summit views.

Follow the driveway east toward the mountain. Bear left around a garage and through a metal gate and ascend steadily on an old tote road. The midsummer undergrowth can be thick here, owing to a lack of shade. Take care to follow the blazes, many of which are painted on rocks underfoot. Your route turns left to cross the top of the field you've been paralleling, then enters an open stand of hardwoods dominated by sugar maples. Pass to the right of a small red pine plantation and meet a well-worn path at the top of a rise. A sign identifies this as the Mattatuck Trail. You'll turn right here, toward Mohawk Mountain.

But before you do, continue on the same path straight ahead to the top of the ski slope. This quick walk offers good views west over the terrain you've traveled. The hill below you again shows the effects of the

1989 storm; the green slopes are dotted gray with damaged trees. You also get your first view of the Riga Plateau in the northwest corner of Connecticut. In early April there may be remnants of human-made snow here. Snowmaking is necessary in Connecticut to supplement our unreliable snowfall. Just north of the lift is a small stone lookout tower that predates both the ski area and, judging by its low height, the forest that surrounds it.

Return to the Mohawk/Mattatuck Trail junction and turn left onto the blue-blazed Mattatuck; soon you reach Toumey Road. Follow it straight (south) and soon bear right onto the blazed path opposite a small picnic area. The trail curves up onto the extensive flat ledges. The ruins of a great stone tower dominate this rocky stretch. While the Civilian Conservation Corps built much of Connecticut's forest stonework in the late 1930s, Seymour Cunningham built this steel-braced tower, with its magnificent fireplace, in 1915, before the state began to acquire land. Mohawk State Forest began with a 250-acre gift to the state from Alain C. White (who also founded White Memorial Foundation with his sister, May W. White—see Hike 30), in 1921.

You soon cross a field being reclaimed by the forest, enter some pine woods, and pass an abandoned well and hand pump. Pass through a swampy area where you will find several large bull pines and scattered spruce and black cherry trees.

On the far side of the swamp you cross a stone wall and follow left beside it. Pass a piped spring; a small cement cistern protects the source, and an adjacent pipe runs with cold, clear water. A friend of ours claims that a hiker should never pass a spring without drinking, even if only a sip— a symbolic thanks for the water, the trail, the day, and the good fortune to be there.

But today untreated water, even from a spring, may be contaminated with microscopic *Giardia* cysts. Even a symbolic drink may cause illness (see Introduction).

Soon you'll pass a clearing to your left where once stood an Appalachian Trail shelter. Climb up to and across a gravel tote road and continue to ascend the north side of the Pinnacle. Near the top you clamber over boulders. Across the valley, Mohawk's summit towers are visible when the trees are leafless. Descend along a stone wall, a remnant of open hillside pastures. Level out and cross a beautiful glade with ferns and a view south to Mohawk Pond. Cross a tote road and then climb a laurel-covered slope to the gravel summit road.

Head to your right up the blue-blazed road to the nearby top of Mohawk Mountain. There, dwarfed by radio towers, a lookout tower rises just high enough to top most of the trees. There are picnic facilities and a paved parking area for motorists who arrive on the gravel road. A March trip will reward you with a clump of pussy willows adjacent to the paved area.

Climb the steep wooden tower steps and enjoy the expansive view. Mounts Everett, Race, and Bear punctuate the Riga Plateau to the north. The Catskills rise on the western horizon. Farther to your left, in the distance, is the mountainous Hudson Highland in New York. The large, flat-topped mass in the middle distance to the right of the Riga Plateau is Canaan Mountain.

When your eyes have drunk their fill, descend the paved road to the east, which loops back west down the north slope of the mountain. Chestnut sprouts are common along the edge of the road. A little way down the road you pass a clearing to your right opposite two imposing stone gateposts flanking a tote road to your left. Look over your right shoulder back to Mohawk. Rejoin the blue blazes of the Mattatuck Trail at the small picnic area on your right and follow them north, taking care to turn left down the Mohawk Trail just before reaching the ski area. Follow the Mohawk Trail back through the Cathedral Pines to your car in Cornwall.

35

Natchaug

Location: Eastford

Distance: 6.6 miles

Vertical rise: 300 feet

Time: 4 hours

Rating: CD

Map: USGS 7.5-minute Hampton

The woods of Connecticut contain many ghosts. Our human and natural histories bear the memories of Native American nations, early settlers and farmers, great forests come and gone many times since the *Mayflower,* and one of our greatest natural calamities, the chestnut blight.

The American chestnut, once comprising nearly one-quarter of all our hardwood forest trees, and particularly favored by farmers due to its tasty nuts, was allowed to grow to great size in their otherwise open fields. The blight was introduced to North America in a shipment of Asian chestnuts (which are immune to the blight) brought to New York City around the turn of the 20th century. By the end of the First World War most of America's chestnuts had succumbed. Despite major efforts at Yale University and elsewhere, no sure solution to the disease has yet been discovered. Although no cure has been found for the blight, our chestnut is a vigorous sprouter, so the once mighty chestnut is now, ironically, a common small tree in Connecticut's hardwood forest. This hike takes you past two ghosts of chestnuts past in the Natchaug State Forest.

From the junction of CT 198 and US 44 in Phoenixville, drive south on CT 198 for 0.5 mile. Turn sharply left onto General Lyon Road; in 0.1 mile turn right onto Pilfershire Road (shown on the map as Pilshire Road), and then turn right again in 1.7 miles onto Kingsbury Road where there is a sign for the state forest unit headquarters. In about a mile this road becomes dirt. Where the blue-blazed Natchaug Trail crosses, take a gravel road left to Beaver Dam Wildlife Management Area. There is a sizable parking lot at the end of this road.

Facing the pond, bear left out of the parking lot to follow the Natchaug Trail. But first explore the earthen dam backing up the pond to your right. A stone-and-concrete apron accommodates the pond's spring overflow, but a vertical corrugated pipe, which also acts as a debris screen, usually handles the summertime water flow. The croak-jump-splash of thousands of frogs here heralds your approach to the water's edge. In the pond near the far shore is a brush, stick, and mud beaver lodge. You may see beaver cuttings along the start of the trail. The pond's surface is almost completely covered in summer with floating and emergent vegetation, especially the rather dull, yellow-blossomed bullhead lily and the exotic white-flowered water lily. Tall, emergent purple spires of pickerelweed line the shallow shoreline.

Return to the trail that parallels the pond. Several highbush blueberry bushes tempt you to dally, and the summer perfume of the pepperbush lightens your way. In late summer the woodland birds are quiet; they anticipate the coming of fall sooner than we do. Swallows line the telephone wires (they are usually gone by Labor Day), and families of flickers and towhees rummage through the woods together.

After passing through a grove of red spruce and unhealthy red pine, you reach Kingsbury Road in about 0.6 mile. Follow the road to your right. There are two kinds of safe three-leafed vines along here: the hog peanut, whose attractive lilac blossoms belie its name, and the virgin's bower.

About 0.8 mile from the start, the trail enters the woods to your left and soon passes through Nathaniel Lyon Memorial Park,

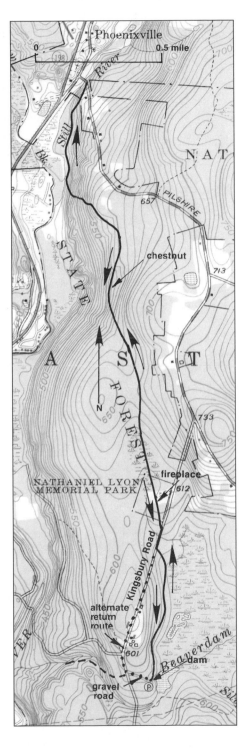

The last standing chestnut trunk.

named for the first Union geneal to die in the Civil War, at the battle of Wilson's Creek in Missouri. Nathaniel Lyon was born in nearby Eastford, Connecticut. The park features picnic tables, outhouses, a water pump, and a great stone fireplace. Midway across this open area, bear left down an old tote road. On this stretch of the trail you wander through mixed hardwood forest, pass occasional stone walls, and finally invade the stillness of a hemlock grove.

In 1.9 miles the remains of a giant chestnut tree, once more than 15 feet in circumference, now lie rotting on the forest floor to your right. Once one of the natural wonders of eastern Connecticut, it has been dead for generations, and its seemingly indestructible wood has finally broken down. The photograph was taken in 1977—compare it to the way the chestnut looks now. Except for a few black birches, the space around the dead patriarch is respectfully empty. The chestnut sprouts nearby probably sprang from the still-living roots of the dead hulk.

While we were admiring this relic of our once most valuable hardwood, a small, chunky, brownish gray form circled a stub and disappeared into a knothole. This was only the second flying squirrel we have seen in broad daylight. This normally nocturnal animal is actually quite common in our woods. Its chunky look derives from the folds of skin joining the front and rear legs, which allow this little creature to glide (not fly!) from high points to lower branches.

A little farther along on the left stands a much smaller, but still huge, dead chestnut. Its lack of massive side limbs has kept much of the trunk intact. It's likely this tree grew in a woodlot, where side limb development was stifled by the competition for sunlight. Identification of dead chestnuts depends upon an unusual dissolution sequence:

Most dead trees rot from the outside in—the chestnut rots from the inside out! The hard, intact surface hides a rotting interior. The chestnut's durability made it highly sought after for beams and lumber.

At 2.3 miles you come to a group of circular piles of stones, many perched on large rocks embedded in the ground. In the days of small hand-tool harvesters like scythes, this was an efficient method of clearing fields, quicker than building a wall; with today's straight-line mowing machines it would be unacceptable. Of course, running a mowing machine on these rocky hillsides would be a feat in itself.

The checkered leaves of the evergreen rattlesnake plantain are common along this section of the trail. Its faded spires of last year's orchids thrust upward here and there. This is one of the few plants whose foliage is more familiar than their flowers.

In about 2.6 miles turn left down a rutted road across from a lean-to. Follow along the edge of a hemlock grove, which offers a welcome break from cold north winds on the hillside. Soon turn right into the woods and bear right again at a wooded, grassy remnant of field dotted with eastern red cedars. Carefully follow the blue blazes through these reforested fields.

Dropping down a bank in a mature hemlock grove remarkable for its thick understory of hemlock seedlings—evidence of this tree's tolerance for shaded conditions—you reach the Still River and follow it upstream. (This trout stream is a tributary of the Natchaug River.) In the next ½ mile you alternately pass through typical woodland and grassy woods featuring the short-lived American hornbeam or musclewood, so called because its smooth, corded branches resemble muscular arms contorted with strain. For some reason, it does not shade out grass, unlike most trees.

After 3.3 miles you reach Pilfershire Road at a bridge. On the upstream corner of the bridge is a large white walnut, or butternut—a not-too-common, short-lived tree. Retrace your steps over the trail.

You may choose to follow gravel Kingsbury Road from Nathaniel Lyon Memorial Park past the Natchaug State Forest headquarters to your car at Beaver Dam Wildlife Management Area, and take in a CCC plaque, another familiar sight in Connecticut's woodlands. FDR's Civilian Conservation Corps did much work in the state's forests and parks during the Great Depression. Dams, trails, shelters, roads, walls, and other similar projects were built by the corps, a unique mix of the Departments of War (now Defense) and Interior. The army ran the camps, and foresters, engineers, and land managers used the workforce to improve the country's abundant natural and recreational resources. You'll pass a marker honoring the workers of Civilian Conservation Corps Camp Fernow, Company No. 183. The marker notes the corps's origin: CREATED BY PRESIDENT FRANKLIN ROOSEVELT, 1933–1942, RENEWING THE COUNTRY'S NATURAL RESOURCES AND CHALLENGING THE HUMAN SPIRIT OF A NATION IN DEPRESSION.

36

Peoples State Forest

Location: Barkhamsted

Distance: 7 miles

Vertical rise: 1,000 feet

Time: 4 hours

Rating: BC

Maps: USGS 7.5-minute Winsted, New Hartford

Good hiking trails do not just happen, nor are they maintained effortlessly. Three groups maintain most of Connecticut's trails. The Connecticut Chapter of the Appalachian Mountain Club does an excellent job of covering the Appalachian Trail. The unpaid volunteers of the Connecticut Forest and Park Association maintain the extensive Blue Trail System. Because each trail section in this system is the domain of a single individual who is subject to the vagaries of time and temperament, occasionally a section of blue-blazed trail is slightly unkempt. But overall, these volunteers do a superb job.

Conditions on state-maintained trails are the most variable, due to the demands of funding and priorities. Peoples State Forest is an example of an excellent trail system that benefits from a combination of volunteers and state funding. Not only are the trails in good shape, but the Stone Museum described at the beginning of this hike has been restored as well, and provides displays and programs for summer visitors.

From the junction of CT 318 and US 44 east of Winsted, proceed east on CT 318 across the Farmington River and take the first left onto East River Road. In 0.8 mile, by the Peoples Forest sign, fork right onto Greenwoods Road, the paved state forest road. You have missed your turn if you come to a picnic area on your left. Then, in 0.2 mile, turn left up a short gravel road to a parking lot by a well-constructed trailside museum, a legacy of the Civilian Conservation Corps of the 1930s. Try to park

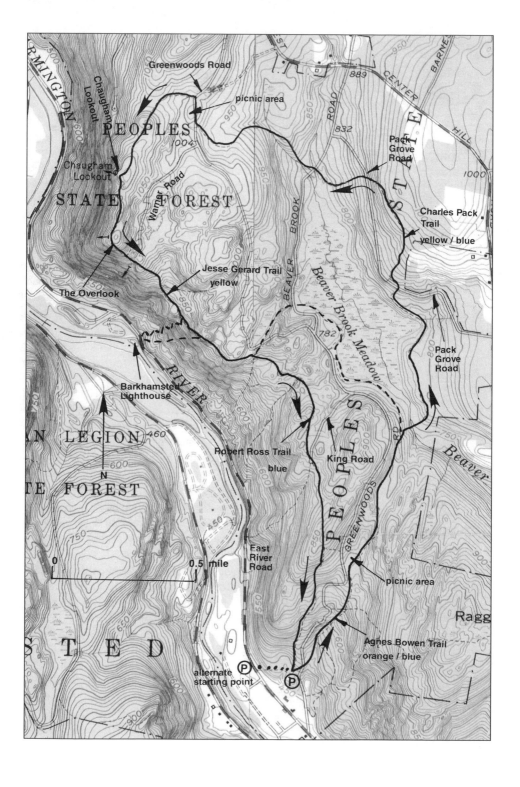

efficiently so others visiting the museum can park here, too. When the forest is busy, and in winter when Greenwoods Road is not maintained, it is recommended that hikers park on East River Road at Matthies Grove and take the blue-blazed Ross Trail directly across the road from the parking lot uphill to the museum.

The Agnes Bowen Trail, named for a leader in the establishment of Peoples Forest and marked by blue blazes with orange dots, starts into the woods here, across the parking lot from the museum. Follow this path through a stand of huge white pines. We found porcupine tracks in the snow near the museum on a recent December visit. Porkies are notable for their waddling gait and are active during warmer stretches of the winter. Shortly the blue-blazed Robert Ross Trail breaks off to your left; stay on the orange-on-blue-blazed trail as it curves downhill to the tar forest road. Turn right and follow the road for a few yards, then go left into the woods. Almost immediately you cross a small stream, which the now rocky trail follows uphill to your left. In ½ mile the trail passes through a roadside picnic area, turns right at a fireplace, and in another ⅔ mile intersects the Charles L. Pack Trail (yellow dots on blue).

Turn right to follow these blazes. In a few yards you reach Beaver Brook, which you cross on a footbridge (use caution: slick when wet) built by the Youth Conservation Corps in 1976. On your right you can see the old high-water double-cable crossing; the cable crossing was used by walking on the lower cable and holding on to the upper one for balance. Here you'll find the red cardinal flower, a really striking midsummer bloom.

After crossing the footbridge, bear left across the hillside, keeping Beaver Swamp on your left, and then curve to your right up-

hill. Beaver Swamp was once a meadow, and some of the Pack Trail follows the wagon path used to haul hay from these fields at the turn of the 20th century. You'll pass a large foundation to your right, all that remains of a dwelling built before 1806 and torn down in 1880. In ⅔ mile from the junction with the orange-on-blue-blazed trail, you cross gravel Pack Grove Road. Climb among the beech trees (Pack Grove) and then descend to join the trail again in another ½ mile. Turn right onto the gravel road and then bear left to leave the road and continue to drop downhill to Beaver Brook Road. Turn left and recross the brook on a bridge. Watch for trout swimming under the bridge. Turn right off the road and reenter the woods on the stream's far side on a woods road, and eventually ford a small feeder brook. Another ½ mile of woods walking brings you to Greenwoods Road, where this trail ends.

Turn right to follow the pavement through Big Spring Recreation Area, and then turn left into the woods. Here you pick up the yellow-blazed Jesse Gerard Trail, which leads you to the escarpment along the Farmington River. Note the delicate spring blooms of Canada mayflower along the path here.

This trail traces an old tote road for a short distance before taking an obscure path uphill. After passing between two huge glacial boulders ⅓ mile from Greenwoods Road, the trail turns right, toward Chaugham Lookout. These open ledges, ½ mile from Greenwoods Road, provide an excellent view northwest across a wide, wild, wooded valley. The canoe-dotted Farmington River winds sinuously below. The village of Riverton in the valley to the north looks very New England–like with its white church steeple. Chaugham was a Native American whose cabin in the valley below, lit up at

Beaver Brook above the meadow

night, was a familiar landmark for stage drivers heading for New Hartford. His cabin, in an old Native American settlement, was called the Barkhamsted Lighthouse.

The well-worn trail continues through hemlocks along the ledge escarpment, reaching another overlook in ⅓ mile. Proceeding steeply down, you find sweet low-bush blueberries flanking the trail over erosion-bared basalt. The yellow-blazed Jesse Gerard and blue-blazed Robert Ross Trails run together here. They split about ¾ mile from Chaugham Lookout. A yellow-blazed trail turns right and descends 299 steps to the river at Barkhamsted Lighthouse. Continue on a yellow-and-blue-blazed trail until the yellow-blazed trail descends also to Barkhamsted Lighthouse; here follow the blue-blazed trail up a steep hill beneath a ledge before resuming the descent. Pass over a rise and reach a wide road coming from your left. Bear right downhill and then turn left into the woods, following blue blazes.

Continue downhill on the blue-blazed trail to the orange-on-blue-blazed trail near the Stone Museum. Follow the blazes to your right back to your car. Take the time to check out the museum if it's open. The chestnut beams (see Hike 35, Natchaug) alone are worth the visit; however, there is plenty of natural and human historical information there to add to your day's enjoyment.

37

West Peak and Castle Crag

Location: Meriden

Distance: 6.4 miles

Vertical rise: 1,200 feet

Time: 4 hours

Rating: B

Map: USGS 7.5-minute Meriden

Save this hike until you're in good shape (it's difficult), your mind is receptive to scenic beauty (the views are very special), and the day is clear and cool (visibility is very important).

This hike starts in Hubbard Park in Meriden, just off I-691. Take exit 4 off I-691 and follow West Main Street east toward downtown Meriden. After about ¾ mile turn left into Hubbard Park. Keeping the pond to your right, bear right at the first intersection to continue around the pond to a stop sign. Turn right toward the highway overpass and then park to your left in front of the concrete roadblocks.

Take the abandoned road north under the interstate highway to Reservoir Road and bear left, continuing north between South Mountain and Merimere Reservoir. This road is open to summit traffic during good weather, so use caution. The reservoir is a public water supply, so you aren't allowed to enter the water, and the poison ivy along the roadside is more than sufficient to reduce the temptation. The view across the water to the west at Castle Crag and its cliffs is outstanding. One mile from the start, turn left to cross the dam at the north end of Merimere Reservoir. Here you can enjoy the fine view of the lake and the notch it sits in.

At the dam's end, turn left to follow the blue-blazed Metacomet Trail up the traprock embankment into the woods. After crossing an attractive rock-bound rill, you edge up the long west side of the reservoir. Then follow near the twisting shore of the lake—the

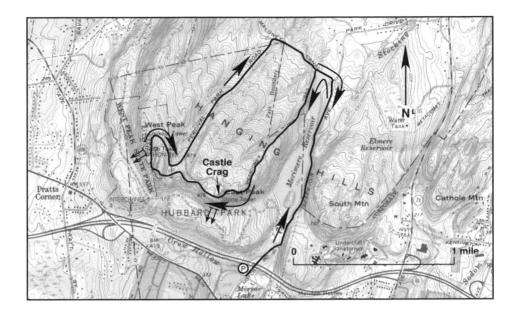

route is peppered with volcanic rocks. After leaving the shore, the way at first is very steep and rocky, but gradually the slope eases.

After 2 miles you emerge on cliffs that rise 400 feet above Merimere Reservoir. Evergreen-covered Mine Island below you seems lifted from the Maine coast. Gerry first saw this island in the early 1960s on an autumn morning as the ground fog was lifting. Some sights plant themselves so firmly in your mind's eye that they are always there to delight you.

South Mountain rises from the far shore of the reservoir, and Mount Higby's northern cliffs poke up at left (see Hike 28). On the far left you can make out the jagged Hartford skyline.

As you continue uphill along the cliff, several unmarked paths on your left lead to similar viewpoints with slightly different perspectives; all are spectacular on a clear day. One last lookout provides a glimpse of Castle Crag's tower. You follow the blue-blazed trail across a final dip before arriving

at the base of the tower, 2.2 miles from your car. Climb the tower on metal stairs for a panoramic view from Castle Crag.

The vista west is blocked by West Peak. Sleeping Giant (see Hike 49) and West Rock lie to the south, and the Metacomet ridges to the north. Talcott Mountain (see Hike 45) is readily identifiable with its Heublein Tower. In the far distance you can see the east-facing cliffs of Mount Tom in Massachusetts, the Connecticut River gap, and the humps of the Holyoke Range.

Leaving the tower, continue on the Metacomet Trail across the parking lot. Be careful here; your route can be hard to locate. The trail goes across the near corner of the lot and continues up the slope near the cliffs. The route crosses more open cliffs and then drops down almost to the tower's access road.

Just before the road, a descending blue-blazed trail that avoids road walking by way of a series of ups and downs bears left away from the road. Take this trail and at the bottom turn right onto a tote road. Soon

Castle Crag

turn right again, climbing diagonally left up an overgrown scree slope. A recent mid-March trip revealed a garter snake enjoying the early-season warmth of the hillside's southern exposure. Bear right and ascend a very attractive draw. Great traprock boulders are "flowing" down the intersection of the scree slopes. Look back—the sides of the draw frame the Sleeping Giant with his head to the right.

Near the top of this draw are a large elderberry bush and a stand of American yew. This is the largest, most southerly stand that we have encountered. A northern shrub, the yew ranges as far south as New England, so this may be one of its more southerly appearances.

The trail levels out before bearing left up the steep side a short way to the plateau top of West Peak. Here, the Connecticut Chapter of the Appalachian Mountain Club was formed in June 1921. The club has held at least two reunions here since then, including one marking its 60th anniversary in June 1981. You emerge onto an old road, which you follow left to a formerly fenced, rocky point. You can see the Tunxis ridge to the west. Several cliffs and headlands invite your careful exploration.

After a leisurely lunch—the surrounding thickets make nice spots for a nap—follow the park road down the north side of West Peak. As with most of Connecticut's traprock ridges, the side opposite the cliffs tends to slope gently as a result of the tipping of the layer of traprock. The break in the traprock is then exposed as a cliff. Be sure to turn left at the road junction that leads right to Castle Crag. When you reach Merimere Reservoir, cross the dam and follow Reservoir Road south, retracing your steps to your car.

38

Bear Mountain

Location: Salisbury

Distance: 6.5 miles

Vertical rise: 1,600 feet

Time: 4 hours

Rating: AB

Map: USGS 7.5-minute Bash Bish Falls (MA-CT-NY)

A rugged, windswept mountain with views into three states awaits you at the high point of this hike. On the way, you hike a portion of the justly famous Appalachian Trail (AT). At the top of Bear Mountain is a once magnificent stone monument that has partially crumbled but is still an imposing landmark. In late 1983 the rubble was stabilized, creating a lower monument. It was erected to proclaim (incorrectly) the highest point in Connecticut. In fact, as has been discovered since World War II, the state's high point is on a shoulder of Mount Frissell, another peak on the Riga Plateau just west of Bear Mountain, whose summit is in Massachusetts.

To reach the start of this hike, drive on CT 41 3.2 miles north from its junction with US 44 in Salisbury. There is a small hikers' parking lot on your left.

The blue-blazed Undermountain Trail, a feeder trail to the AT, starts at the back of the parking lot and soon passes a large bulletin board, which carries the latest trail information. There is also a box with a frequently replenished supply of AT information folders. These provide handy parking, camping, and route information.

Proceed through woods; within our memories this area was an open field. We have watched this area change over the past 30 years. Enter the older woods and soon begin to climb, gently at first, and then more steeply. This trail will present an almost unrelieved climb to its junction with the AT in 1.9 miles. It is a good test of wind and muscle and an excellent place to

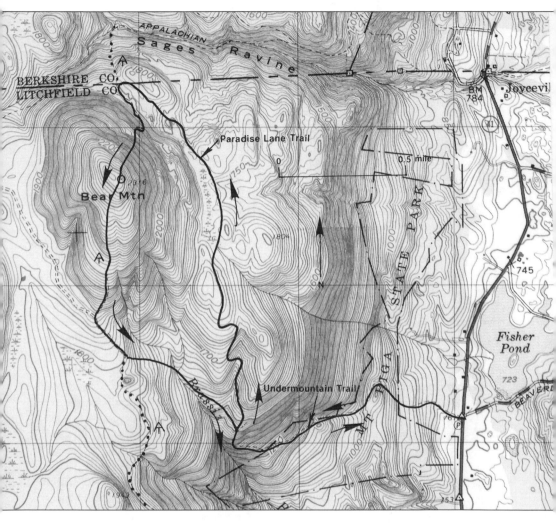

practice the mile-eating trick used by seasoned hikers: Set a pace you can maintain all the way to the top without stopping.

After ¼ mile you pass an eroded gully on your right and the hulks of several large fallen chestnut trees on your left. Although these trees have been dead for at least 70 years, their disintegrating trunks still litter the forest floor. The barkless remains, slowly decomposing, have a weather-beaten look unlike that of any other dead tree. Chestnut trees rot from the inside out, thereby main-

taining their size and apparent integrity longer than most other deadfalls.

As you climb, it becomes more obvious that this trail is an old tote road whose surface has eroded several feet into the hill. This erosion was probably caused by countless horse and wagon trips scoring the surface, with rain and snowmelt doing the rest. Soon you encounter a bad washout. Hikers caused this unsightly scar, at least in part! The constant tramping of feet killed the stabilizing vegetation, and the deeply eroded road prevented the diversion of running water off the trail. Then a real gully washer of a storm, probably in spring when the soil was already saturated and unstable, caused the muddy earth to slide into the ravine at the left, leaving the gouge on the trail you see before you. Since the water now flows into the ravine instead of down the trail, and the Appalachian Mountain Club has rerouted the trail off the worst areas, the rest of the road should be fairly secure.

Two-tenths of a mile above the washout, turn right off the Undermountain Trail onto blue-blazed Paradise Lane. Blazed trails may exhibit many different colors, but the white blazes are reserved for the AT, while AT side trails are blazed with blue. This blue-blazed trail joins the AT north of the summit of Bear Mountain in 2.1 miles. If you continue straight on the Undermountain Trail, you will meet the AT south of the peak of Bear Mountain. You will come back this way on the circuit described here.

Paradise Lane starts roughly parallel to the AT. In a short distance, the trail goes left off the old tote road and zigzags steeply up the hill. This trail has the densest population of chestnut sprouts we've seen in Connecticut, and a couple of them have grown to nearly 4 inches across. You'll soon pass a group camping area on your right. Then, at a relatively flat area on Bear Mountain, the trail levels a bit and even eases gently downhill until it reaches a swampy area.

Along this section of the trail Gerry once had a special experience. A ruffed grouse took off with the usual thunder of wings, without having run a bit, as they usually do. Why did it hold in one spot so long before flying? Having noted where it took off, Gerry went over and found a well-camouflaged, roughly circular nest with nine buff eggs in it.

After going along the level a short way, you will see the very steep south side of Bear Mountain at left. Cross a small seasonal stream and continue curving gently left. Soon you reach a small pond; the water is mostly filled with bushes. After crossing the pond's outlet stream on a log bridge, note the northeast corner of Bear Mountain as you go across an open ledge decorated with laurel and huckleberry. When you cross the yellow blazes along this trail, you enter National Park Service land protecting the Appalachian Trail corridor land in perpetuity.

Descend though hemlocks to the junction with the AT, and then turn left (south). (A right turn would take you to Mount Katahdin in Maine in about 800 miles.) For years, members of the Appalachian Mountain Club used a group of five short-lived white birches to tell them where to turn off onto this end of Paradise Lane from the AT. Now that the National Park Service has bought this land, and this side trail is signed, the trees' role as a landmark has ended; seeming to sense this, they have all died in the past 15 years.

Go diagonally left up the white-blazed, rocky AT on Bear Mountain. Some fine trail work has been done here to stabilize this steep route with large, erosionproof rocks. After a long, steady uphill stretch, you'll turn directly up the steep, ledge-dominated slope. Scramble over several steep pitches where you have to use both hands and feet, and then enter some stunted pitch pines that perch precariously on rather bare open ledges. Almost immediately you will spot the monument on top of Bear Mountain.

While strolling around the open top, watch for large, dark, soaring birds—turkey vultures. These birds, with a 6-foot wingspan, are the largest of North America's vultures. They are common in the adjacent Hudson River Valley and are spreading throughout the Northeast. They use rising columns of air along the edge of the Riga

North from Bear Mountain to Massachusetts' Mounts Everett and Race

Plateau to soar for hours without flapping their wings.

From the summit, the views are superb. To the east lie the Twin Lakes and Canaan Mountain. For the best view to the north, follow the AT north to a ledge on the edge of the stand of scrub pines. From there the mountain with a tower is Mount Everett (2,602 feet), the apex of the second highest mountain mass in Massachusetts. The hulk in front of Everett is Race Mountain (2,365 feet).

When you are ready, follow the AT south off the top. Just as the trail starts seriously downward, there is a grand view to the south and west. Ahead is the relatively level Riga Plateau. To the right the mountains you see are, from left to right, Gridley Mountain (Connecticut), North and South Brace Mountains (New York), and Round Mountain (Connecticut), with Mount Frissell (Massachusetts) behind it; north of Frissell (you will have to go down the path a bit to see past

obstructing trees) is Mount Ashley (Massachusetts). The body of water left of Gridley is South Pond (1,715 feet), and the Catskills can be seen off in the distance on a clear day. It usually takes several visits before these mountains become old friends, but the journeys are definitely worth the effort!

Continue south, passing several pitch pines whose wind-distorted shapes would do credit to a bonsai artist. All lean east, away from the prevailing west winds. The cold, desiccating winds have sheared off any upward shoots that braved the elements so that the tops are flattened and bent eastward—the path of least resistance.

As you progress downward, the various hardy oaks rise slowly to obscure your view. Then you rise into the open again to a partial view of the mountains. Each dip, however, carries you into higher and higher trees until the trees win this game of hide-and-seek.

About 0.6 mile from the summit a tote road comes in on your right from gravel Mount Washington Road; bear left onto the AT. In another 0.2 mile the blue-blazed Undermountain Trail leaves left steeply downhill at the well-signed Riga Junction. Take this trail; it leads you downhill 1.9 miles past the Paradise Lane junction to your car.

39

Macedonia Brook

Location: Kent

Distance: 6.7 miles

Vertical rise: 1,550 feet

Time: 4 hours

Rating: A

Maps: USGS 7.5-minute Ellsworth, Amenia (NY-CT)

A cluster of hills 1,000 to 1,400 feet high, separated by Macedonia Brook, make up Macedonia Brook State Park. This 2,300-acre park boasts 13 miles of trails. The famed Appalachian Trail (AT) used to run through Macedonia Brook, but it was relocated in the late 1980s. Now what was the AT is part of the Connecticut Blue Trail System.

The park began as a 1,500-acre gift from the White Memorial Foundation in 1918 (see Hike 30). This was once the domain of the Schaghticokes, descended from Sassacus's Pequots and dispersed after the 1637 Pequot War, the first of America's Indian Wars. During the Revolutionary War more than one hundred Schaghticoke warriors joined the American cause; serving as a signal corps, they used drums and signal fires to relay messages from Stockbridge, Massachusetts, to Long Island Sound. Macedonia became a thriving community that supported the iron industry in nearby Kent. Because of charcoal production to feed the blast furnaces, all the local timber had been consumed by the 1840s. Competition with the larger Pennsylvania mines closed down the local iron operation in 1865. Macedonia Brook State Park, like many of Connecticut's state forests and parks, was home to a Civilian Conservation Corps company in the 1930s.

Macedonia Brook lies just inside Connecticut's western boundary. From the junction of CT 341 and US 7 in Kent, take CT 341 west for 1.7 miles to Macedonia Brook Road, where a sign directs you to the park down a paved road on your right. Bear left where Fuller Mountain Road turns right

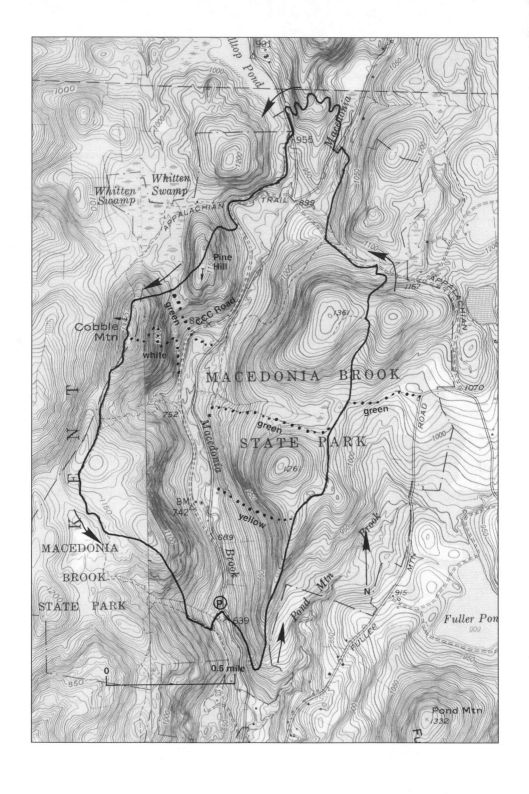

Whittop Pond

991

Whitten Swamp

Whitten Swamp

APPALACHIAN TRAIL 899

955

Macedonia

1050

1100

1167

Pine Hill

green

CCC Road 865

Cobble Mtn

white

K E N T

752

MACEDONIA BROOK

1361

STATE PARK

Macedonia

green

green

1070

ROAD

1000

1200

126

MACEDONIA

BROOK

BM 742

689

yellow

Brook

Pond Mtn

N

915

FULLER MTN

Fuller Pon
909

STATE PARK

1200

P

639

0.5 mile

850

850

Pond Mtn
1332

0.8 mile from CT 341, and reach the blue-blazed Macedonia Ridge Trail at a bridge over the brook after another 0.6 mile. There is parking on both sides of the bridge.

Enter the woods on the east side of the valley (to your right as you drive in from CT 341). Ascend the hillside, turn sharply left, and climb the ridge through open oak forest. On an early-morning hike in July a large hawk flew out of a tree ahead on the ridge. The remnants of an old apple orchard bisect the trail; many of the gnarled, unkempt specimens still bloom each spring.

After 0.9 mile the yellow-blazed trail branches to the left as your trail bends right. Drop down the east side of a hill and join a green-blazed trail that comes in at your left from the park road. The blue- and green-blazed trails run together briefly. At the beginning of the next rise, bear left onto the blue-blazed ridge trail where the green-blazed trail continues down the road and out to Fuller Mountain Road.

A short distance beyond the junction, you walk past several clumps of gray birches on your left. These dowdy cousins of the sparkling white birch have a grayer bark that does not peel with age. A short-lived tree with triangular leaves and black triangular patches beneath the base of each limb, the gray birch is an early colonizer of uncultivated open fields.

Your trail climbs easily and steadily up and over a col between two unnamed peaks. In spring the greenish yellow flowers of the many striped maples here lend a faint but delightful fragrance to the woods. The flower clusters dangle from the branches like exotic earrings.

From the col, the ridge trail drops steeply down to a deeply worn old town road (the former AT); turn left to follow it downhill. At a barricade, turn right off the woods road and cross a stream before climbing over a rise. Turn left to cross over a bridge on dirt Keeler Road. Turn right after crossing the bridge and follow Macedonia Brook before ascending a hill near the northern boundary of the park. We found a box turtle here on one of our recent hikes. The little 6-inch-long specimen was probably better than 60 years old! Adult turtles have relatively few enemies except cars and can live to ripe old ages of more than one hundred years. Pass over the crest of the ridge and drop steeply through a hemlock stand using switchbacks. Turn left onto gravel Weber Road, then turn right to follow blue blazes on the gated old CCC Road at a park sign. Follow the road through gates at its crossing of partially paved Chippewalla Road. Continue on CCC Road following blue blazes, and then turn right off the road to follow a footpath steeply up Pine Hill. Beneath an ash tree on the right we found two morels. Acclaimed as our best-tasting local wild mushroom, this hollow, light brown fungus with its exterior raised latticework is the elusive treasure of the dedicated mycologist. Always make a positive identification with a mushroom expert before nibbling!

At the top of the grade, the trail turns left into the woods, climbing steadily and fairly steeply. In June a few pink azaleas or June pinks spot the trail with color and fragrance. Threading through the laurel undergrowth, the grade eases as you near the top of Pine Hill. As on most Connecticut hills, the steepest slope on Pine Hill is in the middle of the grade. Evidence of the changing nature of our forests is the fact that there are no pines on Pine Hill, which is now covered with oak, birch, and hop hornbeam.

From the ledges on Pine Hill's far side, you have an excellent view down the Macedonia Brook Valley. Close by from right to left are Cobble Mountain, South Cobble Mountain (both of which you climb

Looking south along Macedonia Brook's valley

on this hike), and Chase Mountain. In the center distance are Mounts Algo and Schaghticoke.

Follow the trail down over steep ledges, passing the green-blazed Pine Hill Trail to your left just before reaching the col. Continue uphill, passing through boulders before reaching the ledges above. Scramble over a boulder and climb an 8-foot-high ledge with minimal handholds. This route is not recommended when it is wet or icy. Just above that ledge, follow the blue-blazed trail up a 30-foot sloping ledge. You have to either find a way around or use a crack for traction. This is definitely not recommended in adverse conditions. If you're uneasy with these ledges, you can return to the Pine Hill Trail and follow it ½ mile down to the park road, 1 miles north of your car. Your ascent soon moderates as you pass by several large beds of wild oats with their drooping, bell-shaped flowers.

Be prepared for superb views when you reach the top of Cobble Mountain, for the trail traverses its exposed western escarpment. The ridge across the valley is in New York, and beyond it are the Catskills. By dropping down the ledges a bit you can get a good view of Connecticut's northwest corner, the Riga Plateau. The tallest peak (topped by a fire tower) on your right is Mount Everett in Massachusetts. To its left is Bear Mountain (see Hike 38) in Connecticut.

Continue on these exposed ledges to their far end where the white-blazed Cobble Mountain Trail comes in from your left. Stay on the blue-blazed ridge trail, and drop steeply down the ledges into the col before rising up South Cobble Mountain. The trail passes to the left of the summit. Then follow the steep, rocky route down into the col. Head downhill to the park road and your car.

40

Windsor Locks Canal

Location: Suffield

Distance: 9 miles

Vertical rise: negligible

Time: 4½ hours

Rating: D

Maps: USGS 7.5-minute Windsor Locks,
Broad Brook

By the middle of the 19th century, stiff competition from railroads brought about the collapse of New England's expanding canal system. The Windsor Locks Canal, built in 1829 to bypass the Enfield Rapids on the Connecticut River, was an exception. Here, the canal survived because water diverted from New England's biggest river not only served barge traffic but also provided power to mills, the last of which continued to operate until the 1930s. Today the Windsor Locks Canal still routes an occasional pleasure craft around the rapids, and its old towpath, now paved, offers a pleasant, level trail for walking or bicycling.

To reach the towpath, follow CT 159 south from its southern junction with CT 190 for 0.1 mile to Canal Road on your left. The road ends in about 0.4 mile, with a large parking lot on your left. The size of the lot is not indicative of trail use; it is heavily used by anglers who congregate here from April to June. The famous Enfield Rapids provide the best ocean-run shad fishing in New England.

Head south down the river; pass through the gates and over the canal to the start of the towpath. These gates are locked from mid-November to the beginning of April to preclude towpath use, which could disturb wintering birds of prey. The impressive Enfield Rapids dominate the scene to your left. Your route simply follows the paved way 4.5 miles to its end; there are no side trails to mislead you. The towpath is a designated bicycle trail, so please give cyclists the right-of-way.

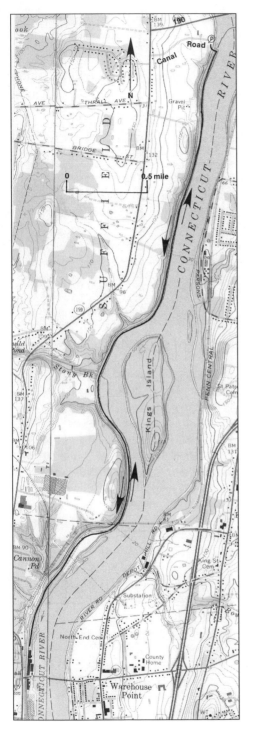

While the plants and wildlife along the way are the chief attractions of this hike, human-made constructions along the canal are not without interest. About 2 miles from the start, the blunt prow of heavily wooded, mile-long King's Island comes into view. Notice here that the banks of the canal are made of the soft Connecticut Valley red sandstone, best known as the rock used to build New York City's brownstone apartments. About ⅓ mile along King's Island you cross the Stony Brook Aqueduct, which was built in 1827 and rebuilt in 1998; this structure allows the water level of the canal to remain higher than that of the Connecticut River below—without it the canal's water would drain into the river via the brook! A quarter mile below King's Island you pass alongside venerable stone abutments supporting a trestle over the Connecticut River; several trains whistled by as we hiked the towpath.

As you walk, maintain an alert eye. This entire trip is a veritable oasis in an urban desert. While humans create monotonous conformity, nature, in all her diversity, moves in wherever possible.

We came upon a young woodchuck caught between the devil (us) and the deep blue sea (the canal). Butterflies were constant companions. Besides the cabbage white (the only butterfly that is a common agricultural pest), we saw various swallowtails, skippers, wood satyrs, and a beloved ally, the red admiral, whose caterpillar ravages nettles.

From a botanical point of view, this walk is one of the best in the state. We identified oxeye daisy, fleabane, yarrow, vetch, two varieties of milkweed, campion, Saint-John's-wort, black-eyed Susan, several goldenrods, mullein, deadly nightshade, thimbleweed, Deptford pink, plantain (American and English), both bull and

Windsor Locks Canal and paved towpath

Canada thistle, roses, gill-over-the-ground, jewelweed, daylily, and lovely sundroplike giant buttercups with cross-shaped stigmas. The clovers, legumes with built-in nitrogen factories on their roots, are well represented. In addition to white and alsike clover, we found at least two varieties of yellow-blossomed hop clovers.

Vines and bushes abound: poison ivy, several varieties of grapes, Virginia creeper, Oriental bittersweet, sweet-smelling Japanese honeysuckle, scrub willow, various types of the smaller dogwoods, elderberry, alder (both smooth and speckled), sassafras, juniper, slippery elm, and smooth and staghorn sumacs with their great masses of red-ripening acidic fruit. On a recent May visit, the white bracts of flowering dogwood punctuated the various shades of green along the canal's edge.

Here also, treetops that you usually see only from below stand open for your scrutiny. These trees growing along the riverbed, or on the canal's steep sides to your left, present their seldom-seen tops for your curiosity. The round buttons that give the sycamore one of its common names (buttonwood) are here at eye level, and the stickiness of the butternut tree's immature nuts can be tested in place. In mid- to late May the fluffs of cotton from the aptly named eastern cottonwood fill the air—in places we have seen a gossamer layer of this cotton 2 inches deep on the ground. In early summer you can pick with ease the tasty fruit of the red mulberry—if you can get there before the birds!

We talk of waste areas, but probably the only true wastelands are those areas sealed with concrete and asphalt—and even these are transitory. A constant rain of seeds awaits the smallest moistened crack, ready to sprout and grow. Near the end of the towpath, we found that a clump of field bindweed had wrestled a foothold in the junction between an old brick building and the asphalt drive. In the wild the small, white morning glory–like flowers of this "weed" have little appeal for most of us, but here they lighten a dingy corner.

A second set of gates 4.5 miles from the first marks the end of the towpath near CT 140. Turn around and retrace your steps to your car.

41

Mansfield Hollow

Location: Mansfield

Distance: 8 miles

Vertical rise: 600 feet

Time: 4½ hours

Rating: CD

Map: USGS 7.5-minute Spring Hill

Because of its proximity to the University of Connecticut at Storrs, Mansfield Hollow Recreation Area is sprinkled with temporary refugees from academia: jogging professors, strolling students, and young families with toddlers. In addition to picnic tables, fireplaces, ball fields, bridle paths, rest rooms, and boat-launching facilities, Mansfield Hollow also encompasses one of the two southern termini of the Nipmuck Trail, which stretches 34 miles north to Bigelow Hollow State Park near the Massachusetts border. This hike follows the blue-blazed Nipmuck Trail through a flood-control area and rolling countryside as far as 50 Foot Cliff, a nice little lookout.

From the junction of CT 89 and CT 195 in Mansfield Center, drive south on CT 195 for 0.5 mile to Bassett Bridge Road and turn left. After 0.8 mile park in the lot to your left, on the right side of the entrance road to Mansfield Hollow State Park.

To reach the start of the Nipmuck Trail, follow the paved entrance road to a gated woods road through the open field fringed with white pine woods, keeping the flood-control causeway to your left and the ball field to your right. Then take the blue-blazed Nipmuck Trail through the gate adjacent to the causeway and enter a forest remarkable for its understory of white pine seedlings, normally a shade-intolerant species. The flood-control reservoir is visible to the east.

The trail starts on sandy soil, where white pines grow very well. It winds through various trail junctions, but your route is marked well, and you should have no problem

following the blue blazes through the woods. You reach a woods road in 0.1 mile; the blazes lead to the right before turning left into the woods. The reservoir is visible beyond the end of the road. Follow the blue blazes carefully through this maze of trails and woods roads. You may encounter recent relocations designed to prevent abrupt meetings between hikers and mountain bikers. On your right are patches of shinleaf, which you can distinguish by their almost round evergreen leaves. Although you will not see their spikes of nodding white flowers until June or July, the flower buds may be found nestled beneath forest litter, here mostly pine needles, in early May. This plant derives its name from the early custom of applying its leaves to sores and bruises—any plaster, no matter where applied, was called a shin plaster.

As you wend your way up onto a flat, the trail touches and then heads left off a bridle path. You will flirt with numerous bridle paths strewn with strawberry plants and cinquefoils through the first part of the hike. The mixture gives you a chance to distinguish between these two plants with similar leaves: The strawberry has three-leafed bunches, and the local cinquefoils, five.

Beneath a blue-blazed white pine you will find the first of many hawthorns along the trail. This shrub is characterized principally by formidable 2-inch thorns, as well as both attractive white flowers with a rather disagreeable odor and fall pomes suitable for making jelly. You encounter and cross a second bridle path, pass through another wooded section, and emerge once again on a bridle path.

At this junction, head right. After curving left through a small patch of woods, the trail continues along the right side of a ball field, Southeast Park, on a gravel road to CT 89, 1.5 miles from the start. Follow paved CT 89 to your left briefly and then cross to a grassy area. Bear right into the woods, and then continue downhill by an old well and cellar hole. Cross the abandoned tar road. Soon the trail goes left on a dirt road to the bottom of a dry dike. In flood times the central gates of the flood-control dam can be closed to limit downstream flow. Several such dikes are found in this area. Bear left to cross the stream beside the flood-control

gate and turn right to return to the Nipmuck Trail.

Reenter the woods. White oaks (the bark is actually light gray) stand sentinel on the trail. Follow a gravel road, then turn right onto another road. The road straight ahead is the alternate white-blazed route. A new steel truss footbridge carries the trail across the Fenton River. After crossing the bridge, bear left over some wet ground before reaching a woods road that follows along the east side of the Fenton River Valley. Blue blazes and painted wooden arrows guide you through this stretch. Robins fly ahead of you in the grass, and the soulful cry of the mourning dove echoes around you.

The path now angles up onto a small gravel ridge deposited by the glacier, with the river below you at left. To your left a small stream widens into swamp pools populated with frogs and painted turtles. Dropping off the ridge, you continue through a meadow brilliant with the yellows of the goldfinch and the swallowtail butterfly. Turn left into the woods just before you reach a second gravel ridge.

Shortly you come to the Fenton River again, which is spanned by another new steel truss footbridge. After crossing, follow this 30-foot-wide trout river upstream (right), keeping a cornfield on your left. The white-blazed alternate route rejoins the Nipmuck Trail on the west side of the bridge. Follow the blue-blazed trail as it winds among numerous anglers' paths along the riverbank—watch the blazes carefully to avoid straying. A variety of ferns grace the low spots, while the aptly named interrupted fern stands tall throughout.

Two miles from CT 89 the trail cuts to your left, away from the river and uphill to Chaffeeville Road. The trail crosses the road and ascends through hardwoods and hemlocks. About 25 yards beyond the second

One of two sturdy trail bridges spanning the Fenton River

stream crossing you reach the old trail junction; continue uphill to the west of the cliffs as the trail winds to the top of the ridge, soon emerging on the uppermost ledges of 50 Foot Cliff. This lookout offers fine views of eastern Connecticut woodlands. Enjoy your lunch with a view and then retrace your steps south. To add variety to your return trip, stay straight at the trail junction before crossing the bridge over the Fenton River. Follow the white-blazed alternate route through a field and then up onto higher ground, eventually joining the blue-blazed Nipmuck Trail again above the flood-control plain on a gravel road. Bear right downhill and follow the blue blazes back to your car.

42

Bigelow Hollow

Location: Union

Distance: 8¼ miles

Vertical rise: 800 feet

Time: 4½ hours

Rating: B

Maps: USGS 7.5-minute Westford, Eastford, Wales (MA-CT), Southbridge (MA-CT)

Connecticut rarely contains lengthy undeveloped vistas. Our picturesque traprock ridges lie within the most intensely developed stretches of the state, and the western highlands' views frequently encompass the fields and pastures of an agricultural setting. Bigelow Hollow's Breakneck Pond provides a sense of undeveloped nature, however, with its long narrow waters bordered by ridges on both sides. This jewel of the Nipmuck State Forest is a special place indeed!

Bigelow Hollow's recreation area was established in 1949; combined with Nipmuck State Forest, it is one of the largest unbroken forests in eastern Connecticut. From I-84's exit 73, follow CT 190 east to CT 171 in Union. Turn right and follow CT 171 south to the park entrance to the north, about 1½ miles from Union. Follow the main park road ½ mile to the picnic area and trail parking at the north end of Bigelow Pond. You'll pass a small parking area reserved for anglers on your left before you reach your destination.

Enter the woods opposite the parking lot beside a bulletin board with trail maps, taking the white-blazed East Ridge Trail. Turn left at a fork onto the blue-and-orange-blazed Ridge Trail over a small hill featuring hemlocks and mountain laurel. Cross a small stream and ascend the ridge on a cushioned surface of tree needles. The acid content of the needles helps the overstory hemlocks outcompete other tree species and helps create a grove of trees. White pine needles contribute to the acidic nature of the soil, but white pines primarily retain their dominance

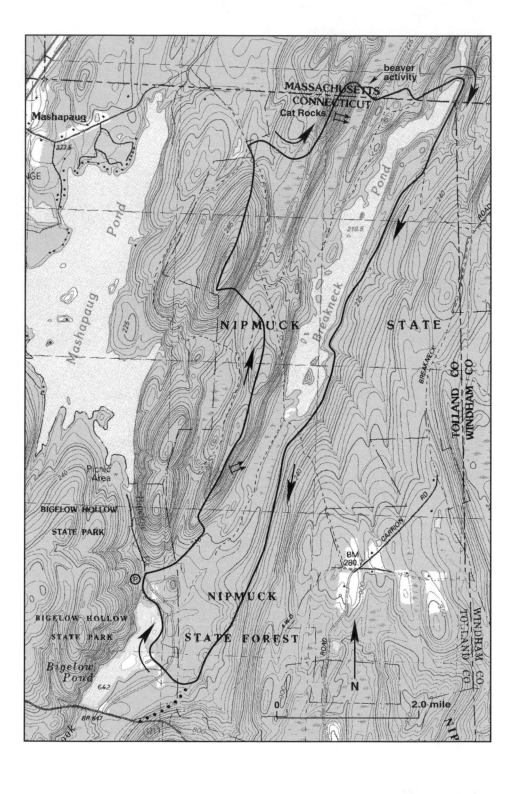

beaver
activity

MASSACHUSETTS
CONNECTICUT
Cat Rocks

Mashapaug

Mashapaug Pond

Breakneck Pond

NIPMUCK   STATE

BREAKNECK

TOLLAND CO
WINDHAM CO

Picnic
Area

BIGELOW HOLLOW
STATE PARK

NIPMUCK

BM
280.7

CARRION

RD

BIGELOW HOLLOW
STATE PARK

Bigelow
Pond

STATE FOREST

ROAD

ROAD

WINDHAM CO
TOLLAND CO

BR 847

N

0   2.0 mile

Breakneck Pond

in the forest by growing faster and taller than New England's other tree species.

Follow the ridge toward Breakneck Pond and enjoy a view of the pond 1.3 miles from the start of your hike. The ridge features rocky soil, oak trees, and an open, parklike understory. Leave the ridge and ascend the 1,020-foot hill west of the pond. After a short, steep climb you'll follow an interesting rocky ridge before you crest the wooded hill. Then descend through the familiar oak-hickory-hemlock forest and see a less common northern tree mixed in: striped maple, probably owing to the hillside's northern exposure. This maple, also called duck's foot maple for the shape of its leaf, does not grow to great size and is easily recognized by its smooth green-and-white-striped bark.

Turn left to follow an eroded woods road that is rutted by four-wheel-drive vehicles. Soon bear right off the road to descend to a

bridge crossing over a brook. From there you ascend to Cat Rocks (the label on the topographic map is off a little; as accurate as they are geographically, topo maps sometimes mislabel features). Cat Rocks has a nice view of the narrow valley that defines Breakneck Pond. The rocky ridge with its pitch pine and sunny exposure is well worth the 3.2-mile hike from Bigelow Pond. Follow the ridge north and cross some boundary markers; one of these is the Masschusetts state line. After passing a boundary line you reach the north lookout and then descend steeply toward a beaver pond. Use care as you follow the blazes to your right before you reach the pond. Otherwise you'll find yourself—as we did—climbing partway back up through the rocks to locate the blazes!

The beavers have made a mess of the trail through this flooded area, so you will have to rely on the blazes. It may be difficult to keep your boots dry through here. Follow the edge of the beaver pond south to your right and reenter Connecticut; cross a double log bridge and then turn left to hike north back into Massachusetts. Bear right away from the wetlands and soon reach a junction with a woods road. Turn left and descend on the white-dot-on-blue-blazed Breakneck Pond View Trail. Cross the pond's outlet and reach a clearing with a beautiful view south down the length of the pond. You'll pass the northern end of the pond and turn right to cross one last time into Connecticut at a stone monument. Here your route becomes the blue-blazed Nipmuck Trail.

Follow the Nipmuck Trail south on the wide unpaved East Shore Road. The white-blazed East Ridge Trail leaves uphill to your left. Continue to follow the blue blazes south along the road, but watch carefully, because your route soon leaves the road to follow the water's edge more closely. The trail becomes a series of gentle ups and downs interspersed with feeder stream crossings from the uplands to the east. You'll pass beaver-gnawed oak and black birch trees along the shore. Beavers tend to drop trees in the direction of the water, although they probably don't do this delib-

erately but rather are aided by a tree's natural tendency to grow toward sunlight, which will be more abundant over open water.

Rejoin East Shore Road and a junction with the East Ridge Trail at the south end of Breakneck Pond, and continue to follow the Nipmuck Trail through a sizable timber cut. Connecticut's forests have regenerated to the point where it has become profitable to harvest trees again. While some folks get upset about cutting forests, the production of sawlogs can help justify setting aside large tracts of woods. Also, as long as people want wooden houses and paper products, we have to grow and harvest trees. The trail is well blazed through the logging operations, so hikers shouldn't have any difficulty following the trail.

After passing through the timber cut you cross a small stream before entering a red pine plantation. Here white pine seedlings dominate the understory, because more sunlight hits the forest floor. Shortly a white-blazed trail is encountered; turn right to follow it downhill to Bigelow Pond. You soon reach the park road, where you walk to the boat launch. From there a yellow-blazed trail leads north to the picnic area and your car.

43

Devils Hopyard

Location: East Haddam

Distance: 7.5 miles

Vertical rise: 800 feet

Time: 4½ hours

Rating: C

Map: USGS 7.5-minute Hamburg

Water dominates the 860 acres of Devils Hopyard State Park: water in the form of the rushing, turbulent Eight Mile River and its tributaries; and water as the agent that shaped this rugged scenic area.

Throughout this state park you pass beneath groves of great trees, primarily hemlocks, with wide boles, straight trunks, and first limbs often 20 feet or more above the ground. They create a brush-free setting for your explorations. The attractions that most people come to see are the spectacular falls and giant trees, but we have added a loop on the other side of the road that, while less spectacular, lets you stretch your legs quite a bit more.

Devils Hopyard became a state park in 1919 and is fully developed, with picnic tables, fireplaces, rainy-weather shelters, a campground, and several miles of hiking trails. The origin of its colorful name is lost in a welter of fanciful stories, ranging from the simple corruption of "Mr. Dibble's hopyard" to tales of mist-shrouded forms seen dancing on the ledges amid spray from the falls.

From the junction of CT 82 and CT 156 in East Haddam, drive east 0.1 mile on CT 82 to Hopyard Road, following signs to the state park. Turn left (north); follow this road 3.4 miles past the picnic area entrance and turn right to the campground (signed) on Foxtown Road. Park in the small paved lot on your left just off Hopyard Road. The campground is just beyond the pond on your left.

Cross the road and go down the trail past the covered bulletin board. Follow the

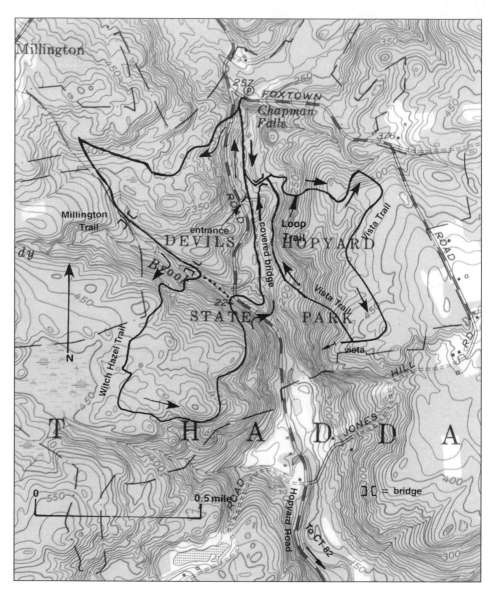

gravel trail past an unmarked trail to your right that passes under a bridge. Shortly you'll pass the Millington Trail going uphill to your right, sporadically blazed red (you'll follow this trail later in this hike). Bear left and descend gently past Chapman Falls to your left. Be sure to save some time to explore the falls area after your hike.

For more than a century prior to its inclusion in the state park, this 60-foot waterfall powered a mill; remains of mills and milldams abound in New England. The sheets of water now fall freely in a series of cascades. To get the full impact of these falls you should view them from both above and below. The rocks beside the trail reveal many circular holes and a smooth, dry chute where the water used to go. The holes were formed when a hard, loose rock got caught in a small indentation in the ledge. The force of the flowing water caused this rock to gyrate in the cavity, eventually wearing a circular hole. After the first rock has worn away, often another one falls in to continue the erosion.

Stop a moment to consider the "why" of a waterfall. It requires a special condition of hard rock overlying a softer rock, so the underlayer will erode at least as fast as the more greatly stressed upper layer. If these conditions do not exist, a waterfall becomes a less dramatic series of rapids or cascades that effectively move the water from a higher to a lower area.

You soon join the park road and continue below the picnic shelter to the covered footbridge. Cross the river (liberally stocked with trout) through the covered bridge and ascend the woods road away from the brook, following blue and orange blazes on the other side. Turn left at a fork onto the blue-blazed Loop Trail. When the trail forks again, bear right and continue climbing, soon passing a large white oak with outstretched side limbs, which indicate that the tree matured in a clearing or pasture. Descend briefly to a T-junction, where you turn right following the sign to the vista, cross a brook, and resume a steady climb marked with white blazes. After topping the rise, come to another T-junction; here you follow another sign leading to the vista, turning right onto an orange-blazed trail.

Cross a brook and ascend to another fork, where you stay to the right. Pass over a rise featuring young, shade-tolerant hemlocks growing under tall pines and oak trees, biding their time for the larger trees to pass away. Descending, you'll pass another tableau of forest succession: large, dead hemlocks interspersed with oaks. The shade

once cast by the tall evergreens no longer blocks out the sunlight. The tall, straight oaks in this stand will spread out their branches some more, and new trees will come in now that sunlight is again plentiful.

Cross another stream and pass over a rise, leveling out until you come to a large, dead hemlock blazed with an orange arrow directing you to your right. Proceed downhill, following the orange blazes toward the vista. Soon follow a footpath that breaks to your left off the main trail. Continue on this path downhill for about 150 yards to a rocky outcropping on the edge of a steep drop.

Eight Mile River Valley lies below you. Hemlocks cloak the steep hillsides. The remains of a dammed pond form the centerpiece of your view; directly beyond, a single farm and a field break the undulating blanket of treetops. A closer look shows that the field is an alluvial fan. Eroding water tore this material from the hills behind it and, when the current slowed, dropped this debris in a fan-shaped area, flattening the valley floor and creating an optimum area for farming.

After enjoying the vista, retrace your steps to the main trail, watching carefully for the junction, and head left downhill. Your orange-blazed trail bears right toward the river and follows it upstream. After passing beneath impressive ledges to your right, the trail passes over a stepped ledge to a hemlock-covered flat. It then runs gently down to the covered bridge, passing the blue-blazed Loop Trail to your right.

Cross the bridge and go right up the road toward the parking lot where you left your car. Just before reaching a rock ledge on your left, turn left onto the sporadically red-blazed Millington Trail. Follow this trail just below the impressive stone embankment and then across the road. The well-used foot trail continues diagonally left, slabbing gently up the hill. Follow the

Eight Mile River Valley from the vista

well-worn path straight through two four-way trail junctions, following occasional ski markers. Follow a ridgetop to a sunken woods road. Turn sharply left to take this road downhill. This junction is marked with an arrow on a huge tulip tree, and the red blazes become more frequent.

Continue on the woods road and eventually you will cross an aging wooden bridge built by a Youth Conservation Corps crew in 1978. Pass a woods road to your left. Stay straight here on the red-blazed woods road. Descend into a hemlock stand and cross a plank bridge over Muddy Brook just below Baby Falls. Immediately on the other side, a yellow-blazed trail cuts in; turn right to climb uphill away from the well-worn woods road. You soon pass the falls, which are on your right and down a steep hill.

When ready, continue following the yellow blazes uphill. You are now on the Witch Hazel Trail. Proceed up the steep grade and move away from the stream. Your climb will level out and cross the top of a rise, passing through an area lush with ferns: Christmas, cinnamon, beech, and New York. The woods here are a mixture of oak, black birch, and hickory.

Turn downward; at one point you pass under a canopy of ancient mountain laurel bushes. The tops are 10 to 15 feet above you, supported by boles almost as thick as one of your legs.

Finally, make a steep descent through a thick grove of hemlocks. Note the almost total lack of undergrowth where these trees grew thickest. Besides the shade, the strong tannin from years of accumulation of fallen needles and other debris prevents most plants from gaining a foothold, creating a practically monocultural grove. Now that these trees are dying out, we'll see how fast new trees and shrubs can move in.

Just as you emerge from the woods you join the red-blazed woods road that you left a mile or so back. Turn right, immediately cross paved Hopyard Road, and proceed down the now dark-red-blazed trail; the yellow blazes ended at the tar road. Pass through another grove of hemlocks, then bear left to join an old tote road. You will soon see the Eight Mile River on your right.

You come again to the stream that you crossed on the other side of the road. Now it is large enough that you may be glad to see the small footbridge a few yards downstream. Follow the red-blazed woods road to a gate at the tar park road that services the park picnic area. Follow this right past several small parking lots and up the hill to your car.

44

Seven Falls

Location: Middletown

Distance: 8 miles

Vertical rise: 900 feet

Time: 4½ hours

Rating: C

Map: USGS 7.5-minute Middle Haddam

Laying out a hiking trail is more an art than a science; the shortest distance between two points does not necessarily provide the most interesting hiking. A trail that is properly laid out directs you to the best of an area's natural features, thus offering you the finest hike possible. This stretch of the Mattabesett Trail, which starts at Seven Falls south of Middletown, does just that. Its corkscrew route approaches, circles, and often climbs the boulders and rock ridges that are so characteristic of the local terrain.

Another attraction of this hike is the number of loop trails. The main trail is blazed with blue rectangles and the loop trails, generally shorter, are marked with blue circles. We suggest that you go out on the main trail and return on the blue-circle loops to maximize hike variety. While our route follows the Mattabesett Trail as far as Bear Hill and returns on several loops for a distance of just over 7 miles, you can shorten the hike by taking only the first or the first two loops for a total distance of 2.5 or 5.5 miles, respectively. This hike is far more difficult to describe than to follow, because the junctions are well signed to assist you in finding your way. The hike is also deceptive, however; you must take care to follow the blazes, and due to the nature of the route (up, over, and around ledges and boulders) you can expect it to take longer than most hikes in this book.

The hike begins by the Seven Falls Roadside Park on CT 154 south of Middletown. Leave CT 9 on exit 10 (Aircraft Road)

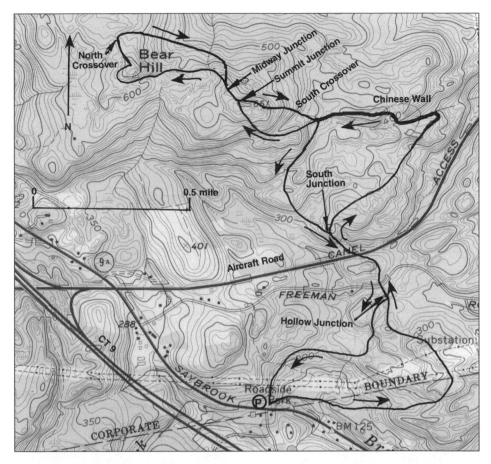

and follow CT 154 south (right) for 0.8 mile. The park is on your left, and roadside parking is available just west of the park, where the Mattabesett Trail enters the woods.

Follow the rectangular blue blazes of the Mattabesett Trail down along the brook to the falls area. To your right, before reaching the brook, you pass the blue-circle trail to your left. Across the brook is the picnic area. About 100 yards from the road, turn left at the double blaze (the upper blaze is displaced in the direction of the turn) by a smaller brook. As we followed this brook upstream in early spring, we watched a water snake wind its way along the brook bottom. Not once did we see it come up for air.

Picnickers have worn an aimless labyrinth of trails through this section; most go nowhere, so be careful to stick with the blue blazes. Shortly you cross this smaller brook near the power-line clearing and wind up on a wooded hill. You soon reach and cross an old tote road; at a second tote road, go left, paralleling the power line. Along this stretch the trail skirts, surmounts, and circles numerous ledges and boulders. In 0.6 mile you pass a Middletown/Haddam boundary marker—a crosspiece with M/H inscribed on a rod set into a rock. From the marker ascend the ledge to your left and follow the faded blue blazes carefully. Several vantage points offer views of the numerous forested,

One of Seven Falls' cascades

rolling hills with only a few houses nestled here and there.

Two high-voltage power lines cut through the woods 0.2 mile farther on. Be careful of this and all such crossings. The route rarely goes straight across the clearing, and except for a possible blaze on the poles there are frequently no markers between the parallel, but widely separated, forest walls. In partial compensation, the blazes on the forest edges are often deliberately made larger. These forest edges are frequently the best place to view wildlife—this was punctuated during a recent fall visit when we flushed two bucks!

When you reach Hollow Junction, 1.4 miles from your car, the blue-circle trail bears uphill to your left, while the blue rectangular blazes continue straight downhill. Go straight here to descend to paved Freeman Road in about 0.1 mile and then, in another 0.1 mile, the busier, paved Aircraft Road (labeled Canal Access on the map). Climb the hill to South Junction (1.7 miles from the start), where a second loop trail bears left. Keep to the main trail, which forks uphill to your right. The path crests a rise and then heads downhill, bearing left at a stream at the edge of a logging operation, then ascending along that stream for a way before crossing it several times and leveling out on a worn woods road. You then climb another ridge about a mile from South Junction. Cross another brook and scramble over ledges and across the top of the Chinese Wall, a long, uniform escarpment that ends at a stream crossing just before reaching South Crossover, 1.2 miles from South Junction. This blue-circle trail crosses the main route here.

Continuing on the main trail, you reach Summit Junction—on an open, rocky hilltop

with a good view west across to Bear Hill—about 0.4 mile from South Crossover. Stay to your left to descend the ledge; in another 0.1 mile bear left onto the main trail at Midway Junction. Climb to the top of Bear Hill (640 feet) on the main trail (rectangles) in another ½ mile, about 3.9 miles from the start. Look for the two U.S. Geological Survey bench markers—one to your right, one to your left. The profusion of huckleberries here would have been a major attraction for bears, hence the probable origin of its name. Continue on the blue-blazed trail, turning left to descend on an old woods road and then bearing left off the road to stay on the ridge. Drop abruptly to another junction ¼ mile from the summit, the North Crossover. Bear right onto this woods road blazed with blue circles. This is the Bear Hill Loop Trail.

Pass through the recovering burned-over north slope of Bear Hill. Many of the oaks and pitch pines bear the scorch marks of a small forest fire. After ½ mile, rejoin the main trail at Midway Junction and ascend to the rocky hilltop and Summit Junction. Bear left to follow the blue-circle trail down to South Crossover. Cross the main trail and descend ½ mile following faded blue-circle blazes through open hardwood forest to the ledges of South Junction. Retrace your steps across Aircraft and Freeman Roads and soon bear right onto the blue-circle-blazed Seven Falls Loop, which passes over and around ledges, then skirts a pond just above a small cascade. Here the trail once again clambers around boulders and rock outcrops. Cross the power-line clearing just before descending to the main trail, which you follow briefly to CT 154 and your car.

Seven Falls

45

Talcott Mountain

Location: West Hartford

Distance: 8½ miles

Vertical rise: 700 feet

Time: 4¾ hours

Rating: C

Map: USGS 7.5-minute Avon

Close by the city of Hartford is a large, attractive area of open reservoir land. Preserved to maintain water purity, areas such as this one in West Hartford are often open to nonpolluting activities. A nice day brings out an endless procession of walkers, joggers, bicyclists, hikers, and—in winter—cross-country skiers. The value of this land is incalculable. This hike will take you over another of Connecticut's traprock ridges. You'll follow the Metacomet Trail over Talcott Mountain, passing by Heublein Tower, one of the state's most prominent landmarks. Metacomet, or King Philip, Wampanoag sachem, gave his name to one of our Indian Wars, the 17th century's King Philip's War.

From the junction of US 44 and CT 10 south in Avon, proceed east for 2.3 miles on US 44. On your left (north), a sign indicates RESERVOIR 6, METROPOLITAN DISTRICT. Turn in here to park.

Walk to the far end of the parking lot, pass a mounted reservoir map, and bear left onto the dirt road that is barred to motor vehicles. Pass through the metal gate and proceed north. This soon becomes the blue-blazed Metacomet Trail. Along your route are the great rhubarblike leaves of the burdock; its nondescript flowers yield the round, multihook burrs that dogs and hikers pick up in fall. These plants usually grow alongside trails and at hikers' campsites, because when hikers stop and remove them from their socks or pants they throw the burrs or seeds down where they are. The fresh green growth of grapevines edges out

Cave

Metacomet Trail

King Phillip
Mtn

Little
Phillip Mtn

BM △ 3

BM △ 178

BM △ 218

Heublein Tower

red dot trail

Radio Tower
(WTIC)

Tower Trail

gas line

875

Hoe Pond

power line

757

N

Talcott

550

406

Hartford Reservoir No 6

0   0.5 mile

BM 527

412

BM △ 599

397

Ely
Pond

652

Metacomet Trail

Ely
Mound

498

BM

Welles Pond

394

Heublein Tower from across Hartford Reservoir No. 6

into the dirt road, where they are soon beaten back by the pounding feet of joggers. Shaded by hemlock, spruce, and pine, this west shore of the reservoir is lovely any time of the year.

The wind-stirred wavelets on the reservoir reflect the sun in a sparkling glitter that adds life to this shifting scene. Along the shallow edges of the water swim numerous species of the sunfish family, including the black bass; this border area provides protection from predators and is handy for snaring land-based insect life.

The shiny-leafed vine on the reservoir side of a cement bridge is the harmless five-leafed Virginia creeper, but the small cement-and-stone bridge abutment used to be covered with great masses of poison ivy. There is still much poison ivy along the way; nestled within its foliage you may find its lovely, greenish yellow blossoms. Along here we saw a pair of 4-foot black rat snakes. Effective rodent eaters, they are now considered a threatened species by the Connecticut Herpetological Society. Like many of our larger creatures, its major enemy is humans!

Farther along, the great torrent of water pouring into Reservoir 6 is ducted from another reservoir in an extensive system. Hartford gets most of its water from the Shepaug and Barkhamsted Reservoirs in northern Connecticut; the West Hartford reservoirs serve largely for holding and storage, rather than as prime sources of water.

Continue along the west shore of the reservoir. Before reaching the north end of the reservoir and its bridge, turn left at double blue blazes to follow a woods road uphill away from the reservoir. Continue uphill on woods roads, walking under a power line and, not long after, through a gas pipeline clearing. After passing through a stand of white birch trees, you'll reach the paved ridge road and bear right briefly before reentering the woods to the west to ascend to the traprock ridgeline.

Pass under a relay tower and continue to the summit development featuring stone garages, picnic pavilions, and a barbecue pit installed to entertain then-general Eisenhower.

Soon you'll pass to the left of Heublein Tower. This 165-foot structure is the most ornate of the four towers situated on this ridgetop. Built in 1914, it was home to the family of Gilbert Heublein, the liquor magnate, for more than 30 years. The tower and almost 600 acres of land were protected by the state of Connecticut in 1966 through a coalition of government agencies and private conservationists, and they presently form Talcott Mountain State Park. The tower has visiting hours from mid-April to November; contact the Connecticut State Parks Division (860-424-3200) for details. The view encompasses nearly 1,200 square miles; on the northern horizon you can pick out New Hampshire's Mount Monadnock (the second most climbed mountain in the world; the first is Fujiyama in Japan) some 80 miles to the north; the Berkshires in western Massachusetts; the hills of eastern Rhode Island; and Long Island Sound to the south.

Follow the woods road north and bear right to remain on the ridgeline. After following the crest with intermittent views to the west, turn right onto the blue-blazed Metacomet Trail, a winding, narrow path through thick mountain laurel. Leave the laurel and follow a woods road down the east side of King Philip Mountain. After a stream crossing, turn right to stay on the trail, climb briefly over a small rise, and descend to a power-line clearing. Enter the clearing and, just before reaching the gravel service road (which the blue-blazed Metacomet Trail follows north to your left), take a sharp hairpin turn to your right onto a grassy woods road back under the power line. This road follows blue blazes with red spots along a fence line on your right. Turn left, away from the fence line, at a fork in the road and follow the sunken woods road uphill. Ascend gently past a solitary stone chimney and continue to the power-line clearing, where you briefly follow the service road to your right before entering the woods on the far side. Please note that if you have difficulty finding the red-spot trail, you can turn right onto the gravel service road in the power-line clearing and follow it until the red-spot trail crosses it. Then turn left and continue with the trail description below.

Cross a stream and then a pipeline clearing. Go straight through a woods road crossing; this is the old tower trail. Soon your woods road reaches the reservoir and passes the bridge at the northern end to your right. Leave the red-spot-blazed trail that crosses the bridge, instead bearing left to follow the road along the reservoir's eastern shore. As you top a hill, the Metropolitan District Commission's filtration plant for Bloomfield comes into view. Beyond is the ever-growing Hartford skyline. From this point on, your route is in the open, fully exposed to cold winds in season. An extra sweater and windbreaker may be necessary. The dirt road joins and briefly follows the plant's tar road along the wooded shore.

Keep along the reservoir, following the lesser-used tar road. This road turns to dirt in a few yards and follows the length of the reservoir bank. As you look back, the Heublein Tower thrusts up above the ridge. The rock riprap lining the banks below you retards erosion.

When you come to a tar road again, stay on the path between it and the water. Eventually you reenter the woods at a chained barrier. At the fork, bear left uphill on the narrow path away from the reservoir. A right turn here will take you out to the end of a point of land, which is worth the detour. After crossing a causeway, you soon emerge on the road within sight of the parking lot.

46

Ragged Mountain

Location: Southington

Distance: Preserve Trail only
(May 15–September 15) 6.0 miles;
Metacomet/Preserve Trail loop 9.1 miles

Vertical rise: 1,000 feet

Time: 5 hours

Rating: A

Maps: USGS 7.5-minute New Britain,
Meriden

Hiking trails in central Connecticut are at the mercy of development, which is staved off by limited parcels of public lands. A key component of these public lands is watershed land, which many of our Blue Trail System pathways use whenever possible. However, water company lands are fragile and at risk from a variety of factors, so there may be restrictions regarding their use. After all, we all want good water to drink from our taps. Portions of the Metacomet Trail on Ragged Mountain are on New Britain Water Department land, which is closed to public use from May 15 through September 15. During this time, the hike over Ragged's traprock ridges is limited to the Preserve Trail loop. The longer hike described here is available for hiking from September 16 through May 14, which we find to be the best times to hike here anyway.

To get to this area of volcanic cliffs, start from the junction of CT 372 and CT 71A in New Britain. From CT 372 (Corbin Avenue), take CT 71A (Chamberlain Highway) south for 1.1 miles. Turn right onto West Lane. Proceed on West Lane for 0.6 mile to Ragged Mountain Memorial Preserve (563 acres) to your right. There is room for parking alongside the road.

Follow the blue blazes with red dots of the Ragged Mountain Preserve Trail about 100 yards to the beginning of the trail loop. You will start out on the left arm of the loop and return on the right.

Immediately bear left off the woods road. Be careful not to continue blithely along a well-defined woods road and miss the trail

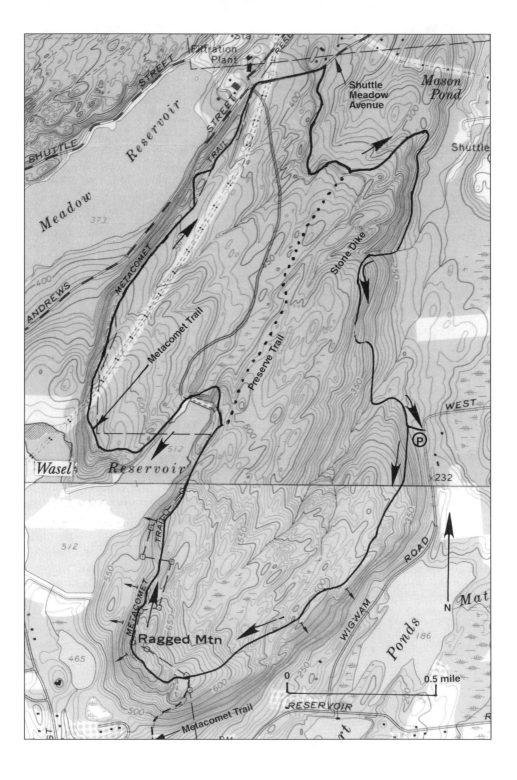

Filtration Plant

STREET

STREET

Shuttle Meadow Avenue

Mason Pond

Shuttle

SHUTTLE

Reservoir

Meadow

TRAIL

400

373

METACOMET

ANDREWS

400

Metacomet Trail

Preserve Trail

Stone Dike

550

350

WEST

512

P

Wasel

Reservoir

232

512

350

ROAD

550

TRAIL

550

600

METACOMET

WIGWAM

N

Ponds

Mat

186

465

Ragged Mtn

Metacomet Trail

0   250   0.5 mile

RESERVOIR

R

turn, which is easy to do. Bear left yet again away from the well-worn path, which continues straight. Climb gently on the trail, which is well marked with red-on-blue blazes. Soon you level out and go due south, then continue climbing past an old woods road on your right, and then level out yet again.

The Connecticut woodlands are crisscrossed with innumerable woods roads; some are easily followed, some have become choked with brush, and some are so faint as to defy certain identification. These roads were cut and used (usually for just a short time) to harvest the wood and charcoal that were major products of our woodlands in the last couple of centuries. The abandoned roads are slowly but surely being obliterated by the healing hand of nature. Pass over a rise and then turn sharply right onto a footpath, which leads to more old woods roads. After another brief stint on a woods road, bear left and climb to a rocky ridge where Hart Ponds are visible through the trees. Continue on the ridge, soon climbing to an excellent lookout above the ponds. Drop down briefly and return to the ridgetop, reaching another fine viewpoint above Reservoir Road. Continue on open ledges with fine views to the south where West Peak (one of the highest traprock ridges in Connecticut; see Hike 37), with its towers, can be seen in the distance.

The trail drops into and then climbs out of another small ravine. Permanent water is rare in traprock—snowmelt and rain soon run off this impervious rock, leaving most ravines stark and dry. Continue south along a small, rocky ridge, and then turn down and left off the end of the ridge before climbing again to more views and a freestanding wall—difficult to describe but unmistakable when you see it—1.2 miles from the start. The tops of central Connecticut's traprock ridges provide exhilarating hiking with excellent views.

Join the blue-blazed Metacomet Trail on top of Small Cliff, south of Ragged Mountain's summit. Follow the blue blazes down into a ravine and then scramble up the traprock to the top of the cliffs, which are largely wooded here. In about another ¼ mile of gentle ups and downs you will come out into the open on the summit of Ragged Mountain. Here, of necessity, many of the blue blazes are painted on rocks instead of trees.

We've sat atop the cliffs and watched three seagulls play follow-the-leader above the reservoir. Large birds often use the thermals associated with cliffs to soar for hours with nary a wing beat. Far below you can see strollers sauntering along the reservoir dike.

Bear right away from the cliffs, drop down, and climb again as the trail undulates along the ridge. A final lookout offers views of the northern end of Wassel Reservoir.

Volcanic ridgetops are usually not good places to find large varieties of flowers, but we have found one especially favorite flower in Connecticut's traprock (though rarely elsewhere): pale corydalis, a member of the poppy family, closely related to bleeding heart and Dutchman's-breeches. Whenever you traverse these ridges, be on the lookout for this striking rose-and-yellow flower.

Wind along the ridge down toward the reservoir's shore. The rugged trail surface requires proper hiking foot gear—not street shoes. Near the end of the reservoir on an open rocky ledge, pass the blue-and-red-blazed preserve loop to your right. This is the summer loop on Ragged Mountain that shortens this hike by 3 miles. Between May 15 and September 15, follow the blue and red blazes north along woods roads for 1.3 miles to a three-way trail junction. To your left is the feeder trail to the Metacomet Trail at Shuttle Meadow Avenue; you follow the

The top of Ragged Mountain's cliffs

Preserve Trail for another 1 ½ miles back to your starting point on West Lane.

Between September 16 and May 14, continue on the Metacomet Trail along the ridge and pass over a rocky promontory directly across from the dam below. Follow the trail east beyond the dam and then steeply descend some step ledges. This part of the trail requires some use of your hands to get down the rock wall. If this kind of hiking is more hair-raising than adventurous for you, we recommend returning to the preserve loop trail.

After reaching the floodplain below the dam, double back toward the dam and then cross the field to your right. Climb to the top of the dam's western end through a cleft in the ledge. Ragged Mountain's cliffs stand in profile across the reservoir. Cross the dam access road and bear left to follow a gravel road on the north side of the reservoir. This road is sparsely blazed, but the subsequent right turn off it in nearly ½ mile is well marked.

Ascend to the top of the ridge and cross a power-line clearing at its highest point. Bear right and soon reenter the woods to follow the northern escarpment over Shuttle Meadow Reservoir. The trail along the ridge is well shaded by pitch pine, red cedar, and hemlock. The thick woods can provide a much-needed windbreak on windy days and can be especially welcome after you've crossed the exposed top of Ragged Mountain. Follow this ridge for a mile, passing vistas over the reservoir, before coming out onto a grassy woods road. Proceed on the road until you reach Shuttle Meadow Avenue. Turn right and follow the pavement, taking care to stay on the edge of this fairly busy road.

Cross a canal and turn right to follow the feeder trail (blue blazes with red dots) south along it. After ½ mile turn left at a well-blazed junction. To your right, the preserve trail leads back to Ragged Mountain. Follow woods roads east and descend toward a meadow before curving right to stay in the woods.

After about ¾ mile your trail turns sharply to the right and climbs alongside a small stream (crossing it once) to a lovely waterfall. Here you will find the remnants of a stone dike. Climb carefully up the loose traprock slope to the ridgetop and turn left as the trail continues south. Here, though not well worn, the trail is well blazed. Descend along the hillside, and descend again. Soon you cross a deeply eroded old road, then a brook, and then descend gradually to an old woods road.

Go right about 0.1 mile to reach the beginning of the loop you started a few hours ago. At the junction, go left to your car.

47

Cockaponset

Location: Chester

Distance: 10.1 miles

Vertical rise: 900 feet

Time: 5½ hours

Rating: CD

Map: USGS 7.5-minute Haddam

Cockaponset State Forest is a 15,000-acre monument to the Civilian Conservation Corps (CCC). In its heyday (1933–1942) Cockaponset forest was home to three camps, with a workforce three times as large as is presently employed in the entire state forest system. The passage of decades has not obliterated the roadside fire holes, stonework ditches, stepped trails, and tasteful plantings.

This hike starts by Pattaconk Reservoir in Chester. From CT 9 take exit 6 to CT 148. Follow this road west 1.5 miles to Cedar Lake Road and turn right. Travel 1.5 miles to the signed entrance to the Lake Pattaconk State Recreation Area and turn left. In 0.4 mile (past the beach) there are parking lots on both sides of the road.

You are at the Filley Road crossing of the Cockaponset Trail. This 10.1-mile hike makes three loops and can easily be shortened to 2.3 or 5.8 miles by taking just the first or the first two loops. The entire trail has been wheeled (distances have been measured accurately using a calibrated wheel), and at all junctions away from the road crossings there are signs posting distances to various spots on the trail. However, signs at junctions are notoriously hard to maintain, as they are too tempting a target for vandals and souvenir hunters. Your hike follows the Cockaponset Trail (blue blazes) north to the Beaver Brook junction and returns using the loop trails (red dot on a blue blaze) wherever possible.

Proceed through the parking lot on the west (to your right as you're coming from

Cedar Lake Road) side of the road, following the blue blazes as the trail leaves the far left end of the parking lot. Your trail soon heads right onto a blue-blazed gravel road to Pattaconk Crossing (junction 4). Bear left to stay on the blue-blazed Cockaponset Trail, heading north to Old County Road. Cross a series of three woodland brooks, each one more lovely than the one before; all three flow into Pattaconk Reservoir.

When we first scouted this trail, thousands of chipmunks enlivened these woods. Six years later we didn't see any. Chipmunks, like many of the small mammals whose numbers are not effectively limited by predators, go through population cycles. From a very low point, their numbers increase steadily year by year until they seem to be everywhere; then disease and/or starvation decimates their population and the cycle starts over again.

After crossing several more streams, the trail climbs and then descends gently to Pattaconk Brook at junction 5 (see map), 1.2 miles from your car. Cross the brook over an arched bridge, which may be slippery when wet. This is where you return on the Pattaconk Trail to your right if you wish to hike only the 2.3-mile option.

Remain on the blue-blazed trail to your left, reaching another brook crossing in 0.3 mile at North Pattaconk, junction 6 (see map). Just before the junction, look for the patch of bright red cardinal flowers. Here you rejoin the original Cockaponset Trail (now the Pattaconk Trail from junction 4 to 6), which is well worn and easy to follow. The Pattaconk Trail to your right ends here.

Follow the blue-blazed Cockaponset Trail north from junction 6 for 0.8 mile through a small logging operation to Old County Road. In spring the ledges in this section are decorated with dwarf ginseng,

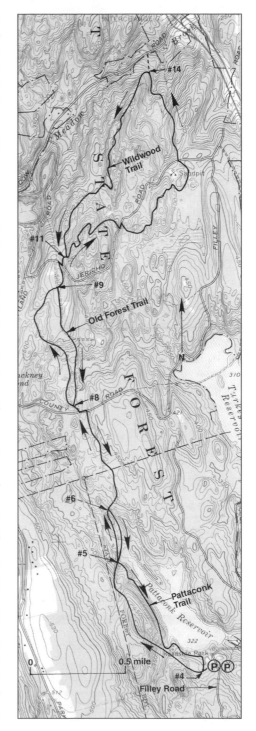

white violet, wood anemone, Solomon's seal, and a profusion of mountain laurel.

Turn left onto Old County Road and proceed for 0.1 mile before turning right at the bottom of a hill on a tote road. Pass Old County Road junction 8 (see map) where the Old Forest Trail blazed with red-spotted blue blazes bears to your right up a woods road. On your left is a laurel-covered hillside, on your right a brushy swamp. Follow the blue blazes north and climb uphill off the tote road, soon passing a small rock outcropping to overlook a dammed-up cattail swamp. Proceed with the swamp pond on your left, soon crossing the old dam. Originally built by the Works Progress Administration in 1936, the dam's height was increased 3 feet in 1979.

Your blue-blazed trail bears left along the pond through azaleas and laurels. Passing a rock jumble to your right, proceed through a lovely laurel tunnel to another large rock jumble on your right. Follow the blue blazes through a recently logged area and cross a skid road. Timber harvesting appears to be increasing in Connecticut's woodlands. So far the hiking trails are still easy to follow. Such collaboration between recreation and resource management can make a difference in favor of land for trails when legislative appropriations for land protection are discussed.

Soon the trail joins a woods road and reaches Jericho junction 9 (see map), 3.1 miles from the start. Here is where you can head back to your right—following the red-dot-on-blue-blazed trail (Old Forest Trail)—if you wish to hike only 5.8 miles.

Just before you reach gravel Jericho Road, you pass a small stand of red spruce; this is the only native spruce found in any numbers in Connecticut. Its needle-covered twigs, when boiled with molasses or a similar sweetener and fermented, yield spruce beer, a good scurvy remedy. The colonists also used spruce to flavor homemade ales before hops were common in America.

Bear right a short distance on Jericho Road past an old CCC water hole on your left, and then turn left back into the woods. Almost immediately you reach Wildwood junction 11 (see map), where the Wildwood Trail goes to your left. Stay straight along the blue-blazed Cockaponset Trail and ascend some stone stairs.

The next mile of trail to the second crossing of Jericho Road is a work of art: trail layout and construction at their best. It is stepped, curbed, graded, and routed by all points of interest. It was constructed only incidentally for the ease and comfort of the hiker; after more than 60 years of use, erosion here is practically nonexistent. Around Memorial Day weekend lady's slippers are in bloom everywhere along this woodland path.

The trail in the midst of this scenic mile climbs and follows a brush-crowned, rocky ridge littered with fallen red pine trees. At one point along this ridge are four spaced concrete blocks to your right, the underpinnings of an old fire tower. These remnants tell two stories: the prominence of this ridge as a lookout and the substitution of modern, efficient fire-spotting planes. To reach a fire tower with its warden standing his lonely vigil was once a favorite goal for hikers, for both good views and good stories.

After crossing Jericho Road again, the trail reenters the mountain laurel woods to your left and passes several low, protruding ledges patched with large clumps of rock tripe. Shortly, the trail skirts a swamp on your left, which is sprinkled with tiny yellow spicebush blossoms in early spring.

About 0.5 mile from the road crossing, watch the blue blazes carefully, because several unmarked trails lead left to a campground. Soon pass a sand pit to your left

A dam in Cockaponset State Forest

and cross Jericho Road again, 5.1 miles from your car. Take the left fork across the road and continue gently downhill, then uphill through the laurel. A recent late-August visit saw the treadway littered with spiny beechnuts. You will first hear, and then see, the brook rushing along to your left. Cross the brook and continue through a small stand of hemlock to a huge downed hemlock on your right—this giant broke off about 15 feet above the ground! Immediately cross another brook before coming to Beaver Brook junction 14 (see map), 5.6 miles from the start.

Here you start your return. You will take the loop trail whenever possible, marked with a red dot on blue blazes. Leave the familiar blue blazes and bear left for a steady ascent on the Wildwood Trail. You meet and then cross a dirt road, turning south and climbing to a wooded hilltop. Descending, you soon level out and continue through a laurel tunnel, then through pines.

Cross Jericho Road for the fourth and last time just south of Wildwood junction 11, about 1.5 miles from junction 14. Follow the Cockaponset Trail to Jericho junction 9 and bear left onto the Old Forest Trail, a deeply rutted tote road. Cross a bridge just before rejoining the blue-blazed Cockaponset Trail at junction 8, proceed south past Old County Road, and bear left on the Pattaconk Trail at North Pattaconk junction 6. Follow this well-worn path, part of the old Cockaponset Trail, past junction 5 to the edge of Pattaconk Reservoir.

The rattling cry of the kingfisher frequently shatters the woodland silence here. From a well-chosen perch these brilliant blue-and-white birds spot a small fish and then plunge headfirst into the water to snare it.

After nearly a mile, pass a beach to your left and bear right uphill away from the reservoir. Soon you'll reach Pattaconk Crossover junction 4. Here take the blue-blazed trail to your left to the parking lot.

48

Tunxis Ramble

Location: Burlington

Distance: 9.5 miles

Vertical rise: 970 feet

Time: 5½ hours

Rating: BC

Maps: USGS 7.5-minute Thomaston, Bristol, Torrington, Collinsville

After hikers gets their "sea legs," short, flat, often comparatively monotonous trails no longer hold the appeal they once did. Aesthetic sense demands a more varied terrain; toughened muscles, more of a challenge. The lengthy Tunxis Ramble with its Mile of Ledges should satisfy both these needs nicely. The loop route described here makes a delightful hike through the forest north of Bristol, particularly in June when the laurel is in flower.

From the junction of CT 4 and CT 72 west in Harwinton, proceed south on CT 72 for 4.4 miles. Turn left onto East Church Road, and after 0.7 mile park on your left just past a gate. Walk around the gate to follow the well-worn tote road. Soon the Tunxis Trail, here marked with solid blue blazes, enters from your right. Continue on the tote road, now the blue-blazed "main line" of the northbound Tunxis Trail. Side trails, marked with blue blazes with a yellow dot in the center and blue blazes with a white dot in the center, will also be used to complete this circuit.

Proceed along the well-beaten tote road. Gill-over-the-ground, a little flower whose fanciful name rivals its delicate purple beauty, is plentiful here. On your left, at the edge of a large planting of red pines, a huge, gnarled maple exudes character. The maple's twisting, wide-spreading limbs overgrown with green plants and fungi are only part of the attraction. Here is the commonplace, blown up to heroic proportions!

Follow the tote road as it passes a swamp filled with skunk cabbage. About 0.6

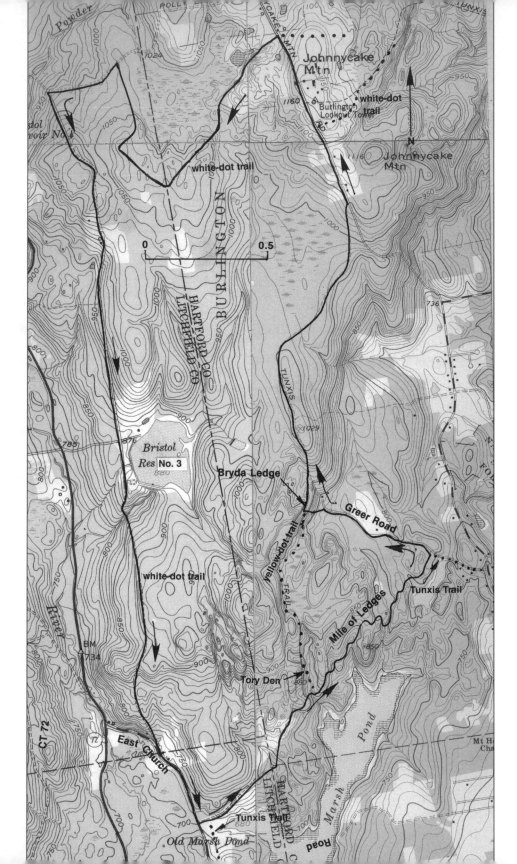

Powder

POLL

YOAKE

100

Johnnycake
Mtn

950

white-dot
trail

1160

Burlington
Lookout Tower

N

1024

1050

white-dot trail

Johnnycake
Mtn

950

1050

950

BURLINGTON

HARTFORD CO
LITCHFIELD CO

0   0.5

950

736

1000

850

TUNXIS

800

1029

785   875

Bristol
Res No. 3
880

Bryda Ledge

Greer Road

800

white-dot trail

Yellow-dot trail

TRAIL

Tunxis Trail

Mile of Ledges

River

BM
1734

900

Tory Den
880

850

Pond

CT 72

72

East Church

300

Mt Hi
Cha

750

Tunxis Trail

Marsh

Road

Old Marsh Pond

HARTFORD
LITCHFIELD

mile from the start, reach a junction with the yellow-dot trail. Follow the yellow-dot trail briefly north to Tory Den, a small set of ledges with nooks and crannies to crawl through. This was a hiding place for Tories when the local Patriots rampaged during the Revolutionary War. Return to the junction and turn left (east) to follow the blue-blazed Tunxis Trail to the Mile of Ledges. This part of the trail is a long series of boulders, ledges, and cleft rocks. You cross a stream over the remains of an old stone dam, climb through a small slot canyon, and climb over a high point with a view south over Marsh Pond. A recent December visit after a light snowfall made this a challenging yet beautiful stretch of trail. In June the faint perfume and showy flowers of mountain laurel growing from dark recesses in moss-cushioned rocks heighten the beauty of each twist and turn. Pass a pond (to your right) sporting a prominent beaver lodge. As you leave the ledges, the *twangs* and *jug-a-rums* of the green frogs and bullfrogs echo through the humid air.

When you reach paved Greer Road near the shore of the pond, 2.2 miles from the start, turn left. After about ½ mile, just before the road ends, turn left to follow the blue-with-yellow-dot-blazed trail into the woods and up the wooded slope to reach a junction at the top of the rise along Bryda Ledge. This route passes near a house to your left. Please respect the rights of property owners; much of our hiking is done on private land and is not a right but a too easily lost privilege.

Here you take the trail marked with blue blazes to your right up the hill. (To your left this trail leads back to Tory Den.) Stout-stemmed bracken fern, a lover of dry ground, and yellow-blossomed whorled loosestrife are prevalent here.

The yellow-dot trail climbs over Bryda Ledge and soon reaches an old road. About a mile from the junction bear left along the south slope of Johnnycake Mountain. After another 0.5 mile you reach gravel Johnnycake Mountain Road; bear left and soon continue straight on the paved road. The next mile of road walking takes you by a private game farm at the top of the hill. Strutting peacocks utter unearthly cries from their pens. (The peacocks' showy beauty is balanced by their loud—and anything but melodious—cry.) The sides of the road are rife with vegetation: meadow rue, angelica, wild geranium, yarrow, and horsemint are common, and orange daylily, an attractive alien escaped from colonial gardens, abounds.

Old Field Road, the white-dot route, turns to your right. Continue north on Johnnycake Mountain Road (no longer following blazes) for another ½ mile. After cresting the hill and walking downhill a way, turn left off the road just before you reach a brick house on your right. The blue-blazed trail crosses the road here, and a register box and trail information are found on the right side of the road. If you miss the turn, Polly Dan Road is 0.2 mile beyond it; turn around to look for the turn, now to your right.

Cross a field to a low point where a white pine and a maple are standing together. Stay to the left of a field along a ledge in hemlock woods. Soon you'll follow on the high ground to the left of swamps. Occasionally you'll catch a glimpse of some trees killed when water from a beaver dam flooded them out.

Bear left on a woods road and gently descend. Soon turn left again onto another tote road and pass over a rise through some recent logging. The trail on the worn road is easy to follow through the work area. Pass through a cluster of standing dead red pine and then cross an old log landing. Shortly you'll pass a house on your right, and the

Along the Mile of Ledges

road you've been walking becomes paved. Follow the paved road downhill, cross Blueberry Hill Road, and pass through a gate. Reservoir 3 is to your left. Continue straight on the gravel road on Bristol Water Department property. When the road bends left, proceed straight into the woods on an overgrown tote road with white-dot blazes. Continue downhill on this trail, cross a brook with steep banks, climb once again, level out, then descend gradually, reaching a driveway that leads downhill to East Church Road. Your car is parked 0.4 mile up the road to your left.

49

Sleeping Giant

Location: Hamden

Distance: Option A—4.8 miles;
Option B—9.0 miles

Vertical rise: Option A—1,600 feet;
Option B—1,900 feet

Time: Option A—3½ hours;
Option B—5½ hours

Rating: A

Maps: USGS 7.5-minute Wallingford,
Mount Carmel

Some hikers belittle the size of the Sleeping Giant, for he rises only 739 feet above sea level. They forget that he is lying down; were he to awaken and get to his feet, he would stand some 2 miles tall!

A series of folded, angular volcanic hills just north of New Haven defines the shape of the reclining titan. Legend has it that the giant was first recognized and named from sailing ships in New Haven Harbor many years ago. From the various parts of his anatomy you can see numerous peaks and ridges that other hikes in this book traverse. The giant is now contained in a 1,500-acre state park. Only a short distance from downtown New Haven, it is a popular spot with campers, picnickers, and hikers. In 1977 the Sleeping Giant Trail System was dedicated as a National Scenic Trail.

From I-91, take exit 10 (Hamden/Mount Carmel) onto CT 40 north. After 2.6 miles on CT 40, follow CT 10 north 1.3 miles to its junction with Mount Carmel Avenue. Turn right and follow it 0.3 mile to the park entrance on your left. There is a large parking lot with a fee.

The 32-mile park trail system, designed by Norman Greist and Richard Elliot, key members of the Sleeping Giant Park Association, is ingeniously laid out in a series of loops. No matter how long or short a hike you wish, you need never retrace your steps. Six east–west trails, marked with blue, white, violet, green, orange, and yellow blazes, join the opposite ends of the park. Five north–south trails marked with red diamonds, squares, hexagons, circles, and

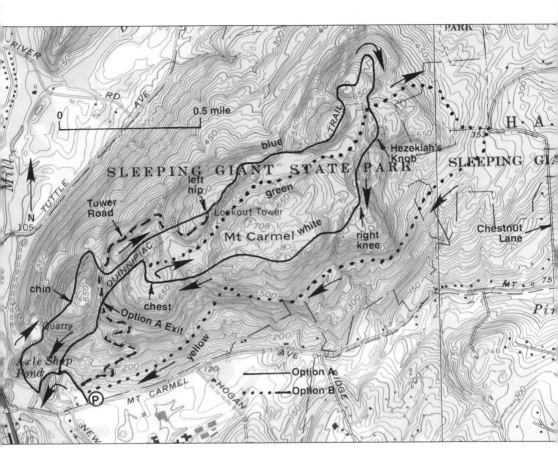

triangles cut across the park. The loop combinations you can devise seem endless.

We have selected two pairs of trails in Sleeping Giant. Since they start at about the same location, you can combine them for a real leg-stretcher. The Connecticut Chapter of the Appalachian Mountain Club has offered all the trails in this state park on a single day to those who want to test their hiking ability!

We favor the blue-white trail combination. It is the most strenuous, covers most of the giant's anatomy, and affords the best views. Alone, the blue-white circuit is Option A. Its combination with the easier green-yellow circuit is Option B.

Start up the right side of the paved picnic loop through the pine-shaded grove. To your right is a cluster of great red oaks. These tall oaks did not "from little acorns grow"; they are stump sprouts from a tree cut long ago. Tree clusters like this one are common in Connecticut's much cutover woodlands.

Follow the blue-blazed feeder trail to the right toward a gully before cutting left across the hillside. You will soon join the main blue-blazed Quinnipiac Trail, the oldest of Connecticut's Blue Trails. Follow it on an old woods road along your right, and then bear right away from the river on a blue-blazed path.

Sleeping Giant

Shortly the first ascent takes you onto the giant's elbow. The trail follows the cedar-spotted basalt ridge of his crooked arm to the right, drops down, and then ascends his head. An old quarry drops off steeply to your left. The Sleeping Giant Park Association was formed in 1924 to protect the mountain from being torn down by a quarrying operation. This stretch is a long, difficult scramble—a good test of your hiking condition. Avoid this area in winter; the slope is usually icy and treacherous. An alternate route around the steepest ledges is available to your right; this route is not recommended in bad weather, either.

Back to your right you will see two ridges. The Quinnipiac Trail runs along the closer mass of shapeless hills; the Regicides Trail follows the long ridge of West Rock farther right. The neat lawns and tastefully spaced buildings of Quinnipiac College lie below.

Continue to the jutting cliff of the giant's chin. The wide path in the valley below is the Tower Trail; beyond it rises the giant's massive chest. Looking north you can see the traprock ridges known as the Hanging Hills of Meriden, where the Metacomet and Mattabesett Trails join. West Peak, a large rock mass with a crown of towers, lies at the left just beyond the rock tower of Castle Crag (see Hike 37). The flat-topped peak to the right is South Mountain. The city of Meriden fills the break in the ridge; the two hills farthest to the right are Mount Lamentation and Chauncey Peak (see Hike 32). Lava flows formed all these traprock peaks and plateaus some 200 million years ago.

The trail zigzags steeply down the north end of the giant's head, crosses the tower road twice, and then climbs his left hip, also known as Mount Carmel, 1.5 miles from the picnic ground. Perhaps the best view in the park is from the top of the summit tower, a ramped rock structure built by the Works Progress Administration in the 1930s. The hilly panorama continues east and south; starting with Mount Lamentation, you see the impressive cliff faces of Mount Higby (see Hike 28), the gap through which US 6 passes, and the long ridge of Beseck Mountain. Like the hills to the north, these ridges are traversed by trails. The barrenness of the land makes landowners more willing to give hiking clubs permission to cut trails on hills than on their more fertile property. Fortunately, hikers much prefer these barren hills to the low-lying fertile fields.

Follow the blue blazes past the tower and continue to the cliff edge, where you can look south to the giant's right hip, right leg, and right knee before dropping down to your right, where you cross the outlet of a swamp. After a level spell through white pines, dip down and then ascend his left leg. Drop again and go up the left knee. Note the pitting that centuries of exposure have produced on the weathered rocks; they contrast sharply with the smooth faces of a few recently uncovered rock surfaces nearby.

Working down the far end of the giant's knee, you encounter the first section of smooth, rolling, rock-free trail. Footing makes a tremendous difference in hiking difficulty, and the angular volcanic-rock ridges of central Connecticut are particularly treacherous. The size of the dogwoods here attests to the depth of the rich soil beneath them.

Begin your ascent of Hezekiah's Knob. As you near the top (3.2 miles from the start), look to the right for early-spring-blooming purple and white hepaticas with their characteristic three-lobed leaves left over from the previous summer's growth. The leaf's shape, supposedly like a liver, was the basis for its medicinal use for various liver problems.

The quarry that led to the creation of Sleeping Giant State Park

The blue- and white-blazed trails meet on the knob. Proceed to your right down the hill on the white-blazed trail. When you reach the top of his right knee, look north across the valley to the giant's rocky left side, where you hiked earlier. Descend the stone-strewn slope and then climb up and down his right leg and right hip. The red-triangle trail cuts across the park by the base of the sleeping titan's chest—this path forms the last climb of this circuit. The trail winds up around the great boulders. In spring you may hear a stream echoing somewhere in the hollows beneath you.

White and green blazes mark the route here. Take a last look across at Quinnipiac College, at a vista marked by a large rock cairn, before reaching the trail junction. Here you leave the green blazes behind and twist down off the giant's chest onto the white-blazed trail, joining the Tower Trail for a short distance. The path leaves the road to your right to follow a course tucked under the giant's chin to the picnic area. At the paved road, head left for the shortest route back to your car.

If you choose to hike Option B, turn right onto the green-blazed trail at its junction with the white-blazed trail—marked with a second, large rock cairn—on the giant's chest. The green-blazed trail crosses the park to the north side of the central spine. During the peregrinations of the trail, your path crosses many red-blazed north–south trails.

If you choose the proper season and year, the mountain laurel display will be magnificent. Almost your entire route is graced with these crag-loving bushes.

It becomes more and more obvious as you proceed that you are on an old tote road. Cross the blue-blazed trail between the left foot and Hezekiah's Knob and descend toward Chestnut Lane. Toward the east end of the park and nearly at the paved road, the green-blazed trail turns right. In just a few yards you come to a great meeting point where all the east–west trails converge at a gate and a bulletin board.

Return on the yellow-blazed trail. Proceed to your right into the woods before the yellow-blazed trail straightens out and parallels the rest of the east–west trails. Even though this route is easier than most in the park, the numerous ups and downs and rough, rocky footing make it fairly tough. A few red "symbol" trails cross your path, but otherwise it is refreshingly uneventful and very quiet until you come within earshot of Mount Carmel Avenue. Near the end, our route was once blocked by the upper part of a fallen hemlock, blasted by lightning. The force of this electrical charge was so powerful that it not only vaporized the sap, which lifted the bark along its path, but also snapped the tree completely off.

Soon the yellow-blazed trail joins a dirt road that goes left and continues to the beginning of the picnic circle, where you go left to reach your car.

50

Ratlum Mountain and Indian Council Cave

Location: Barkhamsted

Distance: 13.0 miles

Vertical rise: 2,250 feet

Time: 8 hours

Rating: B

Map: USGS 7.5-minute New Hartford

Although Connecticut does not have great bodies of water like those in New Hampshire's Lakes Region or the Great Lakes, we once had many lakes, compliments of the ice ages. Most of these have had their levels raised by dams, and additional dams have created many new lakes. Still, bodies of water are transitory. Natural succession proceeds from a lake or pond to a marsh or swamp, to a meadow, and ultimately to a forest. Connecticut is dotted with large, swampy areas that were once lakes and ponds. These continuing processes have occurred over the last 10,000 years since the glaciers retreated.

By building dams, we have temporarily increased our water acreage greatly, but we have only pushed nature back a few hundred, or at most a few thousand, years. Even as we push, nature continues to drop tons of alluvium and rotting vegetation into our lakes and ponds each year. The life of any body of water is dependent on many factors, including the size of inlet streams; the volume of silt and nutrients in the incoming water, which governs the growth rate of water vegetation; and the volume of the water body to be filled.

Some human actions greatly accelerate the filling of the bodies of water that we go to so much trouble and expense to create. Road cuts, developments, and poor farming practices continually supply lake-filling silt. Often the fertilizers put on farm fields and lawns ultimately enhance the growth of choking vegetation in our bodies of water. This hike passes many bodies of water at

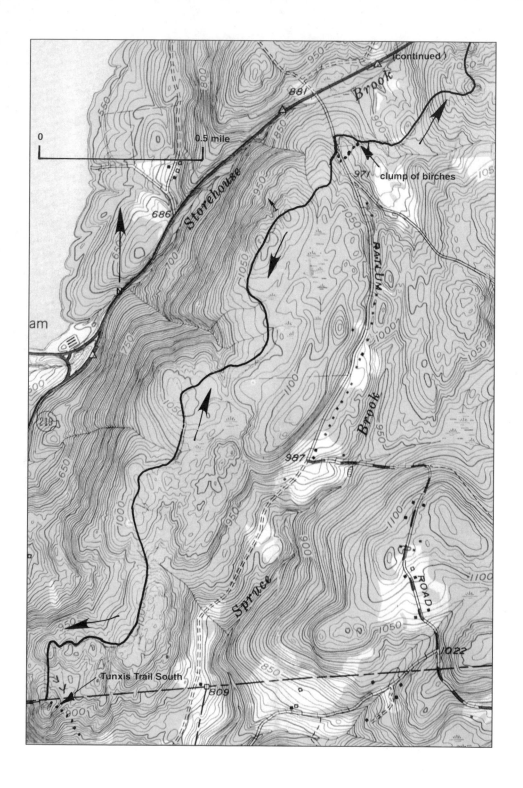

(continued)

clump of birches

Tunxis Trail South

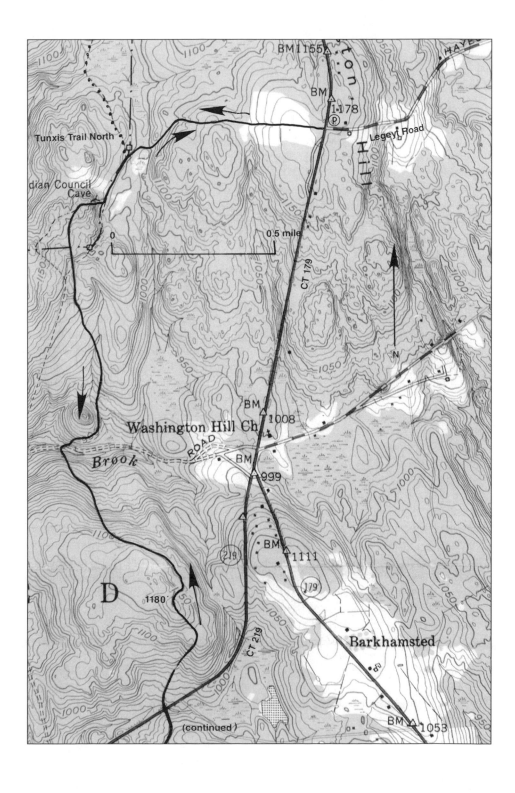

BM 1155△

HAYE

BM
△ 1.178
Ⓟ

Legeyt Road

Tunxis Trail North

dian Council
Cave

0   0.5 mile

CT 179

N

BM
△ 1008

Washington Hill Ch

ROAD

Brook   BM
△ 999

△

BM
△ 1111

219

179

D   1180

Barkhamsted

CT 219

(continued)

BM △ 1053

various stages of succession; no doubt some are now unrecognizable to the layperson's eyes.

Drive to the junction of CT 219 and CT 179 in Barkhamsted. Go north on CT 179 for 1 mile to an old gated town road on your left (west) just opposite Legeyt Road. There is room to park on both sides of CT 179. Do not block the gated road.

Go through the gate and follow the old road as it passes through Metropolitan District Commission land. At the start, you pass several white birch trees with their peeling bark and oval leaves; a single tall gray birch arches over the right side of the road. With its tight bark, large black triangles under its branches, and triangular leaves, this is a very different tree. A good way to learn to distinguish between similar trees is to find two species growing near one another. The white birch is considered a tree of the North, although more than a few are found in northern Connecticut. On the other hand, the gray birch, while not common in northern New England, grows naturally as far south as Virginia's Shenandoah National Park.

Just before a shallow pond at left we found a clump of pearly everlasting—clusters of round white flowers with a dull yellow center, which are popular with dried-flower enthusiasts. This is another northern species; sweet everlasting is more common in Connecticut.

At the bottom of a small hill there is another small pond on your left in the later stages of returning to the land. Try to visualize its original clear beauty. Now it is much smaller; trees are growing in its once open water, especially on the shallower inlet side. Submerged and emergent vegetation is adding to decay—as the pond becomes shallower, its rate of filling increases. In a few hundred years someone may cross this area cussing the swampy wetness underfoot!

Opposite this pond, the blue-blazed Tunxis Trail goes off to your right on its way north to the Massachusetts border. Continue on the old road, now blazed blue, until still another pond appears at left; follow the Tunxis Trail south as it goes off to your right and climbs up through the Indian Council Cave. These are huge boulders reputedly used by Native Americans as a gathering place. Circle left up and around this rock jumble to a lookout on top with views of the surrounding forests. You will take the Tunxis Trail south to Ratlum Mountain.

Follow the blue blazes through this typical northern Connecticut forest over ledges and through laurel, crossing two small streams before reaching the wider Kettle Brook about 1 mile from the caves (2 miles from your car). Cross Kettle Brook on a dirt road, turn left into the woods with the blue blazes, and climb gradually through hemlocks. Enjoy the soft forest floor underfoot here. Cross a dirt road and pass through a small field thick with goldenrod. Soon the trail (now an old road) crosses a small brook and climbs steadily through mixed laurel and gray birch. Bear right off the old road, climb to a rock ledge, join another old road, turn right, and soon zigzag up yet another rock ledge. Although it has no views, this is the highest place around at 1,180 feet. Follow the blue blazes downhill and then cross a stone wall by an immense spreading oak tree. Continue descending on the blue-blazed trail to CT 219 about 3 miles from the start.

Cross CT 219, enter the woods, and follow either blazed trail at a fork to climb gradually through laurel. Both forks join uphill. People have been cutting firewood in this area. Be careful to follow the blue blazes, because many woods roads traverse this section. Pass over a rise before crossing a brook that has swollen into a beaver pond courtesy of a dam downstream. Follow the stream uphill until you can safely cross it, and return downstream on the other side to rejoin the blue-blazed trail. You'll soon reach a clump of four white birches while climbing up to paved Ratlum Road, a bit less than a mile from CT 219. The trail turns right just below the birches and ascends to Ratlum Road. Turn left to follow the paved road to the Tunxis Trail on the other side.

On the west side of Ratlum Road, climb uphill through the woods, soon reaching a lookout with fine views of Barkhamsted Reservoir to the west and northwest. Continue along the edge of the cliff and then roll along the ravines and rises of the ridge's west side. Cross old woods roads at about 1½ and 2 miles from Ratlum Road, then climb an overgrown rocky top, zigzag steeply down and then up, again passing a third woods road. Stay on the blue-blazed Tunxis Trail south and shortly you reach Lookout Point (1,000 feet), about 6.5 miles from your car. Sign in at the trail register. This is an ideal lunch spot, with fine views of Lake McDonough below from ledges that are just downhill to your right.

After enjoying the view, retrace your steps to your car. Pause to admire the evergreen trailing arbutus, or mayflower, between the second and third woods roads on your return.

Index

Let Backcountry Guides Take You There

Our experienced backcountry authors will lead you to the finest trails, parks, and back roads in the following areas:

50 Hikes Series

50 Hikes in the Adirondacks
50 Hikes in the Lower Hudson Valley
50 Hikes in Kentucky
50 Hikes in Coastal and Southern Maine
50 Hikes in the Maine Mountains
50 Hikes in Maryland
50 Hikes in Massachusetts
50 Hikes in Michigan
50 Hikes in the White Mountains
50 More Hikes in New Hampshire
50 Hikes in New Jersey
50 Hikes in Central New York
50 Hikes in Western New York
50 Hikes in the Mountains of North Carolina
50 Hikes in Ohio
50 More Hikes in Ohio
50 Hikes in Eastern Pennsylvania
50 Hikes in Central Pennsylvania
50 Hikes in Western Pennsylvania
50 Hikes in the Tennessee Mountains
50 Hikes in Vermont
50 Hikes in Northern Virginia
50 Hikes in Southern Virginia

Walks and Rambles Series

Walks and Rambles on Cape Cod and the Islands
Walks and Rambles on the Delmarva Peninsula
Walks and Rambles in the Western Hudson Valley
Walks and Rambles on Long Island
Walks and Rambles in Ohio's Western Reserve
Walks and Rambles in Rhode Island
Walks and Rambles in and around St. Louis
Weekend Walks in St. Louis and Beyond

25 Bicycle Tours Series

25 Bicycle Tours in the Adirondacks
25 Bicycle Tours on Delmarva
25 Bicycle Tours in Savannah and the Carolina Low Country
25 Bicycle Tours in Maine
25 Bicycle Tours in Maryland
25 Bicycle Tours in the Twin Cities and Southeastern Minnesota
30 Bicycle Tours in New Jersey
30 Bicycle Tours in the Finger Lakes Region
25 Bicycle Tours in the Hudson Valley
25 Bicycle Tours in Maryland
25 Bicycle Tours in Ohio's Western Reserve
25 Bicycle Tours in the Texas Hill Country and West Texas
25 Bicycle Tours in Vermont
25 Bicycle Tours in and around Washington, D.C.
30 Bicycle Tours in Wisconsin
25 Mountain Bike Tours in the Adirondacks
25 Mountain Bike Tours in the Hudson Valley
25 Mountain Bike Tours in Massachusetts
25 Mountain Bike Tours in New Jersey
Backroad Bicycling in Connecticut
Backroad Bicycling on Cape Cod, Martha's Vineyard, and Nantucket
Backroad Bicycling in Eastern Pennsylvania
The Mountain Biker's Guide to Ski Resorts

Bicycling America's National Parks Series

Bicycling America's National Parks: Arizona & New Mexico
Bicycling America's National Parks: California
Bicycling America's National Parks: Oregon & Washington
Bicycling America's National Parks: Utah & Colorado

We offer many more books on hiking, fly-fishing, travel, nature, and other subjects. Our books are available at bookstores and outdoor stores everywhere. For more information or a free catalog, please call 1-800-245-4151 or write to us at The Countryman Press, P.O. Box 748, Woodstock, Vermont 05091. You can find us on the Internet at www.countrymanpress.com.